Vital Record of Rhode Island

1636 = 1850

FIRST SERIES
BIRTHS, MARRIAGES AND DEATHS

A Family Register For the People

By James N. Arnold
Editor of the Narragansett Historical Register

"Is My Name Written in the Book of Life?"

Volume 4　　　　　NEWPORT　　　　　Part II

Published under the Auspices of the General Assembly

Providence, R. I.:
Narragansett Historical Publishing Company
1893

Notice

In many older books, foxing (or discoloration) occurs and, in some instances, print lightens with wear and age. Reprinted books, such as this, often duplicate these flaws, notwithstanding efforts to reduce or eliminate them. The pages of this reprint have been digitally enhanced and, where possible, the flaws eliminated in order to provide clarity of content and a pleasant reading experience.

Vital Record of Rhode Island 1636-1850: Births, Marriages and Deaths: Newport

Originally published
Providence, Rhode Island
1893

Reprinted by:

Janaway Publishing, Inc.
732 Kelsey Ct.
Santa Maria, CA 93454
(805) 925-1038
www.JanawayGenealogy.com

2000, 2007, 2011

ISBN: 978-1-59641-076-3

Made in the United States of America

INDEX.

NEWPORT.

I.

Names Occurring in Their Natural Order.

Marriages commence with page 8; births and deaths, page 80.

A

Achforth, 3.
Acres, 3.
Adams, 3.
Adlim, 80.
Aiken, 3.
Albro, 3 80.
Allbun, 3.
Alden, 3.
Aldridge, 3.
Allen, 3 4 80.
Allison, 4.
All, 4.
Almy, 4 80 81.
Alsworth, 4.
Ambrose, 4.
Anceaux, 4 81.
Anderson, 4 5 81.
Andrews, 5.
Angell, 5.
Anthony, 5 81.
Armstrong, 5.
Ares, 5.
Arnold, 5 81.
Ash, 5 81.
Asker, 5.
Ashbrook, 5.
Ashley, 5.
Atkinson, 5.
Atkins, 6.
Attwood, 6 81.
Auboyneace, 81.
Auchmutz, 6.
Austin, 6.
Axton, 6.
Ayrault, 81.
Ayres, 6.

B

Babcock, 6.
Bachelor, 6 81.
Baggs, 6.
Bailey, 6.
Baker, 6.
Balch, 6.
Ballard, 6 81.
Ball, 6.
Bannel, 6.
Banks, 7.
Bannister, 7.
Banon, 7.
Bantin, 7.
Baptister, 7.
Barbat, 81.
Barber, 7.
Bardin, 7.
Barill, 7.
Barkenshaw, 7.
Barker, 7 81 82.
Barlow, 7 82.
Barnes, 7.
Barney, 7 82.
Barstow, 7.
Bass, 7.
Barton, 8.
Baskell, 8.
Basil, 8.
Bassett, 8 82.
Bates, 8.
Battey, 8.
Battle, 8.
Batts, 8.
Baxter, 8.
Bayley, 8 82.
Bay, 8.
Beasdin, 8.
Beebe, 8 82.
Beere, 8 82.
Belcher, 8 82.
Belden, 8.
Bell, 8 82.
Benjamions, 8.
Bennett, 8 9 82.
Bernon, 9.
Benson, 9 82.
Bentley, 9.
Berkeley, 82.
Berry, 9.
Bidder, 9.
Biggs, 9.
Bigley, 9.
Billet, 9.
Billings, 9.
Bingham, 82.
Bird, 9.
Bissell, 9 82 83.
Blacon, 9.
Blake, 9.
Blacklin, 9.
Blakewell, 9 83.
Blanchard, 9.
Bliss, 9 83.
Bliven, 10 83.
Block, 10.
Bourk, 10.
Bones, 10.
Bonner, 10 83.
Booker, 10.
Booth, 10.
Borden, 10 83.
Boss, 10.
Bosworth, 10.
Bourk, 10.
Bourse, 83.
Bours, 10.
Bovel, 10.
Bowcott, 10 83.
Bowdin, 10.
Bowen, 10.
Bowers, 10.
Bowler, 10.
Bowles, 10.
Boyd, 10.
Bradford, 10 83.
Braidson, 10.
Brand, 10.
Braman, 10.
Braston, 10.
Brattle, 11.
Brayton, 11 83 84.
Brenton, 11 84.
Brewer, 84.
Brickley, 11.
Bridges, 11 84.
Briggs, 11.
Brightman, 11.
Brink, 11.
Brinley, 11.
Brittain, 11 84.
Bryant, 11.
Bryer, 11.

Brooks, 11 84.
Brophy, 11.
Brownell, 11 84.
Brown, 11 12 84.
Bruff, 84.
Bryer, 85.
Bryn, 12.
Buckmaster, 12 85.
Budlong, 12 85.
Bulliva, 12.
Bull, 12 13 85.
Bunn, 13.
Burden, 13.
Burdick, 13 85.
Burd, 13.
Burgess, 13 85.
Burk, 13.
Burrell, 13.
Burrington, 13.
Burroughs, 13 85.
Burr, 13.
Burtis, 13.
Burt, 13.
Bush, 14.
Butland, 14.
Byles, 14.
Byron, 14.

C

Cabellee, 14 85.
Carrigan, 14.
Cahoone, 14 85.
Callender, 85 86.
Calline, 14.
Calvert, 14.
Calvin, 14.
Campbell, 14 86.
Canterbury, 14.
Candry, 14.
Card, 14 86.
Carey, 86.
Carlton, 14.
Carpenter, 14 86.
Carroll, 14.
Carr, 14 15 86 87.
Carter, 15.
Cartwright, 15 87.
Cary, 15 87.
Casey, 15 87.
Case, 15.
Castoff, 15 87.
Castle, 15.
Caswell, 15 16 87.
Cawdry 16.
Cazenove, 16.
Centre, 16.
Chace, 16 87 88.
Chadwick, 16 88.
Chaffee, 16 88.
Chaffins, 16.
Chaffin, 16 88.
Challoner, 16 88.
Chamberlain, 16.
Chambers, 16.
Champlain, 16 17 88.
Chanders, 17.
Chandler, 17 88.
Channing, 17.
Chantat, 88.
Chaplain, 17 88.
Chapman, 17 88.
Chappell, 17.
Checkley, 17.

Cheesborough, 17.
Child, 17 88.
Chilson, 17.
Chubb, 17.
Church, 17 88.
Claflin, 18.
Claggett, 18.
Clark, 18 19 89.
Clay, 19.
Cleveland, 19.
Coan, 19.
Coburn, 19.
Coddington, 19 89 90.
Codman, 19.
Codner, 19.
Coe, 19.
Coffin, 19.
Coggeshall, 19 20 90 91.
Cogin, 20.
Cohen, 20 91.
Coit, 91.
Coleman, 20 91.
Coles, 20.
Collick, 20.
Collins, 20 91.
Commer, 20.
Comer, 20 91.
Congdon, 20 21.
Conklin, 21.
Connaughton, 21.
Conner, 21.
Conway, 21.
Cookery, 21.
Cook, 21 91.
Corbett, 21.
Cooley, 21.
Coombs, 21.
Cooper, 21.
Corey, 21 91 92.
Cornell, 21 22 92.
Cornwell, 22.
Cosby, 22.
Cottrell, 22.
Coville, 22.
Cowing, 92.
Cowley, 22 92.
Cowdry, 22.
Cox, 22.
Cozzens, 22 92.
Crabb, 22.
Crandall, 22 92.
Cranston, 22 23 92.
Crapon, 23.
Crawford, 23.
Criths, 23.
Crocum, 23.
Crosby, 23.
Crossman, 92.
Crosswell, 92.
Cross, 23.
Crowell, 23.
Culler, 23.
Curry, 23.
Curtis, 23 92.

D

Daers, 23.
Daft, 23.
Daley, 23.
Daggett, 23.
Dana, 23.
Daniels, 23.

Danville, 23.
Danwell, 23.
Darling, 23.
Darrell, 93.
Daten, 23.
Davel, 23.
Davenport, 23 24 93.
Davis, 24 93.
Dawley, 24.
Dawson, 24.
Dayton 24.
Day, 24.
Debey, 24.
Deblois, 24.
Decotay, 24.
Dedwich, 24.
Deering, 24.
Dehane, 24 93.
Delano, 24.
Dell, 24.
Denham, 24.
Dennison, 25.
Dennis, 25 93.
Devallen, 93.
Devens, 25.
Dewich, 25.
Dickens, 25.
Dickinson, 25.
Dicks, 25.
Dillingham, 25 93.
Dill, 25 93.
Dodge, 25.
Dolbear, 93.
Donaldson, 25.
Donnelly, 25.
Dorrell, 25.
Doubleday, 25 93 94.
Douglass, 25.
Dower, 25.
Downer, 25.
Downing, 25 94.
Downs, 25.
Dow, 25.
Doyle, 25.
Drew, 25.
Drinkwater, 94.
Driver, 25.
Dumont, 25.
Dunbar, 26 94.
Dunham, 26 94.
Dunn, 26 94.
Dunscomb, 26.
Dunton, 26.
Dunwell, 26.
Durfee, 26 94.
Dyer, 26 94.
Dykes, 26.

E

Eady, 94.
Earle, 26 94.
Eastman, 94.
Easton, 26 27 94.
Eckstene, 27 95.
Eckstone, 95.
Eddy, 27 95.
Edwards, 27.
Egan, 27.
Elderton, 27.
Eldredge, 27.
Eldred, 27 95.
Elizer, 27 95.
Ellaly, 27.

Ellery, 27 95.
Elliott, 27 95.
Ely, 27.
Emmons, 27.
England, 28.
Erwin, 28.
Esleck, 28.
Essex, 28.
Eustis, 28.
Evans, 28.
Evengs, 28.
Ewen, 28.
Exan, 28.
Exceene, 28.
Eyres, 28.

F

Fairbanks, 28.
Fairchild, 28.
Faisnean, 95.
Fales, 28 96.
Fannett, 96.
Farrell, 28.
Farrens, 28.
Fear, 28.
Feke, 28.
Ferguson, 28.
Field, 28 96.
Finch, 28.
Finley, 28.
Fish, 28 29.
Fisk, 29.
Flagg, 29 96.
Fleet, 29.
Fludder 29 96.
Foreman, 29.
Forrester, 29.
Foster, 29 96.
Fountain, 29.
Fowler, 29 96.
Fox, 29.
Francis, 29.
Franklin, 29 96.
Frank, 96.
Freebody, 29.
Freeborn, 29 96 97.
Freeman, 29 30.
French, 30.
Friend, 30.
Frost, 30.
Fryers, 30.
Fry, 30.
Fullerton, 30.
Fuller, 30.

G

Galledat, 30.
Gardner, 30 31 97.
Garrick, 31.
Gassia, 31.
Gatewood, 31.
Gavitt, 31 97.
Gay, 31 97.
Geissert, 31.
Geoffery, 31.
George, 31.
Gerold, 31.
Gibbons, 31 97.
Gibbs, 31 97.
Gibson, 31 97.
Gifford, 31.

Gilbert, 31 97.
Gillis, 32.
Gill, 32.
Gilman, 32.
Gilpin, 32 98.
Gladding, 32 98.
Glover, 32.
Goddard, 32 98.
Godfrey, 32 98.
Goff, 32.
Goldsmith, 98.
Goldthwait, 32 98.
Goodman, 32.
Goodson, 32.
Goodspeed, 32 98.
Goram, 32.
Goutisam, 32.
Goulder, 32
Goulding, 32 98.
Gould, 32 33.
Grafton, 33 98.
Graham, 33.
Grant, 33 98.
Graw, — 33.
Gray, 33.
Greenborge, 33.
Greene, 33 98 99.
Greenhill, 33.
Greenman, 33 34 99.
Gregory, 34 99.
Greve, 34.
Grice, 34.
Grier, 34 99.
Griffith, 34.
Grinnell, 34.
Grosvenor, 34.
Gubbins, 34.
Guinadean, 34.
Guinedo, 34.
Guild, 34 99.
Gullard, 34.
Gullen, 34.
Guy, 34.
Gyles, 34.

H

Hacker, 34.
Hadwin, 99.
Haiks, 34.
Haix, 34.
Hallock, 34.
Halloway, 34.
Hall, 34 35 99.
Haliburton, 35.
Halverson, 35.
Halyarsan, 35.
Hamblin, 35.
Hamilton, 35.
Hammett, 35 99.
Hammond. 35 99 100.
Hampton, 100.
Handy, 35 100.
Hannah, 35 100.
Hanners, 35.
Hanson, 35.
Harden, 35.
Harman, 35.
Hardin, 35.
Hargest, 35.
Hargill, 35.
Hargreves, 35.
Harkens, 35.
Harley, 35.

Harren, 35.
Harrington, 36.
Harris, 36 100.
Hartshorn, 36.
Hart, 36 100.
Harvey, 36 100.
Hasey, 36 100.
Hastings, 100.
Hatch, 36 100.
Hathaway, 36 100.
Havens, 36.
Hawdon, 36.
Hawkins, 36 100.
Hayden, 100.
Hayhurst, 36.
Haynes, 36.
Hayward, 36.
Hazard, 36 100.
Hazelhurst, 36.
Heath, 36 37.
Heathy, 37.
Hedge, 37.
Heffernan, 37.
Heilman, 37.
Holme, 37.
Hendler, 37.
Hendshaw, 37.
Hewatson, 37.
Hickey, 37.
Hicks, 37.
Hidden, 100.
Higgins, 37 100 101.
High, 37.
Hillsborough, 37.
Hill, 37 101.
Hinckley, 37.
Hindmarch, 37.
Hinyard, 37.
Hiscox, 38.
Hix, 38.
Hodson, 38.
Holden, 38.
Holdredge, 38.
Holman, 38.
Holmes, 38 101.
Holston, 38.
Holt, 38.
Honeyman, 38.
Honeywell, 38.
Hoockey, 38.
Hookey, 38 101.
Hoonsley, 38.
Hooper, 38.
Hoops, 38.
Hopkins, 38.
Horswell, 38.
Houlton, 101.
House, 38.
Hovey, 38.
Howard, 38 101.
Howell, 39 101.
Howland, 39 101.
Hoxsie, 39 101.
Hubbard, 39.
Hubbs, 39.
Huddy, 39.
Hudson, 39 101.
Huffman, 39.
Hughes, 101.
Huling, 39.
Hull, 39 101.
Humphrey, 39.
Humphries, 39.
Hunter, 39.

Huntington, 101.
Hunting, 40.
Hunt, 40.
Husk, 40.
Huxham, 40 101.
Hyer, 40.

I

Ingham, 40.
Ingraham, 40.
Instance, 40.
Ireson, 40.
Irish, 40 101 102.
Isaacks, 40.

J

Jackson, 40.
Jack, 40 102.
Jacobs, 40.
James, 41 102.
Jant, 41.
Jaques, 41.
Jarsey, 41.
Jefferson, 102.
Jeffries, 41 102.
Jencks, 41.
Jenkins, 102.
Jennett, 41.
Jent, 41.
Jepp, 41.
Jersey, 41 102.
Jewett, 41.
Johnson, 41 102.
Jones, 41 42.
Joy, 42.

K

Kaull, 42.
Kay, 42.
Kentley, 102.
Keeling, 102.
Keen, 42.
Kelley, 42 102.
Kelsey, 42.
Kennedy, 42.
Kenney, 42.
Kenyon, 42.
Kilburn, 42.
Kilton, 42.
Kilvey, 42 103.
Kindler, 42.
King, 42 103.
Kinnecut, 42 102.
Kirby, 42.
Kirk, 42.
Kitchen, 43.
Knapp, 43.
Knight, 43.
Knowles, 43 103.
Knox, 103.

L

Ladd, 43 103.
Laird, 43.
Lake, 43.
Lambert, 43.
Lamb, 43.
Lanahan, 43.
Lancaster, 43.
Lanford, 43.
Langley, 43 103.
Langworthy, 43 103.
Larkin, 43.
Lashley, 43.
Latimore, 43.
Lawler, 43.
Lawless, 43.
Lawrence, 44.
Lawson, 44.
Laws, 44.
Lawton, 44 103.
Leach, 44 103.
Lea, 44.
Leatherin, 45.
Leathe, 45.
Ledbetter, 45.
Lee 45.
Legallais, 45.
Legrand, 45.
Leonard, 45.
Leuse, 45.
Levy, 45 103.
Lewis, 45.
Lile, 45.
Lillibridge, 45 103.
Lindsey, 45.
Littlefield, 45.
Little, 45.
Lloyd, 103.
Locke, 45.
Logan, 45.
Lord, 45.
Lovett, 45.
Lovie, 45.
Lowd, 45.
Lowden, 45.
Loyal, 45 103.
Lucas, 45.
Lunt, 45.
Luther, 46 104.
Lyman, 46 104.
Lyndon, 46 104.
Lyng, 46.
Lyon, 46 104.

M

Mackee, 46.
Mackey, 46.
Macomber, 46.
Magee, 46 104.
Magger, 46.
Magrah, 46.
Major, 46.
Malbone, 104.
Malling, 46.
Manchester, 46 104.
Manning, 46 104.
Man, 46.
Marble, 47.
Marshall, 47.
Marchant, 47 104.
Marchngton, 47.
Marcome, 47.
Mark, 104.
Marsh, 47.
Martindale, 47 104.
Martin, 47 104.
Marvin, 104.
Maryatt, 47 104 105.
Mashery, 47.
Mason, 47.
Matteson, 47.
Matthews, 47.
Mawdsley, 105.
Maxson, 47 48 105.
Maxwell, 48 105.
Maylen, 48.
Maynard, 48.
May, 48.
McAlpine, 48 105.
McCone, 48.
McCarrie, 48.
McDaniel, 48.
McDonald, 48.
McGoron, 48.
McGow, 48.
McIntosh, 48.
McMahon, 48.
Mead, 48.
Melville, 48 105.
Mense, 48.
Menhall, 48.
Merryhew, 48.
Messenger, 48.
Messer, 106.
Metcalf, 48.
Mew, 48.
Milbourne, 48.
Miles, 106.
Millerd, 48 106.
Millett, 48.
Millikin, 48.
Miller, 48 106.
Millward, 49.
Minott, 49.
Mitchell, 49 106.
Mock, 49.
Moffatt, 49.
Molton, 49.
Monkhouse, 49.
Monroe, 49 106.
Moody, 49.
Mooney, 49.
Moore, 49 106.
Moran, 49 106.
Morey, 49.
Morgan, 49.
Morran, 49.
Morris, 49.
Morse, 49 106.
Mortimer, 49.
Morton, 49 50.
Moses, 50.
Moshier, 50.
Moss, 50.
Mott, 50.
Moulton, 50.
Moyeon, 50.
Muchnear, 50.
Mulder, 50.
Mulholland, 50 106.
Mullen, 50.
Mullonox, 50.
Mumford, 50 106.
Murphy, 50.
Myers, 50.

N

Naps, 50.
Naptoli, 107.
Nason, 50.
Negre, 50.
Negri, 50.
Newburg, 107.

Newcomb, 50.
Newell, 50.
Newman, 50.
Newton, 51 107.
Nichols, 51 107.
Nicold, 51.
Nicolls, 51 107.
Nicoll, 51.
Niles, 51.
Ninegret, 51.
Nocake, 51.
Norman, 51.
Norris, 51.
Northam, 107.
Northup, 51.
Noyes, 51.
Noyce, 51 107.

O

Odlin, 51 52 107.
Oldfield, 52.
Oldham, 52.
Oliver, 52.
Olyphant, 52 107.
Oman, 52.
Openshaw, 52.
Orne, 52.
Osborne, 52 107.
Oslman, 52.
Othoman, 52.
Otis, 52 108.
Oxx, 52.

P

Paddock, 52.
Paine, 52.
Palmer, 108.
Pang, 52.
Panney, 52 108.
Parker, 52.
Parkinson, 52.
Parrot, 52.
Partelow, 52 108.
Partlow, 52.
Pashley, 52.
Pate, 52 53 108.
Patterson, 53.
Pattison, 53.
Paul, 53 108.
Peabody, 53 108.
Peace, 53.
Peacock, 53.
Pearce, 53, 108.
Peirce, 53.
Pearson, 53.
Pease, 53.
Peckham, 53 54 108 109.
Peck, 54 109.
Pedre, 54.
Peet, 54.
Pelham, 54 109.
Pendleton, 54.
Pengelly, 54.
Perkins, 54.
Perry, 54 55 109.
Peterson, 55.
Peters, 109.
Peter, 109.
Pettis, 55.
Phillips, 55 109.
Pickering, 55 109.
Pike, 55.
Pillsbury, 55.
Pinkney, 55 109.
Pinnegar, 55 110.
Pitcher, 55.
Pitman, 55 56 109 110.
Place, 56.
Platt, 56.
Pocock, 56 110.
Pollard, 56.
Poluck, 56.
Pope, 56 110.
Popplestone, 56.
Potter, 56 110.
Power, 56 110.
Pratt, 56.
Preston, 110.
Price, 56 110.
Prior, 56.
Pritchard, 56.
Proctor, 56.
Puffy, 56.
Purchase, 56 57.
Pyne, 57.

Q R

Randall, 57.
Randolph, 57 110.
Rankins, 110.
Rathbun, 57.
Rawson, 57.
Ray, 57.
Read, 57 110 111.
Records, 111.
Redfield, 57.
Redwood, 57 58 111.
Reed 58.
Reeves, 58.
Kelso, 58.
Remington, 58 111.
Remson, 58.
Retsel, 58.
Reynolds, 58.
Rhodes, 58 111 112.
Rice, 58.
Richardson, 58.
Richards, 58.
Richmond, 58 112.
Rider, 58 112.
Righton, 59.
Riley, 59.
Ring, 59.
Rix, 59.
Robbins, 59.
Roberson, 59.
Robertson, 59.
Robinson, 59 112.
Rodman, 59 112.
Rogers, 59 60 112.
Romand, 60.
Romans, 60.
Ross, 60.
Rotch, 60.
Rouse, 60.
Rumeril, 60.
Runiel, 60.
Russell, 60.
Ryan, 60.
Ryder, 60.

S

Sabin, 60 112.
St. Hlaizes, 113.
Salisbury, 60.
Sammels, 60.
Sampson, 60.
Sands, 60.
Sanford, 60 61 112 113.
Saunders, 61.
Savery, 61.
Sawdry, 61.
Sawdy, 61.
Sawin, 61.
Sayer, 61 113.
Sayes, 61.
Scott, 61 113.
Scranton, 61.
Scudder, 61.
Seabean, 113.
Seabury, 61 113.
Seals, 61.
Searing, 61.
Sears, 61.
Senter, 61.
Sereech, 62.
Sergeant, 62 113.
Servat, 113.
Sevens, 62.
Seymour, 62.
Sharp, 62.
Shaw, 62 113.
Sheen, 62.
Sheffield, 62 113 114.
Sheldon, 62.
Shelley, 62.
Shepherd 62.
Sherburne, 62 113.
Sherman 62 63 114.
Shortbridge, 63.
Short, 63.
Shoul, 63.
Shrieve, 63 114.
Silliman, 63 114.
Silvester, 63 114.
Silvery, 63.
Simmons, 63 114.
Simms, 64.
Sim, 64.
Simpkins, 64 114.
Simpson, 64 114.
Singleton, 114.
Sinkins, 64.
Sinkings, 64.
Sisson, 64 114.
Sitterly, 64.
Skinner, 114 115.
Slocum, 64 115.
Smith, 64 65 115.
Snell, 65.
Snow, 65.
Solasger, 65.
Soule, 65 115.
Southwick, 65 115.
Spars, 65.
Speare, 65 115.
Spencer, 65 66 115.
Spinney, 66.
Spooner, 66 115 116.
Sprague, 66 116.
Springer, 66 116.
Spring, 66.
Squire, 66.
Stacy, 66 116.

Stafford, 66.
Stainer, 66.
Stanhope, 66.
Stanley, 66.
Stanton, 66 67 116.
Stedman, 67.
Stephenson, 67.
Sterns, 67 116.
Stevenson, 67.
Stevens, 67 116.
Steward, 67.
Stewart, 67.
Stiles, 67 116.
Stockford, 67.
Stockman, 67 116 117.
Stoddard, 67 117.
Stonal, 67.
Stoneman, 67.
Story, 67.
Stowers, 67.
Stow, 67.
Strange, 67.
Strengthfield, 67.
Strong, 67.
Sturgess, 68.
Sullivan, 68 117.
Swan, 68 117.
Swasey, 68.
Sweeting, 68.
Sweet, 68 117.
Sylvester, 68.

T

Taber, 68.
Taggert, 68.
Tallid, 68.
Tallman, 68.
Tally, 68.
Tanner, 68 117.
Taylor, 68 69 117 118.
Tays, 69.
Tearney, 69 118.
Tefft, 118.
Telfair, 69 118
Tellforte, 69.
Terfand, 118.
Terry, 69.
Testings, 69.
Tewell, 69.
Tew, 69 118.
Thatcher, 70.
Theobald, 70.
Thiddy, 70.
Thomas, 70 118.
Thompson, 70.
Thorp, 70.
Threadkill, 70.
Thorndike, 118.
Thurston, 70 118 119.
Tibbetts, 70.
Tierney, 70.
Tiffany, 70.
Tiler, 70.
Tilley, 70 71 119.
Tillinghast, 71 119 124.
T sdale, 71.
Tomalin, 71.
Toman, 71 120.
Tomlin, 71.

Tomkins, 71.
Topham, 71.
Torrey, 71.
Tosh, 71.
Tower, 120.
Townman, 71.
Townsend, 71 72 120.
Town, 72.
Treby, 72 120.
Trevitt, 72.
Tribut, 72.
Tripp, 72.
Trowbridge, 72 120.
Tubbs, 72.
Tucker, 72.
Tuel, 72.
Turner, 72 120.
Tuttle, 72.
Tweedy, 73, 120.
Tyler, 73.

U

Udall, 73.
Underwood, 73 120.
Updike, 120.
Upham, 73.

V

Vaughn, 73 120.
Vay, 73.
Veil, 73.
Vernon, 73 120 121.
Verrier, 73.
Vial, 73.
Vickery, 73 121.
V lett, 73 121.
Vinall, 121.
Vinson, 73.
Vinton, 73.
Vose, 73.
Vroom, 73.

W

Wadsworth, 74.
Wady, 74.
Wagner, 121.
Walden, 74.
Walker, 74 121.
Walkman, 74.
Wallace, 74.
Wallen, 74.
Walsham, 74.
Wampsee, 74.
Wanton, 74 121.
Ward, 74 121 122.
Warner, 74.
Warren, 74.
Washburn, 74.
Waters, 74.
Watmaugh, 74.
Watson, 75.
Way, 75.
Weatherdon, 75.
Weatherd, 75.
Weathers, 75.
Weaver, 75 122.

Webb, 122.
Weeden, 75 122.
Weeks, 122.
Weldon, 122.
Welford, 75.
Wells, 75.
Wench, 75 122.
Westcott, 76.
Westgate, 76
Westgorth, 122.
West, 76.
Wetherell, 76 122 123.
Whaling, 123.
Wheaton, 76.
Wheeler, 76 123.
Whiley, 76.
Whipple, 76.
Whitehead, 76, 123.
Whitehouse, 76.
White, 76 123.
Whitfield, 76.
Whiting, 76.
Whitman, 76.
Whittemore, 76.
Wightman, 76 123.
Wight, 76.
Wignell, 76 123.
Wigneron, 76.
Wilbour, 76 77 123.
Wickham 77 123
Wilcox, 77.
Wiles, 77.
Wiley, 77.
Wilkey, 77 123.
W lkinson, 77.
Wilks, 77.
Willard, 77.
Willokey, 77.
Willett, 77.
Williams, 77 78 123 124.
Willing, 78.
Willis, 78.
Wills, 78.
Wilson, 78 124.
Wing, 78.
Winston, 78.
Winsor, 78.
Witherell, 78.
Woodard, 78.
Woodmansee, 78.
Woodons, 78.
Woodroff, 78.
Woodside, 78.
Woodward, 78.
Wood, 78 79.
Woolley, 79.
Wrightington, 79 124.
Wright, 79 124.
Wry, 79.
Wyatt, 79 124.
Wyles, 79.

X Y Z

Yates, 79.
Yeates, 79.
Yeats, 79.
Yeomans, 79 124.
Youldridge, 79.
Young, 79 124.

II

Names Occurring Promiscuously.

A
Adlam, 36 65.
Allen, 70.
Almy, 4 21 119.
Anthony, 77.
Appleton, 27.
Arnold, 18 74.
Avery, 53.

B
Badger, 45.
Balch, 55.
Barker, 7 24 34.
Bissell, 4.
Bliss, 3 6 9 13 28 43 47 48 55 73.
Borden, 53 65.
Bordin, 29 50 70.
Bours, 45 68.
Bradford, 12 14 31 45 52 54 67 71.
Bradley, 37.
Brady, 31.
Braman, 99.
Brierley, 25.
Brightman, 23.
Brisbane, 6.
Bronson, 71.
Brown, 5 19 31 47 76 79 106 117.
Bull, 34 49 60.
Burdick, 103.

C
Callender, 6 8 9 13 14 16 18 19 21 23 26 27 28 29 31 36 39 40 41 44 46 47 48 50 51 53 54 59 60 61 62 64 65 68 70 72 73 74 75 76 77.
Carey, 47.
Card, 45.
Carr, 30.
Chadwick, 123.
Chase, 43.
Choules, 7 44.
Church, 4.
Clarke, 3 4 15 19 20 44 111.
Coddington, 5 10 20 23 24 29 38 40 44 46 47 48 52 54 55 60 68 69 73 78.
Coggeshall, 18 22 26 57 74.
Collier, 6 71.
Cone, 14.
Coon, 19.
Corey, 13.
Cory, 22.

Cranston, 4 5 10 11 19 21 32 35 44 50 51 53 59 60 61 62 64 69 71 74 76 78.
Crocker, 72.

D
Davis, 61.
Dehan, 35.
Dentzel, 4.
Douglan, 34.
Dowling, 4.
Dumont, 3 9 25 57 63.
Dyer, 53 59 73.

E
Easton, 40 41.
Eddy, 3 6 8 11 13 14 15 19 25 27 40 53 54 55 59 62 63 64 66 67 69 70 71 75 76 77.
Ellery, 20 39.
Elton, 57 78.
Ely, 63.
Eyres, 3 5 6 7 8 9 10 11 12 13 14 15 17 18 19 20 21 22 23 24 25 26 27 28 29 30 31 32 33 34 35 36 37 38 39 40 41 42 43 44 45 46 47 48 49 50 51 52 53 54 55 56 57 58 59 60 61 62 63 64 65 66 67 68 69 70 71 72 73 74 75 76 77 78 79.

F
Fallowfield, 35.
Fitton, 5.
Fones, 26.
Foster, 56, 74.
Freeman, 16.
Fry, 13.

G
Gammell, 24 27 76.
Gano, 55.
Gardiner, 24 42 73 111.
Gavitt, 29.
Gibson, 29 32 40 43 44 49 57 58 66 72.
Gould, 6 36 47 49 51 58 75.
Griffin, 68.
Grosvenor, 75.

H
Hall, 45.
Hammett, 111.
Hammond, 80.
Harrison, 110.
Hatfield, 11 16 20 56 57 59 61.
Hazard, 15 123.
Heath, 118.
Heffernan, 41 56.
Hix, 77.
Hopkins, 4 7 13 21 24 28 31 37 40 43 60 62 64 65 69 70 74 76.
Honeyman, 7 10 11 13 16 19 22 24 27 32 35 36 41 49 53 62 68 74 76.
Howard, 8 16 17 28 30 37 41 63 67 72 73 78 79.
Howland, 60.
Hubbard, 29 67 116.
Hudson, 33 96 102.

I J
Jackson, 5 7 12 17 19 23 25 32 43 44 45 50 51 56 62 67 68 79.
Jack, 96.
Jansen, 43.
Jones, 71.

K
Kelley, 44.

L
Lawton, 10 15 18 24 25 38 48 52 56 57 76 118.
Lang, 25.
Leaming, 10.
Leaver, 5 7 10 12 13 14 21 24 30 33 34 38 39 41 47 48 50 53 54 56 60 63 64 65 67 72 74 75 77 78 79.
Leigh, 53.
Livesey, 3 6 12 23 25 31 35 37 43 57 72 75.
Longford, 111.
Long, 60.
Lord, 27 44 63.
Lovejoy, 4.

M

Mason, 6 15 23 30 34 37 39 43 55 66 97.
Matthews, 20.
Maxon, 3 9 13 18 24 27 28 32 33 39 47 58 77.
McAllister, 56.
McKensie, 4 6 7 11 33 35 37 39 42 52 65 68 78 79.
Miller, 78.
Mudge, 20.
Muir, 31.
Murphy, 110.

N

Nichols, 32 64 72.
Northam, 58.

O

O'Conner, 49.
O'Reilly, 49 69 70.
Othman, 3 4 8 10 14 31 32 35 40 48 63 67 73 75 78.

P

Patten, 20 25 49 57 78.
Peirce, 66.
Phelan, 10.
Potter, 4 16 17 33 46 54.

Q R

Richardson, 40 97.
Richards, 81.
Robbins, 39 95.
Rogers, 14 41 53 58 59.
Ross, 7 19 30 63.
Rush, 42.

S

Searing, 3 4 8 9 10 11 12 14 17 20 22 24 25 26 27 28 31 33 34 36 37 38 40 41 42 43 45 46 48 49 50 51 52 53 54 55 56 58 59 60 63 66 67 68 69 70 71 72 77 79.
Sheekey, 21.
Sheffield, 31, 39, 64.
Shepherd, 34, 42.
Sherman, 111.
Silvester, 15 17 19 20 43 54 63 70.
Slocum, 15 69 101.
Smith, 3 12 19 24 25 32 34 36 38 40 45 53 64 68.
Snow, 43.
Spaulding, 58.
Spencer, 75.
Stewart, 72.
Stiles, 3 4 5 6 9 12 13 14 16 17 18 19 22 23 24 25 27 28 29 30 32 33 34 35 36 37 38 39 42 44 47 48 49 51 52 54 57 58 59 60 61 63 64 65 66 67 68 69 72 73 74 75 77 78 79.
Stoddard, 10 38 63 78.
Stone, 59.
Swan, 112.

T

Taylor, 16 60 111 119.
Thayer, 3 5 7 9 12 17 21 22 23 24 25 27 28 29 30 31 33 34 35 36 37 39 40 42 43 44 45 47 48 49 51 52 53 54 56 57 58 59 60 61 65 68 69 70 72 73 75 78.
Thurston, 3 4 5 6 7 8 9 10 11 12 13 14 15 16 17 18 19 20 21 23 24 26 28 29 30 31 32 33 34 35 36 37 39 40 41 42 43 44 45 46 47 48 49 50 51 52 53 54 55 56 57 58 59 60 61 62 63 64 65 66 67 68 69 70 71 72 74 75 76 77 78 79.
Tilley, 110.
Tillinghast, 47, 71.
Towle, 37 41 42 54 55 66 69 75.
Troop, 29.
Truro, 36.
Tucker, 19 29.
Tustin, 29.
Tyng, 57.

U

Updike, 71.
Upham, 9 11 34 35 44 46.

V

Vaughn, 105.
Vernon, 78.
Vesey, 10.
Vinall, 4 5 6 7 8 9 10 11 12 15 17 20 22 23 24 25 26 28 34 35 41 42 45 47 49 52 56 58 61 65 66 71 75 78.
Vinton, 5 6 12 13 16 22 23 25 28 31 35 36 42 55 63 67 73.
Vose, 102.

W

Walden, 56.
Wanton, 21 26 32 68.
Ward, 58 59 67.
Waterhouse, 31 47 52 69.
Webb, 22 39 40.
Weeden, 22.
West, 3 22 44 66.
Wight, 20.
Willard, 50.
Wilson, 77.
Winson, 27.

X Y Z

III

Names of Places.

A

Albany, N. Y., 48.
Alexander Co., 31.
Antigua, W. I., 74 111.

B

Baltimore, Md., 81.
Barbadoes, W. I., 56.
Barrington, R. I., 3.
Berwick, Mass., 49.
Block Island, 71.
Boston, Mass., 6 9 13 14 17 20 24 28 34 48 66 67 69.
Bristol, Conn., 7.
Bristol, R. I., 13 16 22 29 34 52 53 68.
Brooklyn, N. Y., 32 57.
Brunswick, Me., 45.

C

Cambridge, Mass., 27.
Charleston, S. C., 52.

Charlestown, Brooke Co., Va., 119.
Charlestown, R. I., 13 21 27 51 54.
Chester Co., 53.
Chilmarth, Mass., 57.
Clintonville, Mass., 19.
Company C 2d Regt., N. Y. H. A., 118.
Connecticut, 66 78.
Constantinople, Turkey, 8.
County Sligo, Ire., 34.
Coventry, R. I., 44.
Coventry, Warwick Co., Eng., 106.
Cranston, R. I., 5.
Cumberland, R. I., 21.

D

Dartmouth, Mass., 4 23 77 98 105 123.
Demerara, W. I., 50.
Dighton, Mass., 40.
Dossetshire, Eng., 10.
Dublin, Ire., 96.

E

East Greenwich, R. I., 37 39 65 75.
Easton, Mass., 38.
England, 96.
Exeter, R. I., 7 66.

F

Fall River, Mass., 9 10 23 36 39 56 58 77.
Falmouth, Mass., 82.
Foster, R. I., 42.
Foxboro, Mass., 12.
France, 62.
Freetown, Mass., 16 36 53 57 67.
French Co., 77.
Friends Bur'l place Newport, 191.

G

Gardiner, Me., 31.
Gaudeloupe, W. I., 97.
Georgetown, D. C., 59.
Glastenburytown, 17.
Glocester, R. I., 77.
Great Britain, 38.
Greenland, N. H., 55.
Greenwich, 37.

H

Halifax, N. S., 14 98.
Harwich, Mass., 18.
Hopkinton, R. I., 43 54.
Huntington, Conn., 63.

I

Ireland, 5 59.

J

Jamaica, W. I., 29.
Jamestown, R. I., 5 8 15 26 28 38 39 44 51 59 62 64 66 113 116.
Johnston, R. I., 27.

K

Killingly, Conn., 9.
Kings Towne, R. I., 26 51.
Kittery, Me., 120.

L

Lebanon, Conn., 43 103.
Liberty ship, 99.
Little Compton, R. I., 11 23 33 53 62.
London, Eng., 63 77 123.
Los Angeles, Cal., 57.
Lowell, Mass., 5.
Lynn., Mass., 13.

M

Marblehead, Mass., 45.
Mayflower ship, 101.
Middleboro, Mass., 62 79.
Middletown, R. I., 9 12 13 14 16 19 26 29 30 31 33 38 40 42 43 45 46 47 52 53 54 57 64 65 73 75 111.
Milford, Conn., 44.
Morrstown, N J., 25.
Mystic, Conn., 17.

N

Nantes, France, 113.
Nantucket, Mass., 87.
New Bedford, Mass., 3 56 58.
Newburne, N. C., 42.
New Hampshire, 76.
New Haven, Conn., 67.
New Jersey, 12 76.
New London, Conn., 24 43 74 92.
New Providence, Bahama Isle, 6.
New Shoreham, R. I., 4 25 38 49 69 103.
New York, 12 14 38 40 43 47 52 57 58.
Northampton, Mass., 67.
North Carolina, 37 97.
North Kingstown, R. I., 10 26 30 39 40 50 51 54 65 68 72 80 117

Norwich, Conn., 45.

O

Oblong, N. Y., 99.
Orange Co., 41.

P

Pawtucket, R. I., 3
Pennsylvania, 58 65.
Philadelphia, Pa., 29 54 55 78 114.
Plymouth, N. H., 28.
Port au Prince, W. I., 88.
Portland, Me., 35.
Portsmouth, R. I., 3 4 6 15 17 21 27 28 29 34 44 48 50 58 62 64 67 69 89 97 116 118.
Providence, R. I., 5 6 13 16 19 21 23 26 28 29 31 33 36 38 41 42 47 53 54 55 58 59 63 65 72 74 79 95 101.

Q

Quakertown, Pa., 81.
Quincy, Mass., 44.

R

Rehoboth, Mass., 42 81.
Rellngton, Conn., 27.
Richmond, Va., 57.
Roxbury, Mass., 25.

S

St Christopher, W. I., 16.
St Thomas, W. I., 121.
Salem, Mass., 26 60 69 111.
Sandwich, Mass., 3 9 50.
San Francisco, Cal., 25.
Savannah, Ga., 31.
Scituate, Mass., 7.
Scotland, 9 49.
Seekonk, Mass., 23.
Ship Liberty, 99.
Smithfield, R. I., 23 29 58.
Somerset, Mass., 21 22 40 52.
South Carolina, 34 97.
South Kingstown, R. I., 6 7 14 17 31 36 56 62 67 75 76 124.
Stamford, Conn., 94.
Stonington, Conn., 51.
Swansey, Mass., 10 15 27 32 48 53 59 60 78 84 99.
Sweden, 5.
Syracuse, N. Y., 48.

Taa River, China, 105.
Tauton, Mass., 28 59 78.
Tiverton, R. I., 4 6 20 21 29 50 74 84.
Truro, Mass., 5.

U

United States Army, 47.
United States Navy 72.
United States 2d Art., 5.

V

Vermont, 73.
Virginia, 117.

W

Walpole, Mass., 99.
Warren, R. I., 17 29 37 76.
Warwick, R. I., 33 35 53 71 111.
Washington, D. C., 77.
Waterbury Co., Kerry, Ire., 21.
Weathersfield, Conn., 75.
Westerly, R. I., 9 19 22 52 89.
Westfield, Mass., 75.
Westport Mass., 16.
West Williamstown, Mass., 75.
Wickford, R. I., 29.
Windham, Conn., 28 43.

X Y Z

Yarmouth, Mass., 32.

NEWPORT.

MARRIAGES.

A

171	ACHFORTH	Mary, and Samuel Crapon, Feb. 20, 1755.
48	ACRES	Margaret, and Daniel Tosh, Oct. 19, 1686.
1-44	ADAMS	John, of Barrington, son of Samuel and Catherine Burdick, of James; m. by Elder William Bliss, May 10, 1795.
1-54	AIKEN	Joseph, and Rachel Miller (widow); m. at New Bedford, Mass., by Rev. Samuel West, July 20, 1779.
1-54	"	Rachel, and George Monroe, March 6, 1785.
215	ALBRO	Samuel, and Rebecca Weeden; m. by Elder John Maxson, Sept. 13, 1764.
1-104	"	Sarah, and Benjamin Downing, Nov. 9, 1809.
2-2	"	Caleb, J., of Portsmouth, and Martha S. Taylor, of Newport; m. by Rev. A. Henry Damont (also 2-9), June 27, 1839.
1-130	"	John F., of Newport, and Elmira Burden, of Pawtucket; m. by Rev. Michael Eddy, Sept. 26, 1833.
2-13	"	Rhoda J., and Oliver J. Dawler, Feb. 7, 1841.
2-28	"	Silas, and Nancy Murphy; m. by Rev. Thatcher Thayer, Aug. 20, 1844.
2-30	"	Thomas L., of Portsmouth, and Mary G. Mitchell, of Sandwich, Mass.; m. by Rev. Richard Livsey (also 2-32), Aug. 19, 1847.
2-32	"	Samuel M., of Portsmouth, son of Peleg and Mary O. Moulton, of Newport, dau. of Sidney S.; m. by Rev. B. Othman, Nov. 15, 1849.
239	ALLBUN	Patience, and Samuel Corbett, June 15, 1747.
151	ALDEN	Lydia, and James Rem —Aug. 19, 1745.
190	ALDRIDGE	Mary, and George Simpkins, Aug. 25, 1765.
57	ALLEN	Sarah, and Joseph Peabody, Dec. 27, 1711.
148	"	Benjamin, and Sarah Hoockey; m. by Rev. Nicholas Eyres, March 24, 1712-3.
58	"	Rowland, and Miriam Bull; m. by Peleg Smith, Justice, Oct. 30, 1722.
121	"	Elizabeth, and Peleg Clarke, Sept. 25, 1740.
151	"	Timothy, and Alice Anthony; m. by Rev. James Searing, June 17, 1744.
141	"	Susanna, and John Davis, Aug. 20, 1747.
239	"	Mary, and Edward Morse, Sept. 15, 1747.
142	"	William, and —— Franklin, —— 23, 1750.
232	"	——, and Hannah Hammond, recorded May 28, 1751.
229	"	Robert, and Elizabeth Ballard; m. by Jeremiah Clarke, Justice, Dec. 28, 1756.
199	"	Comfort, and Merion Millward; m. by Rev. Gardiner Thurston, Aug. 19, 1759.
188	"	Christopher, and Martha Arnold; m. by Rev. Ezra Stiles, Feb. 10, 1760.
148	"	Elizabeth, and John Shaw, June 21, 1764.
3	"	Richard, and Susanna ——, A— 13, ——.
145	"	Ann, and Richard Hinyard, Aug. 18, ——.
1-52	"	Joseph, and Mary Taggart; m. by Rev. Gardiner Thurston, Jan. 21, 1780.

1-33	ALLEN	William Samuel Newton, and Abigail Westgate; m. by Rev. Samuel Hopkins, June 27, 1784.
1-68	"	William, Jr., and Mehitable Church; m. by Rev. William Potter, June 15, 1806.
1-136	"	Clarissa R., and George Kenyon, March 3, 1839.
2-11	"	John N., and Rosannah R. Dickens; m. by Rev. James A. McKenzie, Nov. 5, 1839.
2-36	"	Mrs. Susan, and George J. Lewis, Oct. 24, 1845.
2-30	"	Eliza, and Thomas Read (also 2-32), July 6, 1847.
2-34	"	Caroline M., and Thomas J. Champlain, Dec. 12, 1848.
2-31	"	William, and Jane R. Thorp; m. by Rev. B. Othman, June 14, 1849.
2-49	"	Jeremiah, of New Shoreham, and Phebe R. Simmons, of Newport; m. by Rev. John Lovejoy, March 5, 1854.
191	ALLISON	Elizabeth, and William Dykes, Jan. 8, 1767.
205	ALL	Isaac, and Elizabeth Franklin; m. by Rev. William Vinall, March 19, 1761.
13	ALMY	——, son of Job, dec., of Portsmouth, and Bridget Sanford, of Peleg, dec., of Newport; m. by Samuel Cranston, Governor, Dec. 6, 1703.
15	"	Christopher, Jr., of Portsmouth, and —— ——, — 8, 1705.
19	"	Ann, and Joseph Whipple, about 1708.
68	"	John, and Anstice Ellery, Aug. —, 1716.
43	"	Christopher, of Job, of Newport, and Elizabeth Almy, of Tiverton; m. at Tiverton, by Thomas Church, Justice, April 30, 1720.
43	"	Elizabeth, and Christopher Almy, April 30, 1720.
59	"	Elizabeth, and William Ellery, Jan. 3, 1722-3.
117	"	Austress, and Thomas Coggeshall, — 30, 1735.
130	"	John, and Mary ——; m. by James Clarke, Justice, Dec. 6, 1739.
121	"	——, and Peleg Barker, June 25, 1740.
183	"	Job, Jr., of Newport, and Alice Slocum, of Holden, of Dartmouth, Mass.; m. by Job Almy, Justice, Jan. 27, 1742-3.
103	"	Joshua, and Mary Bassett, ——, 1725 (?)
1-13	"	Austress, and Benjamin Almy, May 22, 1751.
1-13	"	Benjamin, of John, and Austress Almy; m. by Rev. James Searing, May 22, 1751.
102	"	Benjamin, of John and Austress, and Sarah Coggeshall, of Thomas and Sarah; m. by Rev. James Searing (also 117), May 22, 1751.
188	"	Austress, and —— ——; m. by Rev. Ezra Stiles, ——, 1758.
1-13	"	Benjamin, and Mary Gould; m. by Rev. George Bissell, Oct. 27, 1762.
1-43	"	Jonathan, and Elizabeth Hammond, May 14, 1770.
117	"	Benjamin, and Mary Gould; m. by Rev. George Bissell, April 8, 1772.
1-68	"	Sarah, and William Edward Tillinghast, May 30, 1782.
1-35	"	Elizabeth, and Samuel Vernon Testins, Dec. 31, 1784.
1-43	"	Jonathan, and Elizabeth Perry; m. by Rev. Gardiner Thurston, Jan. 20, 1796.
1-62	"	Elizabeth, and Daniel W. Barker, Aug. 9, 1797.
1-55	"	Mary, and Henry Downing, Aug. 11, 1799.
236	"	Austress, and Thomas Coggeshall, ———.
1-44	"	Phebe, and Paine Hammond, Oct. 19, 1803.
1-103	"	Mary, and Dr. William Richardson, May 4, 1815.
2-52	"	Frances R., and Alexander Barker, Dec. 1, 1831.
2-47	"	Gideon, and Abby B. Freeborn; m. by Rev. John Dowling, Oct. 12, 1834.
2-3	"	C. A., and R. O. Bush, July 3, 1839.
2-33	"	Thomas T., of Middletown, and Frances T. Barker, of Restcome; m. by Rev. B. Othman, March 17, 1850.
118	ALSWORTH	Mary, and Philip Haynes, May 25, 1755.
2-1	AMBROSE	Eliza M., and William D Boss, Dec. 29, 1838.
1-11	ANCEAUX	Nicholas, and Lydia Richardson, of Thomas; m. by Rev. G. H. Dentzel, March 19, 1781.
157	ANDERSON	James, and Ann Champlain (also 204); m. by Rev. Gardiner Thurston, Oct. 20, 1760.

NEWPORT—MARRIAGES.

2-13	ANDERSON Harriet, and Peter Hazard (col.), May 28, **1840**.	
2-26	" Andrew, of Sweden, and Margaret Doyle, of Ireland; m. by Rev. James Fitton, May 4, 1847.	
153	ANDREWS Thomas, and Hannah Williams; m. by Rev. Nicholas Eyres, Aug. 18, 1751.	
2-13	ANGELL Samuel M., of Cranston, and Mary A. Bates, of Newport; m. by Rev. Thomas Leaver, Jan. 6, 1841.	
151	ANTHONY Alice, and Timothy Allen, June 17, 1744.	
169	" Elizabeth, and Gilbert Stewart, May 23, 1751.	
154	" Sarah, and Remembrance Simmons, Sept. 20, 1751.	
205	" Joseph, and Elizabeth Sheffield; m. by Rev. Gardiner Thurston, March 11, 1761.	
148	" Mary, and Benjamin ———; m. by Rev. Nicholas Eyres, May 3, **1763**.	
158	" James, and Elizabeth Cornell, Aug. 15, 1768.	
1-58	" Elizabeth, and John W. Thurston, March 24, 1800.	
1-128	" Mary Ann, and Robert C. Sisson, Oct. 31, 1830.	
2-54	" Elizabeth, and Jonathan Sherman, Nov. 7, 1838.	
2-15	" Henry, and Ann A. House; m. by Rev. Thomas Leaver, Aug. 28, 1842.	
2-24	" Catherine B., and Benjamin H. Peckham, Dec. 25, 1845.	
2-33	" Elizabeth C., and George A. Brown, Dec. 3, 1849.	
153	ARMSTRONG John, and Abigail Thomas; m. by Rev. Nicholas Eyres, July 13, 1749.	
170	" Elizabeth, and Peter Bowden, March 15, 1753.	
1-134	" Alice H., and Dr. Stephen Champlain, Nov. 4, 1838.	
2-30	" Thomas, and Mary Milbourne; m. by Rev. Thatcher Thayer, Feb. 8, 1847.	
82	ARES Peter, and Sarah King; m. by James Brown, Justice, Feb. 26, 1712-3.	
40	ARNOLD Sion, of Benedict, and Mary Ward, of Thomas, dec.; m. by Samuel Cranston, Governor, Feb. 7, 1700.	
6	" Content, and William Coddington, Oct. 12, 1700.	
13	" Abigail, and Jonathan Lewis, ——— 14, 1704-5.	
13	" Benedict, of Benedict, Jr., and Patience Coggeshall, Jan. 23, 1705.	
81	" Ann, and John Chace, Sept. 20, 1713.	
88	" Oliver, and Elizabeth Card, of Joseph; m. by James Brown, Asst., June 15, 1715.	
139	" Elizabeth, and John Thompson, July 29, 1742.	
152	" Abigail, and James Rogers, Sept. 28, 1746.	
102	" Elizabeth, and Nathaniel Taylor, June 7, 1750.	
203	" Eliphal, and John Smith, June 30, 1757.	
203	" Thomas, and Eliphal Wyatt; m. by Rev. William Vinall, Sept. 16, 1757.	
188	" Joseph, and Penelope Bennett; m. by Rev. Ezra Stiles, July 24, 1759.	
188	" Martha, and Christopher Allen, Feb. 10, 1760.	
205, 227	" Mary, and John Carr, July 19, 1761.	
206	" Mary, and Samuel Spooner, ——— 6, 1763.	
1-36	" Josiah, of Jamestown, and Mary Brinley, of Newport; m. by Nathaniel Coddington, Asst., Feb. 12, 1784.	
2-15	" Lewis Golden, U. S. 2d Artillery, and Julia Mandock Lowd; m. by Rev. Francis Vinton, June 27, 1843.	
242	ASH Thomas, and Hannah Vickery, ———, 1749.	
238	" Mary, and Sylvester Johnson, Nov. 23, 1751.	
118	" Elizabeth, and William Exceene, Sept. 13, 1755.	
2-29	ASKER Ann, and James Graham, Nov. 26, 1845.	
2-29	" Mary, and James Monkhouse, Nov. 26, 1845.	
149	ASHBROOK Elizabeth, and William Javery, ———, 1743.	
2-27	ASHLEY Joseph, of Providence, and Lydia Waterman, of Newport; m. by Rev. Thatcher Thayer, Oct. 24, 1843.	
169, 234	ATKINSON Ann, and Cary Dunn, Nov. 1, 1754.	
190	" John, and Hannah Clarke; m. by Rev. Gardiner Thurston, Dec. 26, 1765.	
2-34	" James Henry, of Lowell, Mass., and Sarah D. T. Denham, of Newport; m. by Rev. Henry Jackson, Oct. 23, 1848.	

155	ATKINS Elizabeth, and John Chilson, April 26, 1754.
2-30	" Daniel, of Truro, Mass., and Caroline M. Thurston, of Newport; m. by Rev. Richard Livsey, March 19, 1848.
105	ATTWOOD Edward, and Mary Phillips; m. by Rev. Nicholas Eyres, July 12, 1750.
188	" Thomas, and Lydia Pinckney; m. by Rev. Ezra Stiles, April 23, 1761.
148	" Mary, and Eleazer Read, Oct. 11, 1763.
1-101	AUCHMUTZ Harriet Barton, and Julius Frederick Heilman; May 10, 1814.
121	AUSTIN Esther, and John Barney; Aug. 12, 1739.
119	" Thomas, and Niobe Moss; m. by Rev. Nicholas Eyres, Aug. 14, 1746.
204	" Ann, and Daniel Austin; Aug. 3, 1760.
204	" Daniel, and Ann Austin; m. by Rev. Gardiner Thurston, Aug. 3, 1760.
2-71	" Lucy Ann, and Willett Anthony Barber; Feb. 14, 1840.
119	AXTON John, and Ruth Foster; m. by Rev. Nicholas Eyres, ———, 1746.
239	AYRES Esther, and Benjamin Clarke; Nov. 19, 1749.
102	" Sarah, and Jonathan Jeffries; Sept. 6, 1751.

B

124	BABCOCK Hezekiah, of South Kingstown, and Mary Peckham, of Newport; m. by Daniel Gould, Justice, Jan. 3, 1739-40.
191	" Robert, and Elizabeth Tibbetts; m. by Rev. Gardiner Thurston, Feb. 5, 1767.
1-119	" Brenton E., of South Kingstown, and Rhoda Clarke, of Newport; m. by Rev. Michael Eddy, Oct. 21, 1830.
2-5	" Sarah, and William Henry Marsh, Nov. 14, 1840.
2-14	BACHELOR Thomas Gillmore, of Boston, Mass., and Charlotte Viall Brown, of Newport; m. by Rev. Francis Vinton, March 8, 1842.
1-56	" James Gould Almy, and Martha Matilda Bowles; m. at New Providence, Bahama Islands, by Rev. James Brisbane, Aug. 4, 1792.
187	BAGGS Phebe, and Royal Lawton (also 188), Sept. 23 or 27, 1762.
6	BAILY Sarah, and Samuel Dunn, Oct. 8, 1702.
132	" Anna, and Samuel Vaughn, June 27, 1742.
149	" Joseph, and —— Sanford; m. by Rev. John Callender, Jr., May 26, 1743.
141	" Elizabeth, and Latham Clarke, Dec. 24, 1747.
141	" Barzillai, and Elizabeth Sanford, July 11, 1748.
203	" Lydia, and John Dunscombe, July 17, 1758.
208	" Richard, and Hannah Shrieve; m. by Rev. John Mason, Sept. 7, 1766.
1-33	" Deborah, and Daniel Sheldon, Nov. 28, 1784.
1-47	" Thomas, of Providence, son of Oliver, and Fanny Burdick, of James, of Portsmouth; m. by Elder William Bliss, Sept. 24, 1795.
1-60	" Lemuel, of Tiverton, son of Oliver, and Amey Fry, of John, of Newport; m. by Rev. William Collier, April 28, 1800.
153	BAKER Desire, and Burgess Thomas, Aug. 10, 1749.
188	" Benjamin, and Martha Simpson; m. by Rev. Ezra Stiles, Jan. 23, 1759.
148	" Benjamin, and Mary Pettis; m. by Rev. Nicholas Eyres, Feb. 4, 1764.
232	" Sarah, and William Haliburton ——— 19, ———.
2-33	" David G., and Sarah M. Whiley; m. by Elder James A. McKenzie, July 11, 1839.
203	BALCH Timothy, and Sarah Rogers; m. by Rev. William Vinal, Nov. 29, 1757.
229	BALLARD Elizabeth, and Robert Allen, Dec. 28, 1756.
205	" Elizabeth, and Oliver Beere ——— 21, 1758.
2-16	BALL Elizabeth M., and Joseph J. Holmes, Dec. 27, 1843.
188	BANNEL Sarah, and —— ——; m. by Rev. Ezra Stiles, ———, 1758.

56	BANKS Bathsheba, and Peter Bours, Jan. 6, 1704-5.
2-27	" ——, and John Smith, Feb. ——, 1843.
2-27	" Ann, and William Eustis, March ——, 1843.
3-33	" Fanny, and Stephen C. Jack, Nov. 25, 1849.
1-114	BANNISTER Sylvia, and Benjamin Johnson, July 14, 1816.
190	BANON William, and Ann Humphrey; m. by Gardiner Thurston, ——, 1766.
170	BANTIN John, and Margaret Huffman; m. by Rev. Nicholas Eyres, Feb. 19, 1753.
1-33	BAPTISTER Michael, and Betsey Clarke; m. by Rev. Samuel Hopkins, July 3, 1785.
171	BARBER Thomas, of Exeter, and Mary Barney, of Newport; m. by Rev. Nicholas Eyres, Oct. 22, 1754.
205	" Jerusha, and Jethro Spooner, March 26, 1761.
109	" Mercy, and Jacob Billet, ——, 28, ——.
2-71	" Willett Anthony, of South Kingstown, and Lucy Ann Austin, of Newport; m. by Rev. Arthur A. Ross, Feb. 14, 1840.
2-9	" William, and Phebe R. Simmons; m. by Rev. Thomas Leaver, April 24, 1842.
93	BARDIN Charles, and Ann Coan; m. by Rev. James Honeyman, —— 18, 1735.
154	" James, and Lydia Thomas, Dec. 29, 1751.
177	" Amey, and Samuel Goldthwait, Feb. 12, 1761.
109	BARILL Mary, and Thomas Crosby ——.
2-29	BARKENSHAW Jonathan, and Grace Ingham; m. by Rev. Thatcher Thayer, Dec. 14, 1845.
18	BARKER ——, late of Scituate, Mass., and Anne Carr, of —— and Waite; m. by Edward Thurston, Justice, Jan. 18, 1709.
97	" Prescilla, and John Clarke, Aug. 29, 1728.
235	" Phebe, and William Peckham, Jr., Jan. 22, 1735-6.
121	" Peleg, and —— Almy; m. by Rev. Nicholas Eyres, June 25, 1740.
119	" Sarah, and Joseph Howland, —— 14, 1745.
172	" Jeremiah, Jr., and Elizabeth Coombes; m. by Rev. Nicholas Eyres, Sept. 19, 1756.
203	" Peleg, and Elizabeth Cook; m. by Rev. William Vinal, May 11, 1758.
147	" Peleg, and Mary Stevens; m. by Rev. Nicholas Eyres, —— 21, 1762.
1-41	" Peleg, Jr., and Mary Carr, Dec. 25, 1765.
116	" Peleg, and —— Wilcox; m. by Rev. Gardiner Thurston, April 5, 1768.
1-62	" Daniel W., and Elizabeth Almy, of Jonathan, Aug. 9, 1797.
1-86	" Abraham, and Ruth Fish, May 16, 1802.
1-95	" Mary M., and George Freeborn, Aug. 28, 1808.
2-52	" Alexander, and Frances R. Almy; m. by Rev. Mr. Choules, Dec. 1, 1831.
2-17	" Cynthia M., and George W. Friend, May 28, 1843.
2-2	" David G., and Sarah M. Wiley; m. by Elder James A. McKinsie, July 11, 1839.
2-33	" Frances T., and Thomas T. Almy, March 17, 1850.
2-46	" Patience H., and Philip B. Smith, March 29, 1865.
2-32	BARLOW Thomas, and Mary W. Lawton, Sept. 26, 1847.
147	BARNES Benjamin, and Ann Remington; m. by Rev. Nicholas Eyres, ——, 1762.
2-29	" Joseph, and Eliza Marchington; m. by Rev. Thatcher Thayer, Dec. 25, 1845.
2-37	" Alphonso, and Caroline M. Tuttle, both of Bristol, Conn.; m. by Rev. Henry Jackson, Aug. 5, 1851.
121	BARNEY John, and Esther Austin; m. by Rev. Nicholas Eyres, Aug. 12, 1739.
171	" Mary, and Thomas Barber, Oct. 22, 1754.
169	BARSTOW Elizabeth, and Nathaniel Coggeshall (also 201, 234), Feb. 27, 1755.
1-26	BASS Edward, and Elizabeth Legrand; m. by Peleg Barker, Justice, Oct. 5, 1785.

74	BARTON Sarah, and John Loyall, recorded Nov. 23, 1727.
282	BASKELL Susanna, and Richard Nichols, Nov. 16, ——.
205	BASIL Philip, and Susanna Moses; m. by Rev. Gardiner Thurston, March 15, 1761.
181	BASSETT William, and Mary Hammett; m. by Rev. Nicholas Eyres, Oct. 7, 1736.
103	" Mary, and Joshua Almy, ——, 1745 (?)
200	" Mary, and William Gardiner, Dec. 5, 1759.
2-27	" Susan, and Henry Culler, July 3, 1843
2-4	BATES John, of Newport, and Hannah F. Carr, of Jamestown; m. at Jamestown by Rev. Leland Howard, Nov. 7, 1839.
2-13	" Mary, and Samuel M. Angell, Jan. 6, 1841.
2-31	" William B., and Harriet Simmons; m. by Rev. B. Othman, April 1, 1849.
172	BATTEY Jane, and Benjamin Sayer (also 1-8), May 1, 1757.
234	" Jane, and Benjamin Taylor, May 1, 1757.
204	" John, and Ann Daten; m. by Rev. Gardiner Thurston, Dec. 28, 1760.
2-56	BATTLE Ellen, and Patrick Grier, Jan. 18, 1820.
1-3	BATTS Benjamin, and Barbara Stafford; m. by Rev. Gardiner Thurston, May 23, 1782.
142	BAXTER Sarah, and Peleg Moore, Nov. 6, 1751.
142	" Alice, and Robert Lillibridge, Jan. 28, 1753.
209	" Mary, and Benjamin Wilson, Jan. 4, 1763.
177	" Thomas, and Mary Gubbins, March 13, 1763.
1-39	BAYLEY Thomas, and Margeret Writington, Jan. 20, 1719-20.
1-2	BAY Phebe, and John Phillips, May 10, 1782.
145	BA—— Lewis, and Mary Fry; m. by Rev. Nicholas Eyres, Oct. 15, ——.
157	BEARDIN Elizabeth, and Thomas Weaver, Jan. 27, 1765.
148	BEEBE Sarah, and Job Howland, Sept. 12, 1763.
191	" Daniel, and Lydia Stanton; m. by Rev. Gardiner Thurston, April 26, 1767.
218	BEERE Charles, and Hannah Hoockey, Aug. 6, 1738.
149	" Rachel, and Patrick Farrell, Jan. 14, 1742.
102	" Hannah, and John Cahoone, —— —, 1751.
205	" Oliver, and Elizabeth Ballard; m. by Rev. William Vinal, —— 21, 1758.
141	BELCHER Edward, and Lydia Howland, June 22, 1747.
102	" Joseph, and Hannah Gladding; m. by Rev. James Searing, Feb. 14, 1751.
155	" Phebe, and Henry Perkins, Aug. 8, 1755.
190	" Elizabeth, and Thomas Cox, Aug. 17, 1766.
1-21	" Sarah, and Andre Geoffery, July 24, 1785.
149	BELDEN Thomas, and —— ——; m. by Rev. Nicholas Eyres, Aug. 26, 1742.
205	BELL Edmund and Elizabeth Wady; m. by Rev. Gardiner Thurston, Jan. 4, 1761.
209	" Phebe, and Ezekiel Cundall, March 6, 1763.
191	" William, and Sarah Thurston; m. by Rev. Gardiner Thurston, Dec. 15, 1766.
2-7	" Mary M., and William K. Stanton, Nov. 25, 1841.
2-29	" Jane, and George Theoball, Sept. 25, 1846.
2-33	" Richard Frederick, and Jane Wiley; m. by Rev. B. Othman, March 17, 1850.
1-122	BENJAMIONS Antony, of Constantinople, Turkey, and Emeline Bliven, of Newport; m. by Rev. Michael Eddy, Aug. 31, 1828.
149	BENNETT John, and Lydia Bennett; m. by Rev. Nicholas Eyres, July 20, 1741.
149	" Lydia, and John Bennett, July 20, 1741.
219	" Honora, and Daniel Kinnecutt; (also 140), Aug. 5, 1741.
150	" Job, and Mary ——; m. by Rev. John Callender, Jr., ——, 1741.
151	" William, and Bethia Gardiner; m. by Rev. James Searing, Jan. 16, 1742-3.
149	" Frances, and Benjamin Nichols, —— —, 1743.
153	" Anthony, and Freelove Coggeshall; m. by Rev. Nicholas Eyres, Aug. 16, 1750.
153	" Elizabeth, and Solomon Treby, Sept. 2, 1750.

102	BENNETT Anstress, and Benjamin Ingraham, ——, 1754.
172	" Job, and Abigail Dyer; m. by Rev. Nicholas Eyres; (also 234), April 10, 1757.
172	" Lydia, and Ebenezer Burrell; (also 234), May 1, 1757.
188	" Penelope, and Joseph Arnold, July 24, 1759.
204	" Mary, and James Clarke, Dec. 23, 1761.
147	" ——, and Thomas ——; m. by Rev. Nicholas Eyres, Sept. 5, 1762.
190	" Merebah, and John Clarke, ——, 1766.
191	" Nancy, and Peter Marshall, June 21, 1767.
179	" Job, of Capt. Job, dec., and Patience Burdick (widow), dau. of Edward Bliven, of Westerly; m. by Elder John Maxson, June ——, 1768.
122	" Joseph, and Mary Peckham; m. by Rev. John Callender, Jr., Sept. 25, ——.
2-12	" Tabor, of Fall River, Mass., and Pamelia Harrington, of Killingly, Conn.; m. by Rev. A. Henry Dumont, April 12, 1860.
65	BERNON Jane, and Col. William Coddington, Oct. 11, 1722.
136	BENSON William, and Sarah W——; m. by Rev. John Callender, Jr., June 5, 1740.
150	" Elizabeth, and William Clarke, Oct. 5, 1741.
151	" John Kendrick, and Ann Hinckley; m. by Rev. James Searing, June 13, 1745.
136	" William, and Frances Gardiner; m. by Rev. John Callender, Jr., Oct. 3, 1745.
122	" William, and Sarah Wilson; m. by Rev. John Callender, Jr., —— 5, ——.
203	BENTLEY William, and Sarah Pitman; m. by Rev. William Vinall, Nov. 18, 1756.
44	BERRY Alice, and John Weaver, March 15, 1710.
149	BIDDER Hannah, and George Lawton, April 18, 1742.
209	BIGGS Alexander, of Scotland, and Elizabeth ——, of Newport; m. by Rev. Ezra Stiles, Sept. 9, 1766.
2-27	BIGLEY Martha E., and Stephen A. Gardiner, Sept. 26, 1842.
109	BILLET Jacob, and Mercy Barber; m. by Rev. Nicholas Eyres, —— 28, ——.
205	BILLINGS Samuel Little, and Elizabeth Vinson; m. by Rev. Gardiner Thurston, April 21, 1761.
191	" William, and Phebe Borden; m. by Rev. Gardiner Thurston, May 3, 1767.
1-71	BIRD Clarissa, and Christopher Ellery, Oct. 22, 1792.
209	BISSELL Job, and Martha Stevens; m. by Rev. Ezra Stiles, June 26, 1764.
148	BLACON Michael, and Amey Greenwood; m. by Rev. Nicholas Eyres, Jan. 8, 1764.
155	BLAKE Susannah, and Moses Thompson, March 23, 1755.
2-28	BLACKLIN Charles, of Boston, and Mary Ann Patterson, of Newport; m. by Rev. Thatcher Thayer, May 13, 1844.
187	BLACKWELL Samuel, of Sandwich, Mass., and Chloe Dennis, of Newport; m. by Rev. Ezra Stiles, Oct. 25, 1756.
102	BLANCHARD Caleb, of Boston, and Hale Little, of Newport; m. by Rev. James Searing, ——, 1753.
226	BLISS John, Jan. 24, 1666.
149	" Henry, and Mary Clarke; m. by Rev. Nicholas Eyres, ——, 1741.
190	" Elizabeth, Collins, and James Clarke, Aug. 9, 1766.
206	" Benedict, of Newport, and Sarah Upham, of Middletown; m. by Edward Upham, Justice, Dec. 24, 1766.
172	" Sarah, and Henry Lyon, (also 233), Dec. 30, 1756.
1-1	" Mary, and Caleb Maxon, Oct. 20, 1782.
1-5	" William, of William, of Middletown, and Abigail Lyndon, of Josias, of Newport; m. by Elder William Bliss, Oct. 16, 1783.
1-88	" Thomas Ward, and Sarah Casey Thurston, Nov. 13, 1783.
1-17	" Sarah, and Isaac Pearce, March 14, 1785.
1-86	" Clarke, of Henry, and Abigail Spooner, of Charles, dec.; m. by Elder William Bliss, Dec. 13, 1789.
121	" Elizabeth, and Christopher Clarke, ——.
1-2	" Mary, and Caleb Maxon, March 1, 1807.

204	BLIVEN Patience, and Jonathan Burdick, Aug. 2, 1761.
1-102	" Desire, and George Clarke, Jan. 19, 1800.
1-122	" Emeline, and Antony Benjamions, Aug. 31, 1828.
2-43	" Silena, and Samuel Hunter, Oct. 20, 1836.
2-22	BLOCK Edward G. (seaman), aged 22 years, son of Peter and Ann, and Susan A. Lawton, aged 17 years, dau. of Peleg and Susan; m. at Fall River, Mass., by Rev. Benjamin Phelan, Nov. 30, 1845.
118	BOARK Margaret, and William Commer, May 25, 1755.
2-21	BONES Mary Jane, and William Saunders, July 1, 1844.
211	BONNER Alexander, and Sarah Kerby; m. by Rev. Jeremiah Leaming, Dec. 17, 1741.
171	BOOKER Patience, and John Williams, Oct. 20, 1754.
2-29	BOOTH Mary, and Joseph Openshaw, Dec. 18, 1845.
1	BORDEN Mathew, and Ann ——; m. by Samuel Cranston, Governor, Dec. 1, 1699.
159	" Matthew, and Hannah Clarke, Dec. 21, 1737.
162	" Ruth, and William Smith, Nov. 1, 1739.
200	" Peace, and William Moore, —— 16, 1760.
191	" Phebe, and William Billings, May 3, 1767.
121	" Ann, and William Smith. —— 1, ——.
1-86	" Hannah, and Caleb Corey, May 17, 1804.
153	BOSS Benjamin, of Newport, and Iiathonne Wightman, of North Kingstown; m. by Rev. Nicholas Eyres, Sept. 23, 1750.
102	" Abigail, and Josiah Crandall, Sept. 9, 1753.
2-1	" William D., and Eliza M. Ambrose; m. by Rev. Isaac Stoddard, Dec. 29, 1838.
2-22	" Mrs. Abby DeWolf, and William Guild, Aug. 4, 1845.
154	BOSWORTH Peter, and Amey Spencer; m. by Rev. Nicholas Eyres, March 31, 1752.
102	" Daniel, and Elizabeth Peckham; m. by Rev. James Searing, —— ——, 1752.
203	" Benjamin, and Frances Nichols; m. by Rev. William Vinal, Feb. 14, 1757.
205	BOURK James, and Eleanor Whiting; m. by Rev. William Vinal, June 25, 1761.
190	" Deborah, and Thomas Chadwick, Aug. 11, 1765.
56	BOURS Peter, and Bathsheba Banks; m. by Rev. James Honeyman, Jan. 6, 1704-5.
56	" Bathsheba, and John Hart, Feb. 27, 1721-2.
64	" Peter, and Ann Fairchild; m. by Rev. William Vesey, —— 16, 1723.
1-89	" Elizabeth, and Paris Otis Richmond, May 1, 1809.
200	BOVEL Mary, and Thomas Cosby, Sept. 5, 1748.
72	BOWCOTT Thomas, and Mary Chadwick; m. by Job Lawton, Justice, Aug. 18, 1726.
170	BOWDIN Peter, and Elizabeth Armstrong; m. by Rev. Nicholas Eyres, March 15, 1753.
2-33	BOWEN Melvina, and Henry Hazelhurst; Dec. 16, 1849.
145	BOWERS Philip, of Swansey, Mass., and Mary ——, of Newport; m. by Rev. Nicholas Ayres, ——, ——.
2-33	BOWLER, William T., and Esther Dodge; m. by Rev. B. Othman, Dec. 16, 1849.
1-56	BOWLES Martha Matilda, and James Gould Almy Bachelor; Aug. 4, 1792.
148	BOYD Margaret, and Joseph Pashley; May 27, 1741.
164	BRADFORD Theophilus, of Dorsetshire, Eng., and Ruth Goodspeed, of Newport; m. by John Coddington, Justice, Feb. 24, 1731.
141	" Priscilla, and Moses Norman; July 26, 1750.
2-29	BRADFORD Ann A., and George E. Vernon; June 25, 1845.
200	BRAIDSON Paul, and Jane Sabin; m. by Rev. Gardiner Thurston, Jan. 17, 1760.
199	BRAND Susanna, and Sylvester Greenman; Sept. 10, 1759.
2-7	BRAMAN William, and Sarah Pearce; m. by Rev. Thomas Leaver, Nov. 14, 1841.
2-43	" Elizabeth A., and Joseph J. French; Nov. 30, 1837.
289	BRASTON Michael, and Elizabeth Wilson, July 4, 1749.

102	BRATTLE	Mary, and James Steward, ——, 1753.
206	"	James, and Elizabeth Lawton; m. by Edward Upham, Sept. 28, 1766.
125	BRAYTON	Charity, and James Rogers; Dec. 1, 1734.
131	"	Isaac, and Mary Sanford; m. by Rev. Nicholas Eyres, Feb. 12, 1737-8.
149	"	Francis, and ———; m. by Rev. Nicholas Eyres, Sept. 9, 1742.
141	"	Mary, and Jeremiah Ross; Nov. 27, 1749.
153	"	Elizabeth, and Samuel Robinson, Dec. 6, 1750.
210	"	Patience, and Charles Young, Nov. 20, 1761.
148	"	Israel, and Elizabeth Lawton; m. by Rev. Nicholas Eyres, Oct. 29, 1763.
1-67	"	Lucy, and Job Greenman, Jan. 1, 1766.
1-90	"	Sarah, and Benjamin Clarke Cornell, Oct. 14, 1810.
27	BRENTON	Benjamin, and Sarah Collins; m. by Samuel Cranston, Governor, ——, 24. ——.
203	BRICKLEY	Henry, and Sarah Weeden; m. by William Vinal, Aug. 17, 1756.
152	BRIDGES	Robert, and Hope Peckham; m. by Rev. James Honeyman, Sept. 7, 1729.
204	"	John, and Elizabeth Gardiner; m. by Rev. Gardiner Thurston, Dec. 13, 1760.
190	"	Ann, and Jeremiah Fairbanks, July 1, 1766.
191	BRIGGS	Jethro, and Mary ——; m. by Rev. Gardiner Thurston, Dec. 17, 1767.
2-4	"	Catherine E., and Peleg G. Sweet, Jan. 5, 1840.
2-12	"	Ebenezer, and Mrs. Sarah Eldred; m. by Rev. James A. McKensie, March 8, 1840.
123	BRIGHTMAN	——, and —— ——, ——, 1740.
142	"	Henry, and Ruth Southwick, —— 26, 1750.
1-95	"	Susannah, and John Stevens, April 29, 1807.
153	BRINK	Mary, and Nicholas Lyng (also 173), Aug. 11, 1751.
171	"	Elizabeth, and James Wady, Jan. 1, 1755.
1-36	BRINLEY	Mary, and Josiah Arnold, Feb. 12, 1784.
1-40	"	Elizabeth, and Capt. William Littlefield, March 10, 1785.
1-92	BRITTAIN	William, and Elizabeth Clarke, May 22, 1785.
1-92	"	Margaretta, and John Cozzens, March 4, 1804.
1-115	"	William, and Ann Price; m. by Rev. Michael Eddy, April 5, 1804.
188	BRYANT	Elizabeth, and John Freeman, ——, 1758.
100	BRYER	Elias, and Mary Tillinghast; m. by Rev. Nicholas Eyres, Dec. 6, 1750.
171	"	Jonathan, and Annie Haix; m. by Rev. Nicholas Eyres, Jan. 26, 1755.
2-21	"	Stafford, and Susan F. Gladding; m. by Rev. Robert M. Hatfield, Aug. 18, 1844.
2-21	"	William, and Ann Thiddy; m. by Rev. Robert M. Hatfield, Oct. 13, 1844.
210	BROOKS	Thomas, and Elizabeth, ——; m. by Rev. Gardiner Thurston, Nov. 3, 1761.
2-33	BROPHY	Bridget, and Edward Geissert, Nov. 17, 1849.
1-81	BROWNELL	Sylvester, of Newport, son of William, of Little Compton, and Sarah W. Wilson, of Jonathan, Jr., of Newport; m. by Rev. Michael Eddy, Oct. 14, 1804.
2-30	"	Patience, and William Maynard, Nov. 24, 1846.
32	BROWN	Mary, and John Brown, May 28, 1714.
32	"	John, and Mary Brown; m. by Rev. James Honeyman, May 28, 1714.
84	"	Hope, and Nathaniel Coddington, Jr., March 20, 1718-9.
62	"	Mary, and Daniel Gould, Nov. 17, 1719.
123	"	Benjamin, and Rebecca Graham, Jan. 30, 1737-8.
121	"	Clarke, and Elizabeth Gardiner; m. by Rev. Nicholas Eyres, Dec. 4, 1740.
151	"	Joseph, and Mary Caswell; m. by Rev. James Searing, Nov. 29, 1744.

119	BROWN	Daniel, and —— ——; m. by Rev. Nicholas Eyres, Feb. 1, 1745-6.
167	"	Ann, and Manion Chaloner, March 14, 1747.
141	"	Josiah, and Susanna Coggeshall, Nov. 1, 1749.
153	"	Susanna, and Solomon Mackey, Aug. 16, 1750.
170	"	Elizabeth, and Benjamin Clarke, Jan. 28, 1753.
142	"	Abigail, and John Woodons, March 19, 1753.
170	"	George, and Amey Read; m. by Rev. Nicholas Eyres, May 17, 1753.
170	"	William, and Elizabeth Fear; m. by Rev. Nicholas Eyres, June 24, 1753.
171	"	Hepseba, and William Hall, Jan. 21, 1755.
203	"	Elizabeth, and Benjamin Wilson, Feb. 5, 1756.
172, 233	"	Roger, and Elizabeth Davis; m. by Rev. Nicholas Eyres, April 10, 1757.
188	"	Benjamin, and Elizabeth Fryers; m. by Rev. Ezra Stiles, May 6, 1759.
188	"	Thomas, late of New Jersey, and Mary Pitman, of Newport; m. by Rev. Ezra Stiles, Nov. 19, 1761.
210	"	George, and Mercy Mortimer; m. by Rev. Gardiner Thurston, Dec. 13, 1761.
206	"	Thomas, and Esther Humphries; m. by Rev. William Vinall, Sept. 16, 1762.
190	"	Samuel, Jr., and Katherine Cranston; m. by Rev. Gardiner Thurston, Aug. 17, 1766.
112	"	Martha, and William Pendleton, June, 1770.
1-87	"	Susannah, and Samuel Matteson, July 4, 1790.
1-65	"	Penelope, and Capt. Robert Lawton, Dec. 31, 1799.
142	"	Elizabeth, and —— ——, July ——.
1-101	"	Elizabeth, and Richard Swan, Oct. 29, 1803.
1-107	"	John, and Fanny Ryan, Dec. 31, 1809.
2-13	"	Charles S., of New York, and Julia H. Grinnell (Col.); m. by Rev. Thomas Leaver, Dec. 10, 1840.
2-27	"	Benjamin, and Caroline Spooner; m. by Rev. Thatcher Thayer, March ——, 1841.
2-14	"	Elizabeth Bowen, and William Marshall Stedman, April 14, 1841.
2-14	"	Rebecca W., and Charles Devens, Jr., April 27, 1841.
2-14	"	Charlotte Viall, and Thomas Gillmore Bachelder, March 8, 1842.
2-16	"	Lowell, of Foxboro, Mass., and Eliza Ann Miller, of Newport; m. by Rev. Francis Vinton, Aug. 13, 1842.
2-28	"	Ellen, and Charles G. Freeman, June 24, 1844.
2-28	"	Betsey A., and John C. Chapman, Nov. 14, 1844.
2-36	"	Martha A., and Richard C. Carrigan, June 23, 1845.
2-36	"	George, and Ann Hall; m. by Rev. E. B. Bradford, Aug. 6, 1845.
2-36	"	Caroline, and Joseph W. Parkinson, Sept. 21, 1845.
2-24	"	James B., and Mary Ann Handy; m. by Rev. Richard Livsey, Oct. 28, 1846.
2-32	"	James B., and Mary Ann Hazard, Oct. 28, 1846.
2-33	"	George A., and Elizabeth C. Anthony, both of Middletown; m. by Rev. Henry Jackson, Dec. 3, 1849.
119	BRYN	Michael, and ——, Warren; m. by Rev. Nicholas Eyres, April 9, 1746.
151	BUCKMASTER	George, and Abia Franklin; m. by Rev. James Searing, July 17, 1743.
203	"	George, and Rebecca Taylor; m. by Rev. William Vinall, June 19, 1758.
2-4	BUDLONG	William R., of Amos and Sally, and Ann B. Richardson, of John, and Sally; m. by Rev. Joseph Smith, June 27, 1841.
172	BULLIVA	——, and John Jones, July 8, 1756.
21	BULL	Benjamin, and Content James; m. by Edward Thurston, Justice, Dec. —, 1710.
37	"	Experience, and William Sanford, July 23, 1717.
95	"	Henry, and Phebe Coggeshall, Feb. 1, 1721.
58	"	Miriam, and Rowland Allen, Oct. 30, 1722.

233	BULL Joseph, and Sarah ——; m. by Rev. James Honeyman, —— 20, ——.
2-27	BUNN Ann Elizabeth, and Samuel Phillips Cross, July 5, 1842.
1-55	BURDEN Elizabeth, and Peter Langley, May 17, 1799.
1-130	" Elmira, and John F. Albro, Sept. 26, 1833.
204	BURDICK Jonathan, and Patience Bliven; m. by Elder John Maxon, Aug. 2, 1761.
179	" Patience, and Job Bennett, June —, 1768.
1-29	" Clarke, of Ichabod, of Charlestown, and Lydia Peckham, of Enos, of Newport; m. by Elder William Bliss, Jan. 11, 1789.
1-44	" Catherine, and John Adams, May 10, 1795.
1-47	" Fanny, and Thomas Bailey, Sept. 24, 1795.
1-110	" Benjamin, of John, and Marcy Curry, of Joseph; m. by Rev. Michael Eddy, Nov. 1, 1808.
1-98	" Martha, and Samuel Spencer, Nov. 5, 1813.
1-114	" Capt. Isaiah, and Mary Lake, of Benjamin; m. by Thomas Corey, Jr., Justice, Feb. 15, 1822.
2-6	" Capt. Daniel, and Margaret D. Crandall; m. by Rev. Thomas Leaver, Sept. 19, 1841.
2-10	" Clarke, and Rebecca Robinson Russell; m. by Rev. Francis Vinton, Nov. 6, 1842.
2-28	" Martha A., and James J. Essex, July 16, 1844.
2-29	" Hannah, and Frederick Lewse, March 1, 1846.
2-34	" Susan M., and John Myers, Oct. 14, 1847.
2-34	" Mary Catherine, and Uriah Ladd, Jr., April 5, 1848.
170	BURD Heost, and Thomas James, June 24, 1753.
29	BURGESS James, and Rebecca Davis; m. by Thomas Fry, Justice, May 1, 1712.
140	" Mrs. Rebecca, and Azrikm Pearce, Oct. 29, 1741.
132	" James, and Elizabeth Exceene; m. by Rev. John Callender, July 29, 1842.
141	" Sarah, and Phillip Moshier, Sept. 27, 1750.
142	" Lydia, and Maxon Moshier, ——, 1750.
142	" Benjamin and Hannah ——, March 29, 1753.
148	BURK Mary, and Nathaniel Locke, July 20, 1764.
172, 234	BURRELL Ebenezer, and Lydia Bennett; m. by Rev. Nicholas Eyres, May 1, 1757.
1-33	" Martha, and Dr. Levi Wheaton, Dec. 20, 1784.
1-33	" Ebenezer, of John, of Lynn, Mass., and Phebe Cahoone, of James, of Newport; m. by Rev. Samuel Hopkins, Aug. 3, 1788.
2-39	BURRINGTON Charles B., and Anna B. Peckham, Dec. 12, 1853.
149	BURROUGHS Desire, and Esek Hopkins, Nov. 29, 1741.
132	" William, and Elizabeth Sanford; m. by Rev. John Callender, Sept. 16, 1742.
114	" Amey, and Robert Durfee, May 1, 1746.
153	" James, and Martha Hall; m. by Rev. Nicholas Eyres, Nov. 21, 1750.
148	" Abigail, and William Hookey, Jan. 17, 1762-3.
157	" William, and Katherine Gardiner; m. by Rev. Gardiner Thurston, Nov. 11, 1764.
119	" Samuel, of Newport, and ——Greene, of Middletown; m. by Rev. Nicholas Eyres, ——.
122	" Mary, and James Malling, —— 30, ——.
2-40	" Samuel, and Mary Sherman; m. by Rev. Michael Eddy, Sept. 15, 1822.
2-22	" George, and Susan Steavens; m. by Rev. Thomas Leaver, Oct. 24, 1844.
2-34	" Martha B., and William F. Lawton, May 26, 1847.
1-33	BURR Ezekiel, of Providence, and Lydia Yates of Newport; m. by Rev. Samuel Hopkins, July 9, 1786.
171	BURTIS Benjamin, and Mary England; m. by Rev. Nicholas Eyres, Sept. 1, 1759.
196	BURT John, of Bristol, son of John of Boston, and Ann Ellery, of Hon. William, of Newport; m. by Rev. Ezra Stiles, Nov. 17, 1768.
1-18	" William, and Mahitable Fowler; m. by Rev. Gardiner Thurston, Nov. 18, 1776.
240	" Rev. John, and Abigail Ellery, Aug. 20, ——.

2-3	BUSH R. O., and C. A. Almy; m. by Rev. J. H. Cone, July 3, 1839.
13	BUTLAND ——, and —— Clarke, Jan. ——, 1704.
122	BYLES Josias, of Boston, and Hannah Little, of Newport; m. by Rev. John Callander, —— 7, ——.
141	BYRN William, and Jemima Jant, May 11, 1747.
235	B—— Abigail, and John Carpenter.

C

1-24	CABELLEE Martin, and Alice Wyatt; m. by Rev. Gardiner Thurston, Aug. 5, 1781.
2-36	CARRIGAN Richard C., of Halifax, N. S., and Martha A. Brown, of New York; m. by Rev. E. B. Bradford, June 23, 1845.
111	CAHOONE Joseph, and Sarah Vaughn; m. by John Callender, Jr., Justice, —— 5, 1740.
141	" James, and Mary Yeats, Dec. 20, 1747.
169	" Elmira, and Henry Willis, Aug. 26, 1749.
141	" Abigail, and Erasmus Phillips, Oct. 4, 1750.
102	" John and Hannah Beere; m. by Rev. James Seering, ——, 1751.
204	" Jonathan, and Ruth Phillips; m. by Rev. Gardiner Thurston, Dec. 3, 1760.
206	" Elizabeth, and Gould Marsh, Nov. 11, 1761.
209	" James, and Phebe Wilcox; m. by Rev. Ezra Stiles, Aug. 28, 1763.
1-33	" Phebe, and Ebenezer Burrell, Aug. 3, 1788.
109	CALLINE James, and Mary ——; m. by Rev. Nicholas Eyres, ——.
204	CALVERT John, and Mehitable Thurston; m. by Rev. Gardiner Thurston, Aug. 14, 1760.
2-29	" Rebecca Jane, and Henry Foster, Sept. 10, 1846.
1-37	CALVIN Sarah, and Martin Rogers, July 31, 1790.
205	CAMPBELL Sarah, and Thomas Goodman, May 7, 1761.
2-7	CANTERBURY Stanley, of New York, and Eliza Johnson of Newport (col.); m. by Rev. Thomas Leaver, Oct. 14, 1841.
141	CANDRY Isaac, and Hannah Wilbur, Dec. 28, 1749.
15	CARD Edward, and —— Corey; m. by John Rogers' Asst., July 24, 1709.
33	" Joseph, and Hope ——; m. at King's Towne, July 13, 1710.
88	" Elizabeth, and Oliver Arnold, June 15, 1715.
131	" Joseph, and Mary Weeden; m. by Rev. Nicholas Eyres, Aug. 7, 1736.
118	" Sarah, and John Pate, Nov. 9, 1755.
147	" Phebe, and James Millwood, ——, 1762.
147	" Phebe, and Caleb Coggeshall, ——, 1762.
148	" Richard, and Martha Tripp; m. by Rev. Gardiner Thurston, May 12, 1764.
1-93	" Martha, and Samuel Rawson, April 18, 1813.
2-27	" Abby C., and George A. Hazard, Oct. 3, 1843.
239	CARLTON Edward, and Sarah Merryhew, July 23, 1749.
204	CARPENTER James, and Avis Tillinghast; m. by Rev. Gardiner Thurston, Sept. 15, 1760.
148	" Willett and Ann Gardiner; m. by Rev. Gardiner Thurston, July 1, 1764.
192	" Ann, and Solomon Southwick, June 20, 1769.
1-52	" Jonathan, of Jonathan, of South Kingstown, and Polly Hazard, of Newport, dau. of Simeon, of South Kingstown; m. by Rev. Michael Eddy, Feb. 4, 1798.
235	" John, and Abigail B. ——; m. by Rev. Nicholas Eyres, ——.
2-27	" John A., of William G., of Newport, and Mary J. Slocum of Gardiner, of Middletown; m. by Rev. B. Othman (also 2:31), Aug. 13, 1848.
195	CARROLL Lawrence, and Susannah Holden; m. by Rev. Gardiner Thurston, June 19, 1768.
75	CARR Elizabeth, and John Godfrey, May 28, 1701.
19	" Sarah, and John Hammet, Jan. 10, 1705.
18	" Anne, and —— Barker, Jan. 18, 1709.
76	" Patience, and Joseph Slocum, Sept. 27, 1724.

NEWPORT—MARRIAGES.

74	CARR	Mary, and Josias Lyndon, Oct. 5, 1727.
124	"	John, of Newport, and Mary Hill, of Swansey; m. by Joseph Mason, Justice, Sept. 15, 1735.
121	"	Sailes, and Martha Child; m. by Rev. Nicholas Eyres, June 10, 1740.
149	"	Caleb, and Elizabeth Phillips; m. by Rev. Nicholas Eyres, —— 15, 1741.
218	"	Elizabeth, and Henry Peacock, Nov. 5, 1742.
120	"	Damarias, and Lemuel Carr, June 6, 1745.
120	"	Samuel, of Newport, and Damarias Carr, of Jamestown; m. by Benjamin Hazard, Asst., June 6, 1745.
197	"	Robert, and Mary Wood; m. by Rev. Nicholas Eyres, May 18, 1749.
202	"	Sarah, and Peleg Cranston, Sept. 7, 1749.
153	"	Robe, and James Noyes, Aug. 1, 1751.
102	"	Mary, and James Hickey, ——, 1752.
155	"	Benjamin, and Mary Martindale; m. by Joseph Silvester, Justice, Sept. 5, 1755.
172	"	Mercy, and Henry Hubbs, May 9, 1756.
145	"	Katherine, and John Greene, Sept. 22, 1757.
200	"	Wait, and Ebenezer West, Feb. 23, 1760.
205	"	John, and Mary Arnold; m. by Rev. Gardiner Thurston (also 227), July 19, 1761.
187	"	Ann, and Audley Clarke (also 188), Nov. 24, 1762.
147	"	Elizabeth, and Richard Story, —— 23, 1762.
209	"	Martha, and James Marsh, Aug. 3, 1763.
1-41	"	Mary, and Peleg Barker, Jr., Dec. 25, 1765.
191	"	Samuel, and Mrs. Sarah Thomas; m. by Rev. Gardiner Thurston, Dec. 6, 1767.
1-35	"	Mary, and Joseph Mumford, May 11, 1788.
1-16	"	Samuel C., and Ann Hockey, Dec. 13, 1789.
235	"	Mary, and William Gardiner, July 27, ——.
2-4	"	Hannah F., and John Bates, Nov. 7, 1839.
2-11	"	Sarah R., and Benjamin C. Paull, Nov. 22, 1842.
2-19	"	Amelia, and Whitman Peckham, June 16, 1844.
153	CARTER	Thomas, and Abigail Fry; m. by Rev. Nicholas Eyres, Sept. 10, 1749.
169	"	Dorothy, and William Thurston, Sept. 4, 1754.
1-54	"	Sally, and Benjamin Field, June 10, 1798.
132	CARTWRIGHT	Ruth, and Joseph Hudson, ——, 1742.
190	"	Dorothy, and James Fry, Aug. 4, 1765.
35	CARY	James, and Bridget Pocock; m. by Walter Clarke, Asst., Dec. 1, 1705.
71	"	Rebecca, and Samuel ——; m. by Job Lawton, Justice, July 14, 1726.
144	"	John, and Martha Pitman; m. by Rev. William Vinal (also 203), July 30, 1755.
206	"	John, and Hannah Weaver; m. by Rev. William Vinal, July 4, 1765.
14	CASEY	——, of Thomas and Sarah, and —— Greenman, of Edward and Mary; m. by Giles Slocum, Justice, March 8, 1705-6.
224	"	John, of Thomas of Newport, and Elizabeth Hix, of Thomas, of Portsmouth, April 17, 1719.
223	"	John, of Thomas and Robert, and Mary Stanton, of John and Elizabeth, Feb. 9, 1726.
177	"	Gideon and Elizabeth Johnson, —— 11, 1760.
2-20	"	Elizabeth, and James B. Read, Sept. 4, 1844.
18	CASE	Mary, and Robert Nicholls, Feb. —, 1698.
204	"	Sarah, and William Spencer, Sept. 11, 1760.
1-61	CASTOFF	Henry, of Henry and Mehitable Clarke, of Sherman; m. by Rev. Michael Eddy, Aug. 6, 1799.
121	CASTLE	Sarah, and David Major, Aug. 26, 1739.
123	CASWELL,	Sarah, and Timothy Witherell, Oct. 5, 1738.
151	"	Lydia, and Jarvis Pinkney, Oct. 19, 1743.
151	"	Mary, and Joseph Brown, Nov. 29, 1744.
170	"	Israel, and Amey Crapon; m. by Rev. Nicholes Eyres, May 17, 1753.

199	CASWELL	Deborah, and Matthew Langley, July 22, 1759.
205	"	Jane, and Robert Cozzens, April 4, 1761.
210	"	John, and Hannah West, m. by Rev. Gardiner Thurston, Dec. 31, 1761.
2-21	"	William W. and Ann Elizabeth Pike, m. by Rev. Robert M. Hatfield, Feb. 15, 1843.
2-21	"	Lewis B., and Mary F. Topham, m. by Rev. Robert M. Hatfield, June 27, 1843.
2-23	"	Lewis B., of Newport, and Caroline H. Peabody, of Middletown; m. by Rev. James Taylor, Jan. 27, 1846.
2-35	"	Elizabeth, and William H. Gardner, June 2, 1850.
209	CAWDRY	Mary, and John Robinson, Nov. 15, 1764.
1-108	CAZENOVE	Eliza F., and William C. Gardner, July 13, 1816.
240	CENTRE	Solomon, and Mary ——. —— 11, ——.
81	CHACE	John, and Ann Arnold; m. by Rev. James Honeyman, Sept. 20, 1713.
123	"	Mehitable, and George Lawrence, —— 9, 1738.
123	"	Perkins, and Elizabeth Ireson, —— 9, 1738.
123	"	Jonathan, Jr., and Ann Shelley, June ——, 1739.
123	"	Ann, and John Scott, July 20, 1740.
151	"	Abigail, and John Downs, ——, 1744.
169	"	Seth, of Freetown, Mass., and Phillippe Paine of Newport; m. by Martin Howard, Justice, Nov. 16, 1752.
188	"	Rhoda, and Jonathan Gladding, Aug. 30, 1759.
205	"	Mehitable, and —— Price, July ——, 1761.
190	"	Ann, and Andrew McCarrie, Oct. 27, 1765.
209	"	Benjamin, of Bristol, and Ann Fry, of Newport; m. by Rev. Ezra Stiles, Oct. 16, 1766.
207	"	Delona, and Joshua Irish, April 28, 1767.
1-121	"	Benjamin, and Abby ——; m. at Middletown, Sept, 9, 1797.
109	"	Ann, and Richard Edwards, —— 20, ——.
2-5	"	Sarah Vernon, and William Cornell, Sept. 29, 1840.
2-14	"	William Henry, and Mary Rodman Cornell; m. by Rev. Francis Vinton, May 3, 1852.
2-21	"	Henry, and Elizabeth H. Moulton; m. by Robert M. Hatfield, June 26, 1843.
72	CHADWICK	Mary, and Thomas Bowcott, April 18, 1726.
171	"	Ann, and Joseph Hill, Oct. 21, 1753.
118	"	Mary, and Thomas Chubb, June 15, 1755.
172	"	Sarah, and Francis Dicks, July 25, 1756.
233	"	Sarah, and Francis Dykes, July 25, 1756.
204	"	Thomas, and Dorothy Eldredge; m. by Rev. Gardiner Thurston, July 13, 1760.
147	"	Patience, and Edward Kenney ——, 1762.
190	"	Thomas, and Deborah Bourk; m. by Rev. Gardiner Thurston, Aug. 11, 1765.
1-80	"	Sally and John Williams, Sept. 25, 1785.
1-113	CHAFFEE	Otis, of Providence, and Almy Underwood, of Westport; m. by Rev. William Potter, April 5, 1801.
1-131	"	Mary Ann, and Albert Cottrell, May 18, 1834.
2-3	"	Nathan M., and Harriet Chapman; m. by Rev. Timothy G. Freeman, Oct. 16, 1837.
2-1	"	Evelyn J., and Capt. William H. Langley, March 29, 1839.
206	CHAFFINS	Elizabeth, and Walter Hanners, March 6, 1763.
160	CHAFFIN	George, of St. Christopher's W. I., and Ann Tilley, of Newport; m. by Rev. John Callender, Jan. 16, 1742.
212	CHALLONER	Mary, and James Robinson, Oct. 16, 1740.
136	"	John, and Martha Church; m. by Rev. James Honeyman, Oct. 12, 1746.
167	"	Manlon, and Ann Brown; m. by Rev. James Honeyman, March 14, 1747.
70	CHAMBERLAIN	Mrs. Elizabeth, and —— Martindale, July 29, 1725.
188	CHAMBERS	Mary and —— ——worthy; m. by Rev. Ezra Stiles, —— 23, 1758.
157	CHAMPLAIN	Ann, and James Anderson (also 204). Oct. 20, 1760.

206	CHAMPLAIN	George, and Ruth Wanton; m. by Rev. William Vinall, July 26, 1763.
1-45	"	Christopher Grant, of Christopher and Margaret, and Martha Redwood Ellery, of Benjamin and Mehitable; m. by Rev. William Potter, April 14, 1793.
1-62	"	Sarah, and Giles Pearce, Dec. 22, 1799.
1-134	"	Dr. Stephen of Glastenburytown, and Alice H. Armstrong of Newport; m. by Rev. Leland Howard, Nov. 4, 1838.
2-84	"	Thomas J., of South Kingstown, and Caroline M. Allen, of Portsmouth; m. by Rev. Henry Jackson, Dec. 12, 1848.
239	CHANDERS	Elizabeth, and Nathaniel Grafton, April 24, 1747.
206	CHANDLER	Katherine, and Jonathan Weeden, Dec. 30, 1762.
174	"	William, and Mary Simpkins; m. by Rev. Gardiner Thurston, Nov. 8, 1764.
157	"	William, and —— Hopkins; m. by Rev. Gardiner Thurston, Nov. —, 1764.
152	CHANNING	——, and Mary Robinson; m. by Rev. James Searing, —— —, 1746.
102	"	Mary, and Eleazer Trevitt, —— —, 1752.
1-91	"	Mary, and George Gibbs, Oct. 9, 1768.
83	CHAPLAIN	Joseph, of Newport, and Mrs. Bathsheba Man, of Warren, R. I., Jan. 22, 1705.
40	CHAPMAN	Patience, and Robert Taylor (also 165), Aug. 9, 1711.
55	"	Katherine, and James Sheffield, May 1, 1714.
142	"	——, and Joseph Phillips, May 7, 1751.
170	"	Elizabeth, and Phineas Perry, Aug. 23, 1753.
171	"	Walter, and Elizabeth Dunn; m. by Rev. Nicholas Eyres, July ——, 1754.
169	"	Israel, and Martha Sears, Dec. 23, 1754.
118	"	Edward, and Mehitable Scranton; m. by Rev. Nicholas Eyres, Nov. 25, 1755.
200	"	Mary, and Alexander Mullen, Feb. 14, 1760.
235	"	Mary, and Joseph Sabin, ——
1-100	"	Rebecca, and Edward Easton Taylor, April 14, 1814.
2-3	"	Harriet, and Nathan M. Chaffee, Oct. 16, 1837.
2-28	"	John C., and Betsey A. Brown, both of Mystic, Conn.; m. by Rev Thatcher Thayer, Nov. 14, 1844.
1-124	CHAPPELL	Abby H., and Charles N. Tilley, Nov. 3, 1830.
2-2	"	Sarah, and George Smith, Aug. 1, 1839.
209	CHECKLEY	William, of Boston, and Mary Cranston, of Newport; m. by Rev. Ezra Stiles, Oct. —, 1766.
134	CHEESBOROUGH	Abigail, and Alexander Grant, Oct. 6, 1760.
123	CHILD	Thomas, and Mary Townman, May 17, 1738.
123	"	Esther and David Lindsey, —— 11, 1738.
121	"	Martha and Sailes Carr, June 10, 1740.
205	"	Ann, and Jonathan Fisk, —— 12, 1758.
188	"	Joanna, and Ebenezer Washburn, ——, 1761.
243	"	Jeremiah, and Elizabeth Dyer, July 24, 17—
155	CHILSON	John, and Elizabeth Atkins; m. by Joseph Sylvester, Justice, April 26, 1754.
118	CHUBB	Thomas, and Mary Chadwick; m. by Rev. Nicholas Eyres, June 15, 1755.
140	CHURCH	Lucy, and Pompey Gardiner (col.), ——, 1741.
136	"	Martha, and John Challoner, Oct. 12, 1746.
171	"	Edward, and Hannah Ledbetter; m. by Rev. Nicholas Eyres, May 5, 1754.
187	"	Benjamin and Bathsheba Cranston; m. by Rev. Ezra Stiles, —— 9, 1756.
188	"	Abigail, and Joseph Smith, Jan. 24, 1762.
148	"	Charles, and Elizageth ——; m. by Rev. Nicholas Eyres, April 11, 1763.
148	"	——, and John La——, June 24, 1763.
240	"	Mary, and Eleazer Trevitt, Oct. 18, ——.
1-68	"	Mehitable, and William Allen, Jr., June 15, 1806.
2-28	"	Thomas, and Mary R. Sayles; m. by Rev. Thatcher Thayer, Nov. —, 1843.

8	CLAFFIN	Sarah, and ———, Jan. 25, 1703.
100	CLAGGETT	Mary, and James Wady, May 27, 1736.
150	"	Hannah, and John Threadkill, Nov. 29, 1741.
199	"	Elizabeth, and Joseph Sheffield, June 21, 1759.
61	CLARKE	Cary, and Ann Dyer; m. by Benedict Arnold, Asst., Feb. 14, 1693-4.
2	"	William, and ———, Knight, April 11, 1700.
2	"	———, and Thomas Fry, Dec. 12, 1700.
13	"	———, and ——— Butland, Jan. —, 1704.
45	"	———, and Ezekiel Woodward, June 8, 1716.
39	"	Ann, and Samuel Dunn, 9th m., 1718.
78	"	Weston, and Mary Willett; m. by Thomas Coggeshall, Justice, June 20, 1728.
97	"	John and Pressilla Barker; m. by Job Lawton, Justice, Aug. 29, 1728.
129	"	Benjamin, and Grizzell Sherman, Nov. 3, 1734.
131	"	James, and Ann Fleet; m. by Rev. Nicholas Eyres, Feb. 26, 1737-8.
123	"	Hannah, and Daniel Millett, Sept. 27, 1739.
159	"	Hannah, and Matthew Borden, Dec. 21, 1737.
121	"	Peleg, and Elizabeth Allen; m. by Rev. Nicholas Eyres, Sept. 25, 1740.
150	"	William, and Elizabeth Benson; m. by Rev. John Callander, Jr., Oct. 5, 1741.
149	"	Mary, and Henry Bliss, ———, 1741.
151	"	Mercy, and ——— Leathe, Dec. 25, 1843.
141	"	Latham, and Elizabeth Bailey, Dec. 24, 1747.
239	"	Benjamin and Esther Ayres, Nov. 19, 1749.
154	"	Amey, and Gideon Cornell, Feb. 16, 1752.
170	"	Benjamin, and Elizabeth Brown; m. by Rev. Nicholas Eyres, Jan. 28, 1753.
171	"	Sarah, and James Crandall, Jan. 17, 1754.
171	"	Anna, and John Oldfield, Feb. 18, 1754.
171	"	Hannah, and Maxson Moshier, Aug. 8, 1754.
171	"	Susannah, and John Sinn, Nov. 13, 1754.
171	"	Mary, and William Taggart, Jan. 26, 1755.
118	"	Ruth, and Caleb Gilbert, Aug. 7, 1755.
118	"	James, and Elizabeth Peckham; m. by Rev. Nicholas Eyres, Sept. 11, 1755.
118	"	Sherman, and Katherine Truell; m. by Rev. Nicholas Eyres, Jan. 22, 1756.
172	"	Henry, and Elizabeth Dailey; m. by Rev. Nicholas Eyres (also 233), May 3, 1756.
176	"	Thomas, and ——— ———; m. by Rev. Nicholas Eyres, ———, 1756.
199	"	Lydia, and Jonathan Maxon, Nov. 14, 1759.
200	"	Ann, and Thomas Tew, Dec. 6, 1759.
200	"	Audley, and Margaret Howland; m. by Rev. Gardiner Thurston, Feb. 7, 1760.
204	"	Sarah, and Daniel Wilcox, Oct. 27, 1760.
204	"	Seth, of Harwich, Mass., and Deborah Ladd, of Newport; m. by Elder John Maxon, —— 10, 1760.
200	"	James, and Mary Rogers; m. by Gardiner Thurston, —— 13, 1760.
205	"	Walter, and Abigail Phillips; m. by Rev. Gardiner Thurston, April 19, 1761.
205	"	James, and Ann Moses; m. by Rev. Gardiner Thurston, May 18, 1761.
204	"	James, and Mary Bennett; m. by Elder John Maxon, Dec. 23, 1761.
205	"	Sarah, and ——— Gilbert, ———, 1761.
187	"	Audley, and Ann Carr; m. by Rev. Ezra Stiles (also 188), Nov. 24, 1762.
147	"	Sarah, and Benjamin Vose, ———, 1762.
148	"	Mary, and Joseph Sanford, June 13, 1764.
190	"	Hannah, and John Atkinson, Dec. 26, 1765.
208	"	Almy, and William Pinnegar, June 24, 1766.

NEWPORT—MARRIAGES.

190	CLARKE	James, and Elizabeth Collins Bliss; m. by Rev. Gardiner Thurston, Aug. 9, 1766.
209	"	John, and Mary Peckham; m. by Rev. Ezra Stiles, Oct. 20, 1760.
190	"	John, and Merebah Bennett; m. by Rev. Gardiner Thurston, ——, 1766.
158	"	Mary, and Robert Lawton, Nov. 14, 1773.
1-92	"	Elizabeth, and William Brettain, May 22, 1785.
1-38	"	Betsey, and Michael Baptiste, July 3, 1785.
1-61	"	Mehitable, and Henry Castoff, Aug. 6, 1799.
109	"	John, and Martha Smith; m. by Rev. Nicholas Eyres, —— 29, ——.
121	"	Christopher, and Elizabeth Bliss; m. by Rev. John Callender, Jr., ——.
145	"	Peleg, and Mary ——; m. by Rev. Nicholas Eyres, Oct. 15, ——.
145	"	Ann, and James Daft, Sept. 17, ——.
1-102	"	George, of George, of Newport, and Desire Bliven, of William, of Westerly; m. by Elder Asa Coon, Jan. 19, 1800.
1-77	"	Olive, and Adina Udall, Oct. 13, 1805.
1-121	"	John, and Eliza Taylor; m. by Rev. Michael Eddy, Sept. 7, 1830.
1-119	"	Rhoda, and Brenton E. Babcock, Oct. 21, 1830.
1-124	"	James, and Ann Smith; m. by Rev. Michael Eddy,, Jan. 9, 1831.
1-125	"	Abby M., and Perry M. Peckham, Nov. 27, 1831.
——	"	William, and Mrs. Isadora Fuller; m. by Rev. Joseph Smith, March 26, 1844.
2-28	"	Sarah Ann, and Charles T. Robinson, Oct. 27, 1844.
2-28	"	Mary G., and A. Henry Dumont, Nov. 14, 1844.
2-64	"	Agnes Matilda, and William Gardiner Read, Oct. 21, 1847.
36	CLAY	Mrs. Ruth, and Elkanah ——; m. by James Brown, Asst., Dec. 6, 1716.
141	CLEVELAND	John, and Elizabeth Daers, April 5, 1748.
145	"	John, and Elizabeth ——; m. by Rev. Nicholas Eyres, —— 18, ——.
2-53	"	Seth, of Providence, and Ardelia Nason, of Newport; m. by Rev. Thomas W. Tucker, Oct. 9, 1831.
93	COAN	Ann, and Charles Bardin, —— 18, 1735.
155	COBURN	James, and Mary Odlin; m. by Joseph Silvester, Justice, Feb. 8, 1754.
2-32	"	Lewis, of Clintonville, Mass., and Catherine Jane Williams, of Newport; m. by Rev. Henry Jackson, Dec. 11, 1849.
6	CODDINGTON	William, of Nathaniel, and Content Arnold, Nov. 12, 1700.
48	"	Ann, and Rev. Samuel Niles, Nov. 22, 1716.
84	"	Nathaniel, Jr., and Hope Brown; m. by Weston Clarke, Justice, March 20, 1718-9.
65	"	Col. William, and Jane Bernon; m. by Rev. James Honeyman, Oct. 11, 1722.
137	"	William and Penelope Goulding; m. by Rev. James Honeyman, May 20, 1740.
119	"	Ann, and John Greene, —— 23, 1744.
89	CODMAN	Mary, and Gideon Wanton, Feb. 26, 1717.
2-18	COE	Capt. Erastus P., and Mary E. Ross; m. by Rev. Arthur A. Ross, Aug. 11, 1841.
153	COFFIN	Paul, and Jerusha Tuel; m. by Rev. Nicholas Eyres, Nov. 15, 1750.
13	COGGESHALL	Patience, and Benedict Arnold, Jan. 23, 1705.
15	"	——, of Joshua, and Mary Freeborn, of Gideon, March 11, 1708.
17	"	Elizabeth, and —— Spencer, July ——, 1708.
19	"	Benjamin, of Major John, dec., and Sarah Easton; m. by Samuel Cranston, Governor; (also (25), Dec. 22, 1709.
49	"	Ann, and Clarke Rodman, Jan. 3, 1717.
68	"	Thomas, of Freegift, and Sarah Lancaster; m. by Samuel Cranston, Governor, Jan. 23, 1717.
88	"	Peter, and Elizabeth Goodson; m. by Rev. James Honeyman, Nov. 11, 1719.
43	"	Caleb, of Joshua and Sarah, and —— Easton, of Nicholas, dec., and Mary, May, 19, 1720—(?).
95	"	Phebe, and Henry Bull, Feb. 1, 1721.

63	COGGESHALL	James, and Phebe Turner, of Lawrence, Nov. 24, 1723.
73	"	Martha, and Abraham Redwood, March 6, 1726.
211	"	Elizabeth, and Benjamin Wilson, March 4, 1729.
90	"	Ann, and Christopher Dickenson, Oct. 6, 1730.
87	"	Sarah, and Benjamin Richardson, Jan. 20, 1730-1.
92	"	——, and —— Peckham, July ——, 1731.
117	"	Thomas, and Anstress Almy; m. by Rev. James Searing, —— 30, 1735.
129	"	Alce, and Robert Nichols, Dec. 28, 1738.
165	"	Rebecca, and Robert Taylor, Dec. 30, 1742.
135	"	Catherine, and Jonathan Otis; (also 152), Oct. 16, 1745.
141	"	Susanna, and Josiah Brown, Nov. 1, 1749.
141	"	Nathaniel, and Mary Cranston, Jan. 31, 1749-50.
153	"	Freelove, and Anthony Bennett, Aug. 16, 1750.
103	"	Sarah, and Benjamin Almy (also 117), May 22, 1751.
211	"	——, and Othniel Tripp, July 9, 1751.
135	"	Sarah, and Reville Monroe, May 24, 1752.
169	"	Nathaniel, Jr., and Elizabeth Barstow (also 234); m. by Rev. Nicholas Eyres, Feb. 27, 1755.
201	"	Nathaniel, Jr., and Elizabeth Barstow; m. by Rev. William Vinal, Feb. 27, 1755.
203	"	Nathaniel, and Abigail Wanton; m. by Rev. William Vinal, May 12, 1756.
147	"	Caleb, and Phebe Card; m. by Rev. Nicholas Eyres, ——, 1762.
191	"	Thomas, and Esther Kenyon; m. by Rev. Gardiner Thurston, Nov. 27, 1766.
1-77	"	William, and Elizabeth Moore, Feb. 28, 1771.
1-33	"	Elizabeth, and Benjamin Slocum, Aug. 24, 1783.
1-23	"	Ruth, and James Greene, Nov. 25, 1783.
1-102	"	Mary, and Jeremiah Lawton, Nov. 23, 1788.
236	"	Thomas, and Anstis Almy; m, by Rev. James Searing, ————.
1-61	"	Simeon, of Middletown, and Phebe Taber, of Tiverton; m. by Christopher Ellery, Justice, Jan. 23, 1800.
1-59	"	David Moore, and Elizabeth Hammond; m. by Rev. William Patten, May 2, 1800.
1-89	"	James, and Eliza Lawton; m. by Rev. Henry Wight, Aug. 16, 1810.
1-118	"	Ann, and Henry Wench, Jan. 13, 1812.
2-21	"	Robert D., and Sarah Ann Hunt; m. by Rev. Robert M. Hatfield, Jan. 4, 1844.
155	COGIN	Thomas, and Mary Holsten; m. by Joseph Silvester, Justice, Nov. 16, 1755.
230	COHEN	Zachariah, and Eleanor Phillips; m. by Rev. James Searing, June 12, 1735.
236	"	Zaccheus, and Eleanor Phillips; m. by Rev. James Searing, ————.
46	COLEMAN	Thomas and Mary Mew; m. by Walter Clarke, D. Governor, Feb. 12, 1702-3
9	"	Eleanor, and Thomas Husk, Nov. 8, 1704.
1-109	"	Rev. Ebenezer, of Tiverton, and Abby Pitman, of Newport; m. by Rev. William Patten, Jan. 17, 1819.
155	COLES	Zilpt, and Levi Shearman, Dec. 24, 1755.
188	COLLICK	Sarah, and James Griffeths, Aug. 15, 1759.
21	COLLINS	William, and Sarah Whitman; m. by Walter Clarke, Asst., Ap———, 1697.
206	"	John, of Hannah, of Newport, and Mary Collins (widow), dau. of John Avery, of Boston; m. at Boston by Rev. Jonathan Matthews, May 23, 1757.
206	"	Mary, and John Collins, May 23, 1757.
1-74	"	Huldah, and Samuel Wilkey, June 2, 1796.
27	"	Sarah, and Benjamin Brenton, —— 24, ——.
118	COMMER	William, and Margaret Boark; m. by Rev. Nicholas Eyres, May 25, 1755.
70	COMER	John, and Mrs Sarah ——; m. by John Coddington, Justice, Jan. 20, 1725.
204	CONGDON	Benjamin, and Katherine Taylor; m. by Rev. Gardiner Thurston, Aug. 9, 1760.

NEWPORT—MARRIAGES.

1-94	CONGDON	Frances, and Benjamin Mitchell, Sept. 9, 1810.
206	CONKLIN	Sarah, and James Lewis, July 5, 1763.
2-23	CONNAUGHTON	Honora, and John Ryan, Jan. 16, 1846.
132	CONNER	Mary, and Robert Odlin, Sept. 26, 1742.
118	"	Edward, and Patience ——; m. by Rev. Nicholas Eyres, March 20, 1755.
2-24	"	Margaret T. B., and Calvin H. Town, Aug. 9, 1846.
2-32	"	Margaret R., and Calvin W. Sawin, Aug. 9, 1846.
2-30	CONWAY	Richard, of Somerset, Mass., and Charlotte Nocoke, of Charlestown, R. I.; m. by Rev. Thatcher Thayer, April 6, 1847.
2-58	COOKERY	Dennis, and Kate Kelly; m. at Waterville, Co. Kerry, Ireland, by Rev. Father Sheeky, ——, 1828.
85	COOK	Joseph, and Hannah Peabody; m. by Samuel Cranston, Governor, May 23, 1717.
95	"	John, and Elizabeth Tweedy; m. by Rev. James Searing, Sept. 16, 1734.
168	"	Jane, and Thomas Manchester, Aug. —, 1737.
152	"	Elizabeth, and —— —— m. by Rev. James Searing, ——, 1746.
203	"	Elizabeth, and Peleg Barker, May 11, 1758.
116	"	Job, and Freelove ——; m. by Rev. Gardiner Thurston, July ——, 1762.
1-53	"	Clarke, and Dorcas Tilley; m. by Rev. Gardiner Thurston, Dec. 11, 1791.
2-28	"	D. of Cumberland, and Harriet Millikin, of Newport; m. by Rev. Thatcher Thayer, June 23, 1844.
2-29	"	Mary Elizabeth, and William Metcalf, Oct. 13, 1845.
153	CORBETT	Samuel, and Elizabeth Luther; m. by Rev. Nicholas Eyres, Oct. 14, 1750.
239	"	Samuel, and Patience Allbun, June 15, 1747.
132	COOLEY	James, and Judith Vial; m. by Rev. John Callender, Jr., Feb. 4, 1741-2.
172	COOMBES	Elizabeth, and Jeremiah Barker, Jr (also 233), Sept. 19, 1756.
2-32	"	Susan D., and Ebenezer H. Shaw, Feb. 15, 1850.
149	COOPER	Isaac, and Mary Cranston; m. by Rev. Nicholas Eyres, May 8, 1743.
153	"	Mary, and Thomas Stanley, June 23, 1749.
142	"	Robert, and —— Douglass, —— 12, 1750.
154	"	Christiana Katherine, and John Smith, Sept. 18, 1751.
190	"	Isaac, and Prudence Mortimer; m. by Rev. Gardiner Thurston, Sept. 18, 1766.
109	"	William, and Phebe Morran; m. by Rev. Nicholas Eyres, —— 26, ——.
2-51	"	Mary, and James Pearson, July 5, 1829.
15	COREY	——, and Edward Card, July 24, 1709.
93	"	William, of Newport, and —— ——, of Tiverton; m. by Job Almy, Justice, Feb. 22, 1722-3.
154	"	Hannah, and John Jehckes, Dec. 3, 1751.
171	"	Mary, and John Read, March 17, 1754.
171	"	Caleb, of Newport, and Hannah Manchester, of Portsmouth; m. by Rev. Nicholas Eyres, Aug. 11, 1754.
1-86	"	Caleb, and Hannah Borden, May 17, 1804.
2-16	"	James W., of Providence, and Charrissa Weeden, of Newport; m. by Rev. Thomas Leaver, Nov. 21, 1843.
93	CORNELL	Gideon, and Rebecca Vaughan; m. by William Wanton, Asst., Feb. 22, 1732.
154	"	Gideon, and Amey Clarke; m. by Rev. Nicholas Eyres, Feb. 16, 1752.
169	"	Mary, and Joseph Reed, (also 234), Dec. 5, 1754.
206	"	Rachel, and John Jent, June 29, 1762.
158	"	Elizabeth, and James Anthony, Aug. 15, 1768.
1-33	"	George, and Sarah Townsend; m. by Rev. Samuel Hopkins, Dec. 9, 1784.
1-48	"	Sally, and John Dunwell, Jan. 15, 1797.
1-64	"	Peace, and Jedediah Irish, April 12, 1801.

(Vit. Rec., Vol. 4.) 9

1-90	CORNELL	Benjamin Clarke, of Newport, and Sarah Drayton, of Somerset, Mass.; m. at Bristol, by Rev. Nehemiah Cory, Oct. 14, 1810.
2-69	"	George, and Maria Rodman; m. by Rev. Daniel Webb, Nov. 8, 1815.
2-21	"	Stephen, and Harriet C. Earl; Sept. 28, 1823.
2-5	"	William, and Sarah Vernon Chace; m. by Rev. Francis Vinton, Sept. 29, 1840.
2-7	"	Mary Ann, and Gideon Moshier; Sept. 22, 1841.
2-14	"	Mary Rodman, and William Henry Chace; May 3, 1842.
2-27	"	Catherine, and Nathan Hammett; Nov. 22, 1842.
152	CORNWELL	Ann, and Lemuel Pearson; June 11, 1746.
200	COSBY	Thomas, and Mary Bovel; m. by Rev. Nicholas Eyres, Sept. 5, 1743.
186	COTTRELL	Barbara, and Henry Soule; May 1, 1743.
1-131	"	Albert, and Mary Ann Chaffee; m. by Rev. John West, May 18, 1834.
2-28	"	Ann, and Charles A. Williams; March 10, 1844.
2-29	"	Michael, and Catherine Wallace; m. by Rev. Thatcher Thayer, May 16, 1845.
142	COVILLE	——, and Thomas ——; March 12, 1751.
218	COWLEY	Joseph, and Mrs. Penelope Pelham; m. by Rev. James Honeyman, Nov. 15, 1741.
203	COWDRY	Isaac, and Mehitable Cox; m. by Rev. William Vinall, April 27, 1755.
169	"	Isaac, and Eunice Stacy; Oct. 30, 1754.
172	"	William, and Mary Murphy; m. by Rev. Nicholas Eyres, Aug. 8, 1756.
233	"	William, and Mary Marshal; m. by Rev. Nicholas Ayres, Aug. 8, 1756.
128	COX	Thomas, and Mehit— ——; Sept. 18, 1737.
141	"	Elizabeth, and Elnathan Hammond; Sept. 5, 1750.
203	"	Mehitable, and Isaac Cowdry; April 27, 1755.
190	"	Thomas, and Elizabeth Belcher; m. by Rev. Gardiner Thurston, Aug. 17, 1766.
2-69	"	Elizabeth, and William Kaull, May 26, 1815.
132	COZZENS	Eleanor, and Robert Feke, Sept. 23, 1742.
159	"	Matthew, and Sarah E. ——; m. by Rev. Nicholas Eyres, ——, 1752.
172	"	Gregory, and Mary Fry; m. by Rev. Nicholas Eyres (also 233), July 14, 1756.
171	"	Matthew, and Elizabeth Tillinghast; m. by Rev. Nicholas Eyres, Oct. 17, 1754.
205	"	Robert, and Jane Caswell; m. by Rev. Gardiner Thurston, April 4, 1761.
1-92	"	John, and Margaretta Brittain, March 4, 1804.
2-11	CRABB	Anna, and William Oman, Nov. 28, 1839.
123	CRANDALL	Rebecca, and Peter Marshall, Nov. 26, 1738.
149	"	Charles, and —— ——; m. by Rev. Nicholas Eyres, March 27, 1743.
102	"	Josiah, and Abigail Moss; m. by Rev. James Searing, Sept. 9, 1753.
171	"	James, of Westerly, and Sarah Clarke, of Newport; m. by Rev. Nicholas Eyres, Jan. 17, 1754.
209	"	Ezekiel, and Phebe Bell; m. by Rev. Ezra Stiles, March 6, 1763.
1-67	"	Sarah, and Humphrey Taylor, May 3, 1801.
1-107	"	Abigail, and William Pengelly, June 24, 1819.
2-6	"	Margaret D., and Capt. Daniel Burdick, Sept. 19, 1841.
2-29	"	S. A., and John Smedmore Hicks, June 14, 1846.
21	CRANSTON	Elizabeth, and Charles Tillinghast, May 17, 1711.
33	"	William, and Miriam Martin, May 20, ——. Recorded 1714.
80	"	William, and Mercy Gould; m. by Thomas Coggeshall, Justice, Sept. 12, 1728.
149	"	Mary, and Isaac Cooper, May 8, 1743.
149	"	Eunice, and Daniel Wilcox, June 16, 1743.
119	"	Hart, and Robert Dunbar, ——, 1744.
202	"	Peleg, of Thomas and Patience, and Sarah Carr, of Thomas and Hannah; m. by Daniel Weeden, Warden, Sept. 7, 1749.
141	"	Mary, and Nathaniel Coggeshall, Jan. 31, 1749-50.

187	CRANSTON	Bathsheba, and Benjamin Church, ——. 9, 1756.
204	"	Mary, and Joseph Tillinghast, Oct. 9, 1760.
1-54	"	Rachel, and Henry Hulder, Sept. 29, 1763.
148	"	Rachel, and Henry Miller, Sept. 29, 1763.
148	"	Frances, and Samuel Davenport, March 18, 1764.
190	"	Richmond, and Sarah Hooksey; m. by Rev. Gardiner Thurston, July 15, 1765.
206	"	Abigail, and Daniel Holloway, Nov. 23, 1766.
190	"	Katharine, and Samuel Brown, Jr., Aug. 17, 1766.
209	"	Mary, and William Checkley, Oct. ——, 1766.
121	"	James, and Eunice Richmond; m. by Rev. John Callender, Jr., —— 14, ——.
240	"	Benjamin, and —— ——, Aug. 1, ——.
2-34	"	Margaret, and Henry Crowell, June 1, 1848.
2-34	"	George Edwin, of Providence, and Charlotte W. T. Denham, of Newport; m. by Rev. Henry Jackson, Dec. 20, 1848.
154	CRAPON	Elizabeth, and Joseph Gladding, Feb. 27, 1752.
170	"	Amey, and Israel Caswell, May 17, 1753.
171	"	Samuel, and Mary Achforth; m. by Rev. Nicholas Eyres, Feb. 20, 1755.
204	"	Sarah, and Othniel Tripp, Sept. 29, 1760.
206	"	William, and Priscilla Oxx; m. by Rev. William Vinall, Dec. 7, 1761.
105	CRAWFORD	Freelove, and John Tweedy, July 28, 1735.
187	"	Elizabeth, and Barnabus Hargill, —— 17, 1756.
210	CRITHS	Daniel, and Elizabeth ——; m. by Rev. Gardiner Thurston, Nov. 15, 1761.
170	CROCUM	Elizabeth, and Edward Thurston, April 8, 1753.
109	CROSBY	Thomas, and Mary Barill; m. by Rev. Nicholas Eyres, ——.
206	CROSS	Martha, and Caleb Hacker, July 15, 1765.
2-27	"	Samuel Philip, of Providence, and Ann Elizabeth Bunn, of Newport; m. by Rev. Thatcher Thayer, July 5, 1842.
2-34	CROWELL	Henry, and Margaret Cranston; m. by Rev. Henry Jackson, June 1, 1848.
2-27	CULLER	Henry, of Fall River, and Susan Bassett, of Newport; m. by Rev. Thatcher Thayer, July 3, 1843.
1-110	CURRY	Marcy, and Benjamin Burdick, Nov. 1, 1808.
7	CURTIS	Holland, and Elizabeth Lawton, of George; m. by Henry Brightman, Asst., ——, 1694.
86	"	Obedience Holland, and Ephraim Davis, Oct. 30, 1729.
200	"	Mary Ann, and Joseph Simons, Dec. 19, 1759.
209	C——	William, and Abigail Otis; m. by Rev. Ezra Stiles, Jan. 15, 1764.

D

141	DAERS	Elizabeth, and John Cleveland, April 5, 1748.
145	DAFT	James, and Ann Clarke; m. by Rev. Nicholas Eyres, Sept. 17, ——.
172	DAILEY	Elizabeth, and Henry Clarke, May 3, 1756.
123	DAGGETT	Silvester, and Elizabeth Ellaby, Nov. 6, 1738.
2-6	DANA	James, and Margaret Lance Power; m. by Rev. Francis Vinton, Aug. 4, 1841.
141	DANIELS	Peter, and Tabitha Hayward, Jan. 20, 1749-50.
2-32	DANVILLE	George, and Margaret W. Melville, Jan. 10, 1848.
2-30	DANWELL	Leander M., of Seekonk, Mass., and Elizabeth Prior, of Newport; m. by Rev. Richard Livesey, March 23, 1848.
2-28	DARLING	James A., of Smithfield, and Georgianna Shaw, of Newport; m. by Rev. Thatcher Thayer, April 30, 1844.
204	DATEN	Ann, and John Battey, Dec. 28, 1760.
207	DAVEL	Joseph, Jr., of Dartmouth, and Martha Southwick, of Newport; m. by Rev. John Mason, Aug. 16, 1765.
88	DAVENPORT	Eleazer, and Mary Pitman; m. by Nathaniel Coddington, Asst., Feb. 12, 1713-14.
123	"	Thomas, of Little Compton, and —— ——, July 22, 1737.

151	DAVENPORT	Mary, and Nathan Townsend, July 1, 1745.
102	"	Ebenezer, and Hannah Smith; m. by Rev. James Searing, —— —, 1751.
169	"	Mercy, and Joseph Silvester, June 10, 1754.
148	"	Samuel, and Frances Cranston; m. by Rev. Nicholas Eyres, March 18, 1754.
240	"	Charles, and Mary Shaw, Jan. 21, ——.
2-13	"	Abby E., and Freeman M. Hoxsie, April 12, 1840.
29	DAVIS	Rebecca, and James Burgess, May 1, 1712.
88	"	James, and Sarah Lile; m. by John Coddington, Justice, Oct. 6, 1729.
86	"	Ephraim, and Obedience Holland Curtis; m. by Job Lawton, Justice, Oct. 30, 1729.
114	"	John and Elizabeth May, —— 23, 1733.
95	"	Sarah, and Thomas Weaver, May 1, 1735.
141	"	John, and Susanna Allen, Aug. 20, 1747.
141	"	Martha, and Thomas Sammels, March 22, 1749-50.
141	"	Elizabeth and George Stainer, April 20, 1749.
153	"	John, and Sarah Sisson; m. by Rev. Nicholas Eyres, May 16, 1751.
171	"	Arthur, and Bathsheba Sanford; m. by Rev. Nicholas Eyres, Oct. 4, 1753.
203	"	Henry, and Mary Weeden; m. by Rev. William Vinall, Sept. 9, 1756.
172	"	Elizabeth, and Roger Brown (also 233), April 10, 1757.
177	"	William, and Elizabeth ——, —nary 23, 1759.
146	"	May, and Mrs. Ann Fish; m. by John Gardiner D. Governor, May 23, 1762.
206	"	John, and Martha Pease; m. by Rev. William Vinall, —— 6, 1763.
190	"	Elizabeth, and William Hall, Dec. 5, 1765.
191	"	Ann, and —— Smith, Jan. 5, 1769.
1-29	"	James, of John, Esq., and Rebecca Easton, of John; m. by Rev. John Maxson, Sept. 4, 1776.
1-33	"	Arthur, and Desire Hathaway; m. by Rev. Samuel Hopkins, Dec. 28, 1783.
240	"	Solomon, and Abigail ——, —— 29, ——.
2-54	"	Anna A., and Frederick A. Potter, Aug. 3, 1851.
141	DAWLEY	Mary, and James Young, Sept. 7, 1749.
2-13	"	Oliver J., and Rhoda J. Albro; m. by Rev. Thomas Leaver, Feb. 7, 1841.
141	DAWSON	William, and Mary Kelsey, ——, 1750.
154	DAYTON	Abraham, of New London, and Ann Jones, of Newport; m. by Rev. Nicholas Eyres, Sept. 21, 1751.
191	DAY	William, and Sarah Jennett; m. by Rev. Gardiner Thurston, Dec. 20, 1766.
239	DEBEY	Basteen, and Rebecca Kennedy, Nov. 12, 1749.
2-13	DEBLOIS	Silas D., of Stephen and Sarah E., and Sarah A. Tew, of Josiah and Christiana; m. by Rev. Joseph Smith, April 2, 1841.
2-29	"	John S., and Henrietta M. Tew.; m. by Rev. Thatcher Thayer, Oct. 2, 1845.
205	DECOTAY	Elizabeth, and David Nichols, Feb. 15, 1761.
177	DEDWICH	Elizabeth, and Joseph Pike, March 14, 1762.
187	DEERING	Thomas, of Boston, and Mary Silvester, of Newport, late of Shelter Island; m. by Rev. Ezra Stiles, —— 9, 1756.
56	DEHANE	Jacob, and Bathsheba Morton; m. by Rev. James Honeyman, Feb. 27, 1721-2.
1-23	DELANO	Jethro, and Rhoda Evans; m. by Peleg Barker, Jr., Justice, Sept. 14, 1785.
2-34	DELL	Mary Elizabeth, and Francis Silvey, Nov. 20, 1845.
102	DENHAM	Benjamin, and Mary Johnson; m. by Rev. James Searing, Dec. 15, 1750.
206	"	Abigail, and Joseph Price, April 8, 1762.
2-41	"	Daniel C., of Daniel, and Sarah L. Sherman, of William; m. by Rev. William Gammell, May 2, 1824.
2-34	"	Sarah D. T., and James Henry Atkinson, Oct. 28, 1848.
2-34	"	Charlotte W. T., and George Edwin Cranston, Dec. 20, 1848.

191	DENNISON Daniel, and Amey Murphy, Oct. 16, 1766.
1-39	DENNIS Sarah, and Thomas Wrightington, Jan. 7, 1728-9.
187	" Chloe, and Samuel Blackwell, Oct. 25, 1756.
190	" Jane, and Jonathan Finley, Nov. 24, 1765.
2-35	" Frances, and Samuel Young (also 2-1), Aug. 6, 1839.
2-17	" Elizabeth, and David Melville, Dec. 10, 1843.
2-34	" John D., and Mary P. Hazard; m. by Rev. Henry Jackson, Sept. 27, 1847.
2-41	" Capt. William H., of San Francisco, Cal., and Leone Nigri, of said place; m. by Rev. Benjamin Brierley, Feb. 18, 1857.
2-14	DEVENS Charles, Jr., and Rebecca W. Brown; m. by Rev. Francis Vinton, April 27, 1841.
170	DEWICH Susanna, and Joseph Wilbor, Sept. 2, 1753.
2-24	" Oliver, and Elizabeth J. Hammond; m. by Rev. A. Livesey (also 32), Sept. 10, 1846.
149	DICKENS James, and —— ——; m. by Rev. Nicholas Eyres, May 12, 1743.
142	" Merian, and John ——, Sept. 18, 1751.
177	" Hannah, and Isaac Lawton, May 8, 1760.
2-11	" Roannah R., and John N. Allen, Nov. 5, 1839.
90	DICKINSON Christopher, and Ann Coggeshall; m. by Job Lawton, Justice, Oct. 6, 1730.
111	" Hannah, and Isaac Lawton, Jr., May 8, 1760.
172	DICKS Francis, and Sarah Chadwick; m. by Rev. Nicholas Eyres July 25, 1756.
150	DILLINGHAM Mercy, and Bartholomew Jackson, Nov. 29, 1741.
47	DILL Joseph, and Mary Tubbs; m. by Rev. Nicholas Lang, Dec. 12, 1715.
2-2	DODGE Stephen G., and Harriet S. Stowers; m. by Rev. A. Henry Dumont (also 9), Aug. 1, 1839.
2-25	" Andrew V., of Roxbury, Mass., printer, aged 24 years, son of Noah and Catherine, of New Shoreham, and Sarah A. Milliken, of Newport, aged 23 years, dau. of Absalom and Zeba; int. May 19; m. June 2, 1847, by Rev. Joseph Smith.
2-33	" Esther, and William T. Bowler, Dec. 16, 1849.
238	DONALDSON William, and Mary ——, July 13, 1743.
141	DONNELLY Elizabeth, and John Vial, May 5, 1747.
141	" John, and Jane Mense, Aug. 12, 1747.
141	" ——, and Daniel McGow, —— 13, 1747.
123	DORRELL William, and Sarah——, May 8, 1737.
206	DOUBLEDAY Benjamin, and Mary Ladd; m. by Rev. William Vinall, March 3, 1763.
1-67	" Dorcas, and Thomas Evans, March 8, 1801.
142	DOUGLASS ——, and Robert Cooper, —— 12, 1750.
171	" Elizabeth, and John —anoll; m. by Rev. Nicholas Eyres, June 9, 1754.
2-6	DOWER Margaret Lance, and James Dana, Aug. 4, 1841.
119	DOWNER John, and Sarah Weatherdon; m. by Rev. Nicholas Eyres, —— 1, 1744.
190	" Dorcas, and Benjamin Tuel, ——, 1766.
153	DOWNING Ruth, and John Peet, April 21, 1751.
1-55	" Henry, and Mary Almy; m. by Rev. William Patten, Aug. 11, 1799.
1-38	" Rebecca, and Joseph Snow, July 17, 1785.
1-76	" Merebah, and John Woodmansee, Oct. 18, 1803.
1-104	" Benjamin, of Nicholas, and Sarah Albro, of Henry; m. by Rev. Michael Eddy, Nov. 9, 1809.
2-15	" Eliza, and John Weaver, Aug. 16, 1842.
151	DOWNS John, and Abigail Chace; m. by Rev. James Searing, ——, 1744.
149	DOW John, and Eliza ——; m. by Rev. Nicholas Eyres, Jan. 27, 1742-3.
2-26	DOYLE Margaret, and Andrew Andrewson; May 4, 1847.
188	DREW James, and Elizabeth Tew; m. by Rev. Ezra Stiles, March 30, 1759.
123	DRIVER Sarah, and William Moyeon; Dec. 31, 1738.
2-28	DUMONT Rev. A. Henry, of Morristown, N. J., and Mary G. Clarke, of Newport; m. by Rev Thatcher Thayer, Nov. 14, 1844.

119	DUNBAR Robert, of Newport, and Heart Cranston, of Jamestown; m. by Rev. Nicholas Eyres, ——, 1744.	
221	" Elizabeth, and John Huxham, Nov. 21, 1762.	
1-136	" Mary A., and Capt. Joseph B. Harkins, March 10, 1839.	
123	DUNHAM John, and Mary Lucas, —— 29, 1738.	
151	" Joseph, and Elizabeth Orne; m. by Rev. James Searing, Oct. 21, 1744.	
152	" Mercy, and Benjamin Mortimer, May 8, 1746.	
199	" John, and Elizabeth Phillips; m. by Rev. Gardiner Thurston, Sept. 20, 1759.	
177	" Robert, and Elizabeth Spooner, Aug. 26, 1762.	
6	DUNN Samuel, of Richard, and Sarah Bailey, of Joseph, Oct. 8, 1702.	
39	" Lemuel, of Newport, and Ann Clarke, of Kings Towne; m. at Kings Towne, 9 m., 1718, by Samuel Fones, Justice.	
195	" Richard, and Mary G——; m. by Rev. John Callender, Jr., Aug. 16, 1745.	
171	" Elizabeth, and Walter Chapman, July ——, 1754.	
169	" Cary, and Ann Atkinson, (also 234); m. by Rev. Nicholas Eyres, Nov. 1, 1754.	
2-40	" Joanna, and John Sullivan, June 15, 1851.	
203	DUNSCOMBE John, and Lydia Bailey; m. by Rev. William Vinall, July 17, 1758.	
190	DUNTON Sarah, and William Langley, April 17, 1766.	
1-48	DUNWELL John, of Providence, and Sally Cornell, of Newport; m. by Rev. Gardiner Thurston, Jan. 15, 1797.	
119	DURFEE Robert, and Amey Burroughs; m. by Rev. Nicholas Eyres, May 1, 1746.	
1-22	" Oliver, of Middletown, and Elizabeth Longley, of Newport; m. by Rev. Gardiner Thurston, Oct. 13, 1782.	
1-103	" Rebecca and Jordan Sprague, Aug. 14, 1814.	
80	DYER Nathaniel, and Elizabeth Parrot, of Simon; m. by John Coggeshall, Asst., Aug. 9, 1688.	
61	" Ann, and Cary Clarke, Feb. 14, 1693-4.	
171	" John, and Mary Hickey; m. by Rev. Nicholas Eyres, Oct. 25, 1754.	
172	" Edward, of North Kingstown, and Abigail Pate, of Newport; m. by Rev. Nicholas Eyres, (also 233), Jan. 27, 1757.	
172	" Abigail, and Job Bennett, (also 234), April 10, 1757.	
145	" Mary, and Daniel Hunter, Oct. 9, 1757.	
204	" Jerusha, and Caleb Jeffries, Oct. 17, 1760.	
147	" Charles, and —— ——; m. by Rev. Nicholas Eyres, ——, 1762.	
190	" Mary, and Thomas Townsend, Dec. 20, 1765.	
243	" Elizabeth, and Jeremiah Child, July 24, 17—.	
102	DYKES Mary, and Robert Nichols, ——, 1754.	
233	" Francis, and Sarah Chadwick; m. by Nicholas Eyres, July 25, 1756.	
191	" William, and Elizabeth Allison; m. by Rev. Gardiner Thurston, Jan. 8, 1767.	
154	D—— Niobe, and Daniel Lambert, June 3, 1753.	

E

191	EARLE Thomas, and Mary Tripp; m. by Rev. Gardiner Thurston, May 14, 1767.	
2-21	" Harriet C., and Stephen Cornell, Sept. 28, 1823.	
19	EASTON Sarah, and Benjamin Coggeshall, (also 25), Dec. 22, 1709.	
43	" —— and Caleb Coggeshall, May 19, 1720 (?).	
134	" Patience, and Christopher Townsend, Dec. 26, 1723.	
73	" Mary, and John Taylor, May 10, 1724.	
79	" Margaret, and Henry Tew, Oct. 2, 1728.	
174	" Freelove, and Francis Pope, Sept. 17, 1729.	
128	" John, of Stephen, and Patience Redwood, of Abraham, late of Salem, Mass., dec.; m. by John Wanton, Governor, April 17, 1735.	

125	EASTON	Marian, and Fones Hazard, Oct. 11, 1739.
132	"	John, and Elizabeth Wallen; m. by Rev. John Callender, Jr., Nov. 25, 1742.
102	"	John, and Susannah Gerold; m. by Rev. James Searing, June 10, 1750.
169	"	Mary, and Capt. Christopher Gardiner, Sept. 16, 1753.
148	"	Freelove, and William Gubbins, April 26, 1764.
209	"	Ann, and Daniel Spencer, Sept. 18, 1764.
190	"	Walt, and Rouse Potter, Dec. 20, 1765.
1-29	"	Rebecca, and James Davis, Sept. 4, 1776.
109	"	William, and Freelove Gardiner; m. by Rev. Nicholas Eyres, —— 12, ——.
217	"	Hannah, and William ——, June 23, ——.
2-84	"	Edward, and Abby S. Howard; m. by Rev. D. H. Lord, Jan. 4, 1846.
171	ECKSTENE	Gottlieb, and Katherine Bonnoway; m. by Rev. Nicholas Eyres, Aug. 19, 1754.
152	EDDY	Mary, and Zebulon Spinney, May 11, 1746.
1-132	"	Michael, of Michael, of Swnen, Mass., and Mary Wilbor, of Joseph, of Johnston, R. I.; m. at Johnston, by Elder Samuel Winsor, Sept. 27, 1787.
2-23	"	Joseph W., and Anna M. Robbins, of Asher; m. by Rev. Michael Eddy, May 5, 1822.
1-135	"	Sarah Ann, and Micah W. Spencer, Sept. 5, 1836.
2-27	"	William, of Rellington, Conn., and Harriet C. Tripp, of Newport; m. by Rev. Thatcher Thayer, Aug. 8, 1843.
169	"	Edmund's Ann, and Richard Humphries, Nov. 1, 1753.
210	"	Katherine, and James Smith, Nov. 15, 1761.
109	EDWARDS	Richard, and Ann Chace; m. by Rev. Nicholas Eyres, —— 20, ——.
1-118	"	Daniel, Jr., of Charlestown, R. I., and Clarissa Gifford, of Jeremiah, of Portsmouth; m. by Rev. William Gammell, Jan. 29, 1826.
151	EGAN	Timothy, and Hester Wilson; m. by Rev. James Searing, Sept. 1, 1745.
123	ELDERTON	Nathaniel, and Priscilla ——, July 2, 1738.
121	ELDREDGE	Randolph, and Freelove Fry; m. by Rev. Nicholas Eyres, Dec. 18, 1744.
172	"	Benjamin, and Mary Gardiner; m. by Rev. Nicholas Eyres, Aug. 22, 1756.
204	"	Dorothy, and Thomas Chadwick, July 13, 1760.
233	ELDRED	Benjamin, and Mary Gardiner; m. by Rev. Nicholas Eyres, Aug. 22, 1756.
116	"	—— and Mary Maryott; m. by Elder John Maxson, Nov. 19 ——.
2-12	"	Mrs. Sarah, and Ebenezer Briggs, March 8, 1840.
222	ELIZER	Isaac, and Richa Isaacks, Feb. 28, 1758.
123	ELLALY	Elizabeth, and Silvester Daggett, Nov. 6, 1738.
68	ELLERY	Anstice, and John Almy, Aug. —, 1716.
59	"	William, and Elizabeth Almy; m. by Rev. James Honeyman, Jan. 3, 1722-23.
220	"	William, Jr., of Newport, and —— Remington, of Cambridge, Mass.; m. by Rev. Nathan Appleton, Oct. 11, 1750.
188	"	Christopher, and Mary Vernon; m. by Rev. Ezra Stiles, Nov. 26, 1760.
196	"	Ann, and John Burt, Nov. 17, 1768.
240	"	Abigail, and Rev. John Burt, Aug. 20, ——.
1-71	"	Christopher, and Clarissa Bird, Oct. 22, 1792.
1-45	"	Martha Redwood, and Christopher Grant Champlain, April 14, 1793.
1-45	"	Benjamin, of Hon. William, and Mehitable Redwood, of Hon. Abraham; m. by Rev. Ezra Stiles, Jan. 22, 1769.
196	ELLIOT	Robert, and Abigail Searing, of Rev. James, dec. (also 209); m. by Rev. Ezra Stiles, July 21, 1765.
1-82	ELY	Hepsa, and Gold Selleck Silliman, Sept. 17, 1801.
123	EMMONS	Ebenezer, and Sarah Tiffany, —— 6, 1738.
1-37	"	Elizabeth, and James Gouffran, Feb. 4, 1781.

171	ENGLAND Mary, and Benjamin Burtis, Sept. 1, 1754.
104	ERWIN Edward, of Boston, and Abby Stanhope, of Newport; m. by Rev. Ezra Stiles, Dec. 30, 1759.
2-17	ESLECK Phebe A., and William Sisson, Aug. 4, 1843.
2-28	ESSEX James J., of Windham, Conn., and Martha A. Burdick, of Charles E., of Newport; m. by Rev. Thatcher Thayer, July 16, 1844.
2-27	EUSTIS William, of Plymouth, N. H., and Ann Banks, of Newport; m. by Rev. Thatcher Thayer, March —, 1843.
1-24	EVANS Rhoda, and Jethro Delano, Aug. 5, 1781.
1-67	" Thomas, of Evan, and Dorcas Doubleday, of Benjamin; m. by Elder William Bliss, March 8, 1801.
62	EVENGS Mary, and Joseph Peckham, —— 3, 1705.
203	EWEN John, and Mary Hayward; m. by Rev. William Vinall, Sept. 22, 1756.
1-15	EXAN Sarah, and Richard Moore, Nov. 12, 1754.
182	EXCEENE Elizabeth, and James Burgess, July 29, 1742.
171	" Sarah, and Richard Moore, Nov. 12, 1754.
118	" William, and Elizabeth Ash; m. by Elder John Maxon, Sept. 13, 1755.
199	EYRES Thomas, and Amey Tillinghast; m. by Rev. Gardiner Thurston, July 12, 1759.
122	E—— John, Jr., and Elizabeth Hall, both of Portsmouth; m. by Rev. John Callender, Jr., Feb. 5, 1740-1.
154	E—— Sarah, and Matthew Cozzens, ——, 1752.
2-28	E—— Jane, and Charles H. Watson, Oct. 20, 1844.

F

123	FAIRBANKS Deborah, and Richmond Hillsborough, March 13, 1740.
151	" Mary, and John Lamb, Aug. 5, 1744.
188	" John, and Amey Heffernan; m. by Rev. Ezra Stiles, April 27, 1760.
190	" Jeremiah, and Ann Bridge; m. by Rev. Gardiner Thurston, July 1, 1766.
1-83	" Benjamin, and Abigail Huddy; m. by Rev. Samuel Hopkins, Dec. 23, 1789.
64	FAIRCHILD Ann, and Peter Bours, —— 16, 1723.
195	" Phebe, and John Magee, Aug. 3, 1758.
2-45	FALES Nathaniel, of Taunton, Mass., and Elizabeth A. Shaw, of Newport; m. by Rev. Leland Howard, July 6, 1839.
149	FARRELL Patrick, and Rachel Beere; m. by Rev. Nicholas Eyres, Jan. 14, 1742.
2-5	FARRENS William, and Eliza Laird; m. by Rev. Francis Vinton, Nov. 14, 1840.
170	FEAR Elizabeth, and William Brown, June 24, 1753.
132	FEKE Robert, and Eleanor Cozzens; m. by Rev. John Callender, Jr., Sept. 23, 1742.
2-27	FERGUSON Henry, of Providence, and Jane Shortbridge, of Newport; m. by Rev. Thatcher Thayer, March 16, 1842.
1-54	FIELD Benjamin, of Providence, and Sally Carter, of Newport; m. by Rev. Gardiner Thurston, June 19, 1798.
102	FINCH William, and Margaret Topham; m. by Rev. James Searing, Nov. 1, 1753.
190	FINLEY Jonathan, and Jane Dennis; m. by Rev. Gardiner Thurston, Nov. 24, 1765.
149	FISH Freelove, and James Sisson, Nov. 12, 1741.
170	" ——— and Stephen ——; m. by Rev. Nicholas Eyres, Sept. 16, 1753.
118	" Jeremiah, of Newport, and Alice Platt, of Jamestown; m. by Rev. Nicholas Eyres, July 7, 1755.
205	" Jonathan, and Ann Child; m. by Rev. William Vinall, —— 13, 1758.
204	" Michael, and Samuel Marycott, Sept. 13, 1761.
146	" Mrs. Ann, and Moy Davis, May 23, 1762.

1-59	FISH John, of Warren, R. I., and Rachel Reed, of Newport; m. by Rev. Gardiner Thurston, Sept. 5, 1790.
1-86	" Ruth, and Abraham Barker, May 16, 1802.
2-11	" Amey, and Levi Johnson, Nov. 21, 1842.
1-21	FISK Samuel, of Smithfield, and Sabrina Wright; m. by Rev. Gardiner Thurston, Aug. 13, 1785.
242	FLAGG Conrad, and —— Hull; m. by Rev. Gardiner Thurston, March —, 1768.
122	" Ebenezer, and Mary Ward; m. by Rev. John Callender, Jr., — 8, —.
66	FLEET Elizabeth, and Samuel Vernon, April 10, 1707.
181	" Ann, and James Clarke, Feb. 26, 1737-8.
154	" Esther, and Joseph Sanford, Sept. 18, 1751.
179	" Elizabeth, and Samuel Freebody, Jan. 6, 1760.
1-122	" Melanchon, of Jamaica, L. I., and Esther Freebody, of Newport; m. at Bristol by William Troop, Justice, May 25, 1829.
2-66	FLUDDER William, of John and Jane, and Catherine Sherman Jack, of Alexander and Sarah Hudson; m. by Rev. Thomas W. Tucker, Jan. 26, 1832.
2-35	FOREMAN George W., of Philadelphia, Pa., and Elizabeth Francis, of Newport; m. by Rev. Josiah P. Tustin, Sept. 28, 1846.
1-58	FORRESTER Elizabeth, and Benania M. Shaw, Feb. 3, 1793.
119	FOSTER Ruth, and John Axton, ——, 1746.
2-29	" Henry, and Rebecca Jane Calvert; m. by Rev. Thatcher Thayer, Sept. 10, 1846.
177	FOUNTAIN Mary, and Edward Thurston, June 17, 1764.
141	FOWLER James, and Ann James, June 28, 1750.
170	" Samuel, and Mary Gardiner; m. by Rev. Nicholas Eyres, Sept. 6, 1753.
157	" William, and Phebe Hopkins; m. by Rev. Gardiner Thurston, May 12, 1765.
1-18	" Mehitable, and William Burt, Nov. 18, 1776.
9	FOX Sarah, and John ——; m by Nathaniel Coddington, Asst., ——, 1704.
239	" Dorothy, and John Youldbridge, March 9, 1748-9.
188	" James, and Sarah Pitman; m. by Rev. Ezra Stiles, Aug. 6, 1761.
2-28	FRANCIS Elizabeth, and George S. Reed, June 17, 1844.
2-35	" Elizabeth, and George W. Foreman, Sept. 28, 1846.
151	FRANKLIN Abia, and George Buckmaster, July 17, 1743.
142	" ——, and William Allen, —— 23, 1750.
205	" Elizabeth, and Isaac All, March 19, 1761.
179	FREEBODY Samuel, and Elizabeth Fleet; m. by Charles Bardin, Justice, Jan. 6, 1760.
2-40	" Benjamin T., and Elizabeth Ann Romans; m. by Rev. Esek Mudge, Feb. 3, 1826.
1-122	" Esther, and Melanchon Fleet, May 25, 1829.
15	FREEBORN Mary, and —— Coggeshall, March 11, 1708.
171	" Gideon, of Portsmouth, and Martha Joy, of Newport; m. by Rev. Nicholas Eyres, April 25, 1754.
205	" Sarah, and Alexander Huling, May 14, 1761.
1-64	" Joseph, of Newport, and Elizabeth Wood, of Middletown; m. by Rev. Gardiner Thurston, July 12, 1776.
1-117	" William W., and Sarah Weaver; m. by Rev. Reuben Hubbard, Oct. 19, 1806.
1-95	" George and Mary M. Barker; m. by Rev. John B. Gibson, Aug. 28, 1808.
2-47	" Abby B., and Gideon Almy, Oct. 12, 1834.
2-1	" Mary, and Samuel Hopkins, Aug. 4, 1839.
2-8	" Joseph B., of Newport, and Mary A. Short, of Wickford; m. by Rev. Franklin Gavitt, April 14, 1842.
2-36	" Ann, and Elias Gibson, June 25, 1845.
2-29	" Michael, 2d, of Newport, and Rhoda ——, of Providence; m. by Rev. Thatcher Thayer, April 6, 1846.
2-31	" Phebe B., and Elijah Sherman, 3d, (also 2-20), May 7, 1848.
188	FREEMAN John, of Tiverton, and Elizabeth Bryant, of Newport; m. by Rev. Ezra Stiles, ——, 1758.

2-28		FREEMAN Charles G., and Ellen Brown; m. by Rev. Thatcher Thayer, Jun. 24, 1844.
2-43		FRENCH Joseph J. and Elizabeth A. Braman; m. by Rev. Arthur A. Ross, Nov. 30, 1837.
2-58		FRIEND Catherine E., and Edwin Peabody, Oct. 25, 1832.
1-126	"	Mary Jane, and John J. Stacy, Feb. 3, 1833.
2-17	"	George W., and Cynthia M. Barker; m. by Rev. Thomas Leaver, May 28, 1843.
188		FROST George, and Mary Russell; m. by Rev. Ezra Stiles, April 9, 1761.
188		FRYERS Elizabeth, and Benjamin Brown, May 6, 1759.
2		FRY Thomas, and —— Clarke, of Latham, Dec. 12, 1700.
90	"	Sarah, and Thomas Leach, July 5, 1709.
121	"	Freelove, and Randolph Eldredge, Dec. 18, 1740.
239	"	Abigail, and John Monroe, Aug. 16, 1749.
153	"	Abigail, and Thomas Carter, Sept. 10, 1749.
172	"	Mary, and Gregory Cozzens, July 14, 1756.
233	"	Mary, and Gregory Cozzens, July 15, 1756.
188	"	Elizabeth, and John Wills, Nov. 8, 1759.
199	"	John, and Ann Millward; m. by Martin Howard, Justice, Oct. 8, 1760.
190	"	James, and Dorothy Cartwright; m. by Rev. Gardiner Thurston, Aug. 4, 1765.
208	"	Stephen, and Ann Johnson; m. by Rev. John Mason, April 21, 1766.
209	"	Ann, and Benjamin Chace, Oct. 16, 1766.
145	"	Mary, and Louis Ba——, Oct. 15, ——.
1-60	"	Amey, and Lemuel Bailey, April 28, 1800.
109		FULLERTON Edward, and Anne Howard; m. by Rev. Nicholas Eyres, —— 21, ——.
2-89		FULLER Mrs. Isadora, and William Clarke, March 26, 1844.

G

141		GALLEDAT John, and Hannah Rouse, April 5, 1748.
22		GARDINER Joseph, and Catherine Holmes; m. by Caleb Carr, Governor, Nov. 30, 1693.
235	"	Elizabeth, and Samuel Lynden, Dec. 22, 1734.
131	"	James, and Eliza Sanford; m. by Rev. Nicholas Eyres, Jan. 19, 1737-8.
121	"	Elizabeth, and Clarke Brown, Dec. 4, 1740.
140	"	Pompey, servant of Caleb and Lucy Church, servant of Mrs. Martha (col.), —— 1741.
151	"	Bethia, and William Bennett, Jan. 16, 1742-3.
113	"	Mary, and Benjamin Wickham (also 149). Dec. 25, 1743.
136	"	Frances, and William Benson, Oct. 3, 1745.
179	"	Catherine, and Thomas Redman, July 6, 1750.
154	"	William Thurston and Mary Men—eli; m. by Rev. Nicholas Eyres, Sept. 19, 1751.
170	"	Mary, and Samuel Fowler, Sept. 6, 1753.
169	"	Capt. Christopher, of North Kingstown, and Mary Easton, of Middletown; m. at Middletown by Martin Howard, Justice, Sept. 16, 1753.
172	"	Mary, and Benjamin Eldredge, Aug. 22, 1756.
200	"	William, and Mary Bassett; m. by Rev. Gardiner Thurston, Dec. 5, 1759.
204	"	John, and Mary Gardiner; m. by Rev. Gardiner Thurston, Aug. 14, 1760.
204	"	Mary, and John Gardiner, Aug. 14, 1760.
233	"	Mary, and Benjamin Eldred, Aug. 22, 1756.
204	"	Susanna, and William Greenman, Nov. 27, 1760.
188	"	Sanford, and Ann Newton; m. by Rev. Ezra Stiles, Dec. 4, 1760.
204	"	Elizabeth, and John Bridge, Dec. 13, 1760.
210	"	John Grinnall, and Abigail King; m. by Rev. Gardiner Thurston, Nov. 27, 1761.

179	GARDINER	Sarah, and William Ladd (also 210), Dec. 27, 1761.
147	"	Mary, and Charles Spooner, ——, 1762.
148	"	Ann, and Willett Carpenter, July 1, 1764.
157	"	Katherine, and William Burrough, Nov. 11, 1764.
209	"	Elizabeth, and David Moore, Nov. 20, 1765.
190	"	Catherine, and Thomas Gardiner, ——, 1766.
190	"	Thomas, of South Kingstown, and Catherine Gardiner, of Newport; m. by Rev. Gardiner Thurston, ——, 1766.
109	"	Freelove, and William Easton, —— 12, ——.
114	"	Lydia, and William Rodman, ——.
235	"	William, and Mary Carr; m. by Rev. Nicholas Eyres, July 27, ——.
240	"	Lucy, and Benjamin Sherbourne, Sept. 5, ——.
1-108	"	William C., of Newport, and Eliza F. Cazenove, of Alexander Co.; m. by Rev. James Muir, July 13, 1816.
2-63	"	Clarissa, and Oliver Read, Dec. 1, 1822.
2-10	"	Robert Hallowell, of Gardiner, Me., and Sarah Fenwick Jones, of Savannah, Ga.; m. at Newport by Rev. Francis Vinton, June 28, 1842.
2-27	"	Stephen A., and Martha E. Bigley; m. by Rev. Thatcher Thayer, Sept. 26, 1842.
2-9	"	Clarissa, and Oliver Read, Dec. 1, 1842.
2-24	"	Harriet A. or F., and Jacob W. Lamb (also 2-132), Nov. 9, 1846.
2-25	"	Jeffrey, and Julia E. Spooner; m. by Rev. Richard Livesey (also 2-32), Dec. 13 or 18, 1846.
2-35	"	William H., and Elizabeth Caswell; m. by Rev. Theron C. Brown, June 2, 1850.
2-43	GARRICK	Thomas, and Mary Lawler; m. by Rev. John Brady, Nov. 14, 1847.
171	GASSIA	John, and Esther Thomas; m. by Rev. Nicholas Eyres, Nov. 25, 1753.
2-15	GATEWOOD	Eliza A. D., and Jerome Sherman, Oct. 12, 1842.
39	GAVITT	John, and Sarah Stephenson; m. by Nathaniel Sheffield, Asst., Sept. 13, 1714.
132	GAY	Peace, and —— ——; m. by Rev. James Searing, —— —, 1746.
2-33	GEISSERT	Edward, and Bridget Brophy; m. by Rev. B. Othman, Nov. 17, 1849.
1-21	GEOFFERY	Andre, and Sarah Beleher, of Joseph, dec.; m. by Rev. Timothy Waterhouse, July 24, 1785.
181	GEORGE	Eliza, and William Mackey, Aug. 14, 1737.
102	GEROLD	Susannah, and John Easton, June 10, 1750.
1-10	GIBBONS	Hen. William, and Valerie Richardson; m. by Rev. Samuel Hopkins, Nov. 7, 1773.
168	GIBBS	Elisha, Jr., and Elizabeth Howland; m. by Rev. John Callender, Jr., April 7, 1737.
152	"	Elisha, of Newport, and Lydia Peckham, of Middletown; m. by Rev. James Searing, Dec. 19, 1745.
155	"	Sarah, and Charles Sherman, Nov. 21, 1753.
157	"	Rebecca, and William Lawton, Nov. 20, 1764.
1-91	"	George, and Mary Channing, Oct. 9, 1768.
1-33	"	Rebecca, and George Hunt, July 24, 1785.
1-33	"	Elizabeth, and Benjamin Tewel, Nov. 6, 1787.
109	GIBSON	Benjamin, and Mary Warner; m. by Rev. Nicholas Eyres, —— 31, ——.
236	"	Elias, of Providence, and Ann Freeborn, of Newport; m. by Rev. E. B. Bradford, June 25, 1845.
2-24	"	George W., and Eliza Sitterly; m. by Rev. Richard Livesey, May 24, 1846.
36	GIFFORD	Ann, and William Swan, June 26, 1716.
1-118	"	Clarissa, and Daniel Edwards, Jr., Jan. 29, 1826.
2-26	"	Ann E., and Martin R. Kenyon, Feb. 8, 1848.
118	GILBERT	Caleb, and Ruth Clarke; m. by Rev. Nicholas Eyres, Aug. 7, 1755.
205	"	——, and Sarah Clarke; m. by Rev. Gardiner Thurston, —— —, 1761.

200	GILLIS	Alexander, and Ann Sabin; m. by Rev. Gardiner Thurston, Jan. 27, 1760.
171	GILL	John, and Sarah Sweet; m. by Rev. Nicholas Eyres, Dec. 12, 1754.
2-8	GILMAN	Mrs. Elizabeth, and Edward C. Locke, Dec. 29, 1841.
1-106	GILPIN	John Bernard, and Mary Elizabeth Miller, of John and Ruth, Nov. 20, 1803.
239	GLADDING	Rebecca, and Benedict Taber, Aug. 5, 1747.
102	"	Hannah, and Joseph Belcher, Feb. 14, 1751.
154	"	Joseph, and Elizabeth Crapen; m. by Rev. Nicholas Eyres, Feb. 27, 1752.
154	"	Elizabeth, and Thomas West, Feb. 28, 1752.
187	"	Priscilla, and Benjamin Oxx, Nov. 11, 1756.
188	"	Jonathan, and Rhoda Chace; m. by Rev. Ezra Stiles, Aug. 30, 1759.
208	"	Ann, and Restcome Helme, Oct. 13, 1765.
2-21	"	Susan F., and Stafford Bryer, Aug. 18, 1844.
2-38	"	John, of Edward, and Mary Ann Holt, of Easton; m. by Rev. B. Othman, Dec. 23, 1849.
2-31	GLOVER	Charles Henry, of Brooklyn, N. Y., son of Charles, and Maria Gardiner Othman, of Newport, dau. of Rev. Bartholomew; m. by Rev. Bartholomew Othman, Aug. 29, 1849.
185	GODDARD	John, of Daniel and Mary, and Hannah Townsend, of Job, Aug. 7, 1746.
237	"	James, of Daniel and Mary, and Susanna Townsend, of Job and Rebecca, Jan. 17, 1750.
142	"	John, and Olive Wood, June 19, 1753.
190	"	Remembrance, and Anthony Shaw, July 25, 1765.
190	"	John, and Mary Nichols; m. by Rev. Gardiner Thurston, Aug. 8, 1765.
2-9	"	Catherine and William Gray, Dec. 5, 1841.
75	GODFREY	John, and Elizabeth Carr; m. by Samuel Cranston, Governor, May 28, 1701.
18	"	Mary, and Isaac Sherman, Nov. —, 1709.
147	"	Joshua, and —— ——; m. by Rev. Nicholas Eyres, —— 27, 1762.
148	"	William, and Freelove Pearce; m. by Rev. Nicholas Eyres, Nov. 20, 1763.
2-14	GOFF	Robert, of John and Sarah, and Catherine S. Tew, of Joshua; m. by Rev. Joseph Smith, Dec. 5, 1841.
148	GOLDTHWAIT	Samuel, and Amey Bordin, Feb. 12, 1761.
205	GOODMAN	Thomas, and Sarah Campbell; m. by Rev. Gardiner Thurston, May 7, 1761.
88	GOODSON	Elizabeth, and Peter Coggeshall, Nov. 11, 1719.
88	"	John, and Elizabeth Peckham; m. by Rev. James Honeyman, May 19, 1731.
2-66	"	John W., and Dorcas D. Martin; m. by Rev. John B. Gibson, May 26, 1841.
2-3	"	Anna S., and Joshua W. Tripp, Dec. 9, 1839.
164	GOODSPEED	Ruth, and Theophilas Bradford, Feb. 24, 1731.
88	"	William, and Ann M. Jewett; m. by Rev. Henry Jackson, Sept. 18, 1848.
15	GORAM	Samuel, late of Yarmouth, Mass., and Elizabeth Hedge, of Newport; m. by Samuel Cranston, Governor, June 22, 1708.
1-37	GOUFFSAM	James, and Elizabeth Emmons; m. by Rev. Gardiner Thurston, Feb. 4, 1781.
191	GOULDER	Mary, and Robert Shoul, July 5, 1767.
37	GOULDING	George, of Roger, dec., and Mary Scott, of John; m. by William Wanton, Asst., Aug. 17, 1707.
137	"	Penelope, and William Coddington, May 20, 1740.
62	GOULD	Daniel, of Thomas and Elizabeth, of Newport, and Mary Brown, of John, of Swansey, Mass.; m. by Jonathan Nichols, Asst., Nov. 17, 1719.
80	"	Mercy, and William Cranston, Sept. 12, 1728.
93	"	Isaac, and Ann Slocum. Recorded Feb. 26, 1732-3.
1-13	"	Mary, and Benjamin Almy, Oct. 27, 1762.
215	"	Joseph, and Martha Rogers; m. by Elder John Maxon, Feb. 5, 1765.

117	GOULD	Mary, and Benjamin Almy, April 8, 1772.
2-12	"	John, and Anne E. Peckham; m. by Rev. James A. McKensie, March 9, 1840.
2-13	"	Mary, and William Gyles, Nov. 22, 1840.
2-15	"	James C., of Middletown, and Deborah M. Littlefield, of Newport; m. by Rev. Thomas Leaver, Oct. 16, 1842.
239	GRAFTON	Nathaniel, and Elizabeth Chambers, April 24, 1747.
102	"	Jane, and John Jones, ——, 1752.
123	GRAHAM	Rebecca, and Benjamin Brown, Jan. 30, 1737-8.
2-29	"	James, and Ann Asher; m. by Rev. Thatcher Thayer, Nov. 26, 1845.
134	GRANT	Alexander, and Abigail Cheeseborough; m. by Rev. Thomas Potter, Oct. 6, 1760.
205	"	Mary, and Gideon Tomlin, Feb. 3, 1761.
145	"	Robert, and Mary Thomas; m. by Rev. Nicholas Eyres, Oct. 8, ——.
169	GRAN——	Mrs. Mary, and Andrew Heatley, July 26, 1750.
234	GRAY	Mary, and Russell Hubbard, Jan. 30, 1755.
190	"	Mary, and Joshua Stacy, Oct. 27, 1765.
2-9	"	William, and Catherine Goddard; m. by Rev. Thomas Leaver, Dec. 5, 1841.
148	GREENBORGE	Oliver, and Mary Slocum; m. by Rev. Nicholas Eyres, Nov. 13, 1763.
131	GREENE	Eliza, and John Hookey, April —, 1737.
123	"	John, of Warwick, and —— ——, of Newport, Dec. 8, 1737.
149	"	Zebulon and Sarah Tripp; m. by Rev. Nicholas Eyres, April 1, 1742.
119	"	John, and Ann Coddington; m. by Rev. Nicholas Eyres, —— 23, 1744.
152	"	Hope, and —— ——; m. by Rev. James Searing, ——, 1746.
141	"	Mary, and Ephraim Macumber, Jan. 11, 1749-50.
154	"	Samuel, and Elizabeth Stan—; m. by Rev. Nicholas Eyres, March 19, 1752.
145	"	John, of Middletown, and Katharine Carr, of Newport; m. by Rev. Nicholas Eyres, Sept. 22, 1757.
200	"	Sarah, and Obed Wing, Jan. 17, 1760.
204	"	Mary, and Daniel Shrieve, Oct. 1, 1760.
188	"	Nathaniel, of Providence, and Keziah Richardson, of Newport; m. by Rev. Ezra Stiles, Jan. 14, 1761.
198	"	Catherine, and John Langley, Aug. ——, 1762.
190	"	Elizabeth, and James Thompson, Oct. 2, 1765.
190	"	Martha, and Anthony Wilbor, April 3, 1766.
190	"	Edward, and Rhoda Wilcox; m. by Rev. Gardiner Thurston, Oct. 1, 1766.
116	"	Deliverance, and Thomas Hudson (also 1-14), Jan. 8, 1768.
1-33	"	James, and Ruth Coggeshall; m. by Rev. Samuel Hudson, Nov. 25, 1783.
119	"	——, and Samuel Burroughs ——.
1-123	"	Phebe C., and Benjamin B. Howland, Aug. 3, 1817.
2-5	"	Clarrissa, and John Hudson, Nov. 4, 1839.
2-27	"	Solomon, of Providence, and Mary B. Munchester, of Newport; m. by Rev. Thatcher Thayer, Jan. 15, 1843.
233	GREENHILL	Isaiah, and Katherine Hill, (also 234); m. by Rev. Nicholas Eyres, Jan. 30, 1757.
205	"	Zebedee, of Little Compton, and Sarah Reider, of Newport; m. by Rev. Gardiner Thurston, May 28, 1761.
14	GREENMAN	——, and —— Casey, March 8, 1705-6.
41	"	Ann, and Benjamin Wilson, Jan. 9, 1719-20.
99	"	Lois, and John Mitchell, June 19, 1720.
131	"	Abigail, and Matthew Pate, Dec. 30, 1733.
153	"	Jeremiah, and Amey Wyles; m. by Rev. Nicholas Eyres, Aug. 13, 1749.
105	"	Job, and Elizabeth Stanton; m. by Rev. Nicholas Eyres, May 24, 1750.
199	"	Sylvanus, and Susanna Brand; m. by Elder John Maxon, Sept. 10, 1759.

204	GREENMAN William, and Susanna Gardiner; m. by Rev. Gardiner Thurston, Nov. 27, 1760.
148	" Amey, and Michael Blacon, Jan. 8, 1764.
1-67	" Job, and Lucy Brayton, Jan. 1, 1766.
154	" Esther, and —— ——; m. by Rev. Nicholas Eyres, ——.
240	GREGORY John, and Sarah Morris, Oct. 24, ——.
207	GREVE John Tripp, and Mary Southwick; m. by Rev. John Mason, Oct. 3, 1765.
206	GRICE Michael, and Silvia Wampsee; m. by Rev. William Vinall, May 1, 1763.
2-56	GRIER Patrick, and Ellen Battle; m. at Co. Sligo, Ireland, by Rev. Father Peter Doudian, Jan. 18, 1820.
102	GRIFFITH Amos, and Abigail Tollid; m. by Rev. James Searing, June —— 1751.
188	" James, and Sarah Collick; m. by Rev. Ezra Stiles, Aug. 19, 1759.
147	GRINNELL William, and Lydia Tillinghast; m. by Rev. Nicholas Eyres, June 17, 1762.
2-13	" Julia H., and Charles S. Brown, (col.), Dec. 10, 1840.
2-29	GROSVENOR Daniel, of Boston, and Hannah J. Pearce, of Newport; m. by Rev. Thatcher Thayer, Oct. 21, 1845.
141	GUBBINS William, and Francis Mayhew, May 7, 1747.
177	" Mary, and Thomas Baxter, March 13, 1763.
148	" William, and Freelove Easton; m. by Rev. Gardiner Thurston, April 26, 1764.
123	GUINADEAN Lewis, and —— ——, Dec. 14, 1737.
203	GUINEDO Catherine, and Robert Morey, March 23, 1758.
2-22	GUILD William, and Mrs. Abby De Wolf Boss; m. at Bristol, by Rev. Thomas Sheperd, Aug. 4, 1845.
1-1	GUILLARD Claudias, of South Carolina, and Sarah Mumford, of Newport; m. by Peleg Barker, Justice, May 18, 1783.
181	GULLEN Phebe, and Daniel ——; m. by Rev. Nicholas Eyres, July 8, 1787.
239	GUY Abigail, and John Osborne, June 17, 1747.
204	" George, and Hannah Smith, m. by Rev. Gardiner Thurston, Oct. 23, 1760.
241	" George, of Newport, and Hannah Smith, of Bristol, —— 23, ——.
2-13	GYLES William, of Newport, and Mary Gould, of Middletown; m. by Rev. Thomas Leaver, Nov. 22, 1840.
195	G—— Mary, and Richard Dunn, Aug. 16, 1745.

H

206	HACKER Caleb, and Martha Cross; m. by Rev. William Vinall, July 15, 1765.
1-33	" Hannah, and Amos Warner, Dec. 9, 1787.
119	HAIKS George, and Anne ——; m. by Rev. Nicholas Eyres, May 15, 1746.
171	HAIX Anne, and Jonathan Bryer, Jan. 26, 1755.
50	HALLOCK Peter, and Bathsheba Terry; m. by Henry Bull Justice, July 13, 1719.
206	HALLOWAY Daniel, and Abigail Cranston; m. by Edward Upham, Nov. 23, 1766.
74	HALL George, of Portsmouth, and Elizabeth Smith; m. by Peleg Smith, Justice, March 25, 1725.
122	" Elizabeth, and John E——, Jr., Feb. 5, 1740-41.
153	" Martha, and James Burroughs, Nov. 21, 1750.
153	" Peleg, and Mary Rider; m. by Rev. Nicholas Eyres, May 19, 1751.
171	" William, and Hepseba Brown; m. by Rev. Nicholas Eyres, Jan. 21, 1755.
206	" Isaac, and Mary Wood; m. by Rev. William Vinall, —— ——, 1763.
177	" Abigail, and George Sears, Jan. 2, 1765.
190	" William, and Elizabeth Davis; m. by Rev. Gardiner Thurston, Dec. 5, 1765.
191	" Benjamin, and Catherine Pinnegar; m. by Rev. Gardiner Thurston, Oct. 16, 1766.

206	HALL George, and Elizabeth Peckham; m. by Edward Upham, March 22, 1767.
1-32	" Abigail, and Thomas Gilbert Pitman, May 4, 1788.
1-38	" Sally, and Paul Thurston, Jan. 2, 1791.
2-13	" Clarissa, and Jeremiah Peabody, Jr., June 6, 1841.
2-21	" Elizabeth, and Benjamin Pitman, April 18, 1844.
2-36	" Ann, and George Brown, Aug. 6, 1845.
232	HALIBURTON William, and Sarah Baker, —— 19, ——.
1-17	HALVERSON Lucina, and John Langley, Jan. 31, 1779.
191	HALYARSON Goodman, and Lucretia Lowden; m. by Rev. Gardiner Thurston, June 11, 1767.
191	HAMBLIN James, and Hannah Wilkey; m. by Rev. Gardiner Thurston, Dec. 7, 1766.
1-12	HAMILTON Alexander, and Sarah Lake; m. by Rev. Gardiner Thurston, Feb. 15, 1784.
2-17	" John, and Sarah Wooley; m. by Rev. Francis Vinton, Jan. 28, 1844.
19	HAMMETT John, and Sarah Carr, of Gov. Caleb; m. by Samuel Cranston, Governor, Jan. 10, 1705.
131	" Mary, and William Bassett, Oct. 7, 1736.
151	" Jane, and Benjamin Holt, April 24, 1743.
152	" Sarah, and William Wilbor, May 29, 1746.
147	" Constant, and —— ——; m. by Rev. Nicholas Eyres, —— 13, 1762.
2-12	" Catherine, and Oliver Read, July 6, 1840.
2-27	" Nathan, and Cath Cornell; m. by Rev. Thatcher Thayer (also 2-63), Nov. 22, 1842.
2-35	" James H., of Charles E., and Elizabeth R. Tilley, of Dea. George; m. by Rev. B. Othman, Oct. 31, 1849.
84	HAMMOND Elnathan, and Mary Wignel; m. by Rev. James Honeyman, Dec. 27, 1728.
141	" Elnathan, and Elizabeth Cox, Sept. 5, 1750.
232	" Hannah, and —— AllenRecorded, May 28, 1751.
164	" John Arnold, and Mary Scott, June 6, 1754.
205	" Abigail, and Jacob Richardson, Sept. 13, 1759.
187	" Anna, and George Nichols (also 188), Sept. 25, 1762.
1-43	" Elizabeth, and Jonathan Almy, May 14, 1770.
232	" William, and Mercy Scranton, Nov. 19, ——.
1-59	" Elizabeth, and David Moore Coggeshall, May 2, 1800.
1-44	" Paine, and Phebe Almy; m. by Rev. Theodore Dehan, Oct. 19, 1803.
2-24	" Elizabeth J., and Oliver Dewich (also 2-32), Sept. 10, 1846.
2-24	HANDY Mary Ann, and James B. Brown, Oct. 28, 1846.
187	HANNAH William, and Rebecca Peckham; m. by Rev. Ezra Stiles, —— 12, 1756.
188	" Rebecca, and George Manchester, Dec. 11, 1760.
206	HANNERS Walter, and Elizabeth Chuffins; m. by Rev. William Vinall, March 6, 1763.
118	HANSON Abigail, and Jonathan Hull, Aug. 10, 1755.
154	HAN—— John, and Patience Hull; m. by Rev. Nicholas Eyres, Nov. 7, 1751.
2-47	HARDEN William, of Oldham, and Jane Little; m. by Rev. S. Fallowfield, Jan. 25, 1833.
157	HARMAN Jacob, of Philadelphia, Pa., and —— Stevens, Nov. 9, 1772.
161	" HARDING Sarah, and Peter James, April 5, 1741.
143	HARDIN Abraham, and Ann Vinson; m. by Rev. Gardiner Thurston, June 26, 1764.
123	HARGEST Richard, and Mary Tellforte, —— 30, 1738.
187	HARGILL Barnabus, and Elizabeth Crawford; m. by Rev. Ezra Stiles, —— 17, 1756.
2-30	HARGREVES John, and Mary Stoddard; m. by Rev. Richard Livesey (also 2-32), June 6, 1847.
1-136	HARKENS Capt. Joseph, of Portland, Me., and Mary A. Dunbar, of Newport; m. by Elder James A. McKensie, March 10, 1839.
2-13	HARLEY Elizabeth J., and Albert Pollard, Oct. 25, 1840.
2-29	HARREN Edwin W., of Newport, and Lucretia A. Whitman, of Warwick; m. by Rev. Thatcher Thayer, Oct. 14, 1845.

2-12	HARRINGTON Parmelia, and Taber Bennett, April 12, 1840.
128	HARRIS Joseph, and Sarah Sweet, June 15, 1738.
151	" George, of Freetown, Mass., and Sarah Lamb, of Newport; m. by Rev. James Searing, Jan. 23, 1743-4.
148	" Elizabeth, and John Pufly, Aug. ——, 1763.
188	HARTSHORN Stephen, of Providence, and Silence Ingraham, of Newport; m. by Rev. Ezra Stiles, Nov. 20, 1760.
56	HART Bathsheba, and Franklin Morton, June 3, 1717.
56	" John, and Bathsheba Bours; m. by Rev. James Honeyman, Feb. 27, 1721-2.
141	" Jonathan, and Margaret Lawless, Oct. 29, 1747.
154	" Andrew, and Jemima Hill; m. by Rev. Nicholas Eyres, Feb. 18, 1752.
177	" Mary, and Gideon Sisson (also 193), Nov. 14, 1762.
219	" Isaac, and Hannah Pollock; m. by Rev. Isaac Truro, June 1, 1763.
206	" Ruth, and John Casper Oslman, Sept. 16, 1766.
154	HARVEY Seth, and Ruth Sheffield; m. by John Callender, Jr., Oct. 19, 1746.
97	HASEY Jacob, and Johanna ——; m. by Rev. James Searing, Jan. 9, 1734.
236	HATCH Mary, and Jeremiah ——; m. by Rev. James Searing, ——, ——.
171	HATHAWAY Martha, and Jeremiah Hill, Nov. 29, 1753.
1-83	" Desire, and Arthur Davis, Dec. 28, 1783.
1-65	" Abner, of Freetown, Mass., and Amey Lawton, of Newport; m. by Rev. Gardiner Thurston, June 28, 1795.
2-27	" Lydia, and Jonathan Pattison, Sept. 30, 1842.
205	HAVENS Merebah, and Sumner Smith, May 18, 1761.
172	HAWDON James, and Martha Tillinghast; m. by Rev. Nicholas Eyres, (also 233), Aug. 19, 1756.
151	HAWKINS James, and Amey Higgins; m. by Rev. James Searing, June 19, 1743.
154	" Ann, and Samuel Marryatt, July 25, 1751.
153	" ——, and Samuel Ma——, —— —, 1751.
2-27	" Dianna L., and John W. Belso, Feb. 28, 1843.
119	HAYHURST Mary, and John Arthur Johnson, ——, 1744.
118	HAYNES Philip, and Mary Alsworth; m. by Rev. Nicholas Eyres, May 25, 1755.
141	HAYWARD Tabitha, and Peter Daniels, Jan. 20, 1749-50.
203	" Mary, and John Ewen, Sept. 22, 1756.
125	HAZARD Fones, and Marian Easton; m. by Daniel Gould, Justice, Oct. 11, 1739.
152	" George, and Martha Wanton; m. by Rev. James Searing, Nov. 24, 1745.
132	" Elizabeth, and Christopher Potter, May 19, 1751.
148	" George, of South Kingstown, and Sarah Taylor, of Newport; m. by Rev. Nicholas Eyres, —— 17, 1762-3.
148	" Nicholas, and Mary ——; m. by Rev. Nicholas Eyres, —— 17, 1762-3.
215	" Hannah, and James Tanner, Jr., July 7, 1771.
1-52	" Polly, and Jonathan Carpenter, Feb. 4, 1798.
1-99	" Sarah, and Alexander Peterson, March 14, 1814.
1-182	" Hannah Mary, and Cyrel C. Wheeler, May 9, 1827.
2-18	" Peter, and Harriet Anderson, (col.); m. by Rev. Francis Vinton, May 26, 1840.
2-27	" George A., and Abby O. Card; m. by Rev. Thatcher Thayer, Oct. 8, 1843.
2-32	" Mary Ann, and James B. Brown, Oct. 28, 1846.
2-26	" George M., of Mumford and Sarah, and Almira Sweet, of Oliver and Sarah Ann; m. by Rev. Joseph Smith, Feb. 1, 1847.
2-34	" Mary P., and John D. Dennis, Sept. 27, 1847.
2-33	HAZELHURST Henry, and Melvina Bowen, both of Fall River; m. by Rev. Samuel Adlam, Dec. 16, 1849.
203	HEATH Ann, and Job Weeden, Nov. 20, 1755.
169	" Patience, and Uriel Lyon, Sept. 19, 1754.

157	HEATH Zephaniah, and Elizabeth Langworthy; m. by Rev. Gardiner Thurston, Dec. 20, 1764.
2-31	" Elizabeth W., and James M. Mead, June 12, 1849.
169	HEATHY Andrew, and Mrs. Mary Graw; m. by Martin Howard, Justice, July 26, 1750.
15	HEDGE Elizabeth, and Samuel Goram, June 22, 1708.
168	HEFFERNAN Elijah, an Ba———, Feb. 20, 17—. Recorded, 1737.
118	" Jeremiah, and Elizabeth Mackee; m. by Rev. Nicholas Eyres, Oct. 26, 1755.
188	" Amey, and John Fairbanks, April 27, 1760.
1-101	HEILMAN Julius Frederick, and Harriet Barton Auchmuty; m. by Rev. Samuel Towle, May 10, 1814.
22	HOLME Catherine and Joseph Gardiner, Nov. 30, 1693.
123	" Thomas, and Mary James, ———, 1740.
157	" John, and ——— ———; m. by Rev. Gardiner Thurston, Oct. 4, 1764.
208	" Restcome, and Ann Gladding; m. by Rev. John Mason, Oct. 13, 1765.
1-33	" James, and Judah Sprague; m. by Rev. Samuel Hopkins, Dec. 30, 1787.
2-14	" Abby Packard, and Benjamin Ward Underwood, Nov. 2, 1841.
209	HENDLER Elizabeth, and Lliphas Marcome, Aug. 15, 1764.
205	HENSHAW Elizabeth, and John Seabury, — 17, 1758.
231	HEWATSON Martha, and Job Snell, ———, 1736.
102	HICKEY James, and Mary Carr; m. by Rev. James Searing, ———, 1752.
171	" Mary, and John Dyer, Oct. 25, 1754.
204	HICKS John, and Ann Thompson; m. by Rev. Gardiner Thurston, Oct. 9, 1760.
2-29	" John Smedmore, and S. A. Crandall; m. by Rev. Thatcher Thayer, June 14, 1846.
151	HIGGINS Amey, and James Hawkins, June 19, 1743.
170	" M———, and Thomas Jones, Sept. 9, 1753.
31	" Richard, and Edith Hiscox, April 2, ———.
109	" Amey, and Edward ———; m. by Rev. Nicholas Eyres, ———.
121	HIGH Elizabeth, and Michael Sullivan, March 19, 1740.
123	HILLSBOROUGH Richmond, and Deborah Fairbanks, March 13, 1740.
124	HILL Mary, and John Carr, Sept. 15, 1735.
121	" Esther, and Edward Lillibridge, July 19, 1738.
154	" Jemima, and Andrew Hart, Feb. 18, 1752.
171	" Joseph, and Ann Chadwick; m. by Rev. Nicholas Eyres, Oct. 21, 1753.
171	" Jeremiah, and Martha Hathaway; m. by Rev. Nicholas Eyres, Nov. 29. 1753.
171	" Daniel, of East Greenwich, and Patience Kelley, of Newport; m. by Rev. Nicholas Eyres, Jan. 8, 1755.
187	" Ruth, and Ebenezer Richardson, — 23, 1756.
172	" Katherine, and Isaiah Greenhill (also 233), Jan. 30, 1757.
199	" Katherine, and Joseph Pyne, Dec. 18, 1757.
188	" Robert, Jr., of Newport, and Percy Reeves, of Greenwich; m. by Rev. Ezra Stiles, Feb. 1, 1759.
200	" Burnett, and Mercy Rogers; m. by Rev. Gardiner Thurston, Feb. 10, 1760.
205	" ———, and Mary Wilbor; m. by Rev. Gardiner Thurston, ———, 1761.
188	" Nancy, and Alexander McDaniel, Feb. 5, 1762.
209	" Mary, and Thomas Willekey, June 20, 1764.
157	" Mary, and Clothier Peirce, Dec. 26, 1764.
2-30	" Henry B. or R., and Emily Perry; m. by Rev. Richard Livesey, (also 2-32), June 15, 1847.
1-87	" Bernard, of Warren, R I., and Sally Moore, of Newport; m. by Rev. Joshua Bradley, Sept. 21, 1806.
151	HINCKLEY Ann, and John Kendrick Benson, June 13, 1745.
2-12	HINDMARCH George, and Mrs. Susan Hull; m. by Rev. James A. McKensie, April 19, 1840.
145	HINYARD Richard, of North Carolina, and Ann Allen, of Newport; m. by by Rev. Nicholas Eyres, Aug. 18, ———.

31	HISCOX Edith, and Richard Higgins, April 2, ——.
224	HIX Elizabeth, and John Casey, April 17, 1719.
171	HODSON Robert, and Mary Thomas; m. by Rev. Nicholas Eyres, Sept. 10, 1754.
205	HOLDEN Judith, and John Spring, May —, 1761.
195	" Susannah, and Lawrence Carroll, June 19, 1768.
9	HOLDREDGE John, and —— ——; m. by Nathaniel Coddington, Asst., ——, 1705.
140	HOLMAN John, and Mrs. Arabella Pelham, Sept. 24, 1741.
74	HOLMES Lydia, and Samuel Rogers, Jan. 31, 1705-6.
188	" John, of Middletown, and Mary Vose, of Newport; m. by Rev. Ezra Stiles, Dec. 4, 1757.
1-25	" Jane, and Thomas Weaver, Jr., June 30, 1783.
2-16	" Joseph J., of Easton, Mass., and Elizabeth M. Ball, of New Shoreham; m. by Rev. Thomas Leaver, Dec. 27, 1843.
155	HOLSTON Mary, and Thomas Cogin, Nov. 16, 1755.
100	HOLT Rebecca, and Ichabod West, Aug. 12, 1736.
132	" Sarah, and John M. ——, Sept. 13, 1742.
151	" Benjamin, and Jane Hammett; m. by Rev. James Searing, April 24, 1743.
191	" Abigail, and Christopher Sylvester, Nov. 6, 1766.
2-17	" ——, and Pardon Smith, Dec. 26, 1843.
2-25	" Johanna, and James L. Weaver (also 2-32), Dec. 17, 1846.
2-33	" Mary Ann, and John Gladding, Dec. 23, 1849.
1-30	HONEYMAN Susanna, and Abraham Redwood, March 8, 1770.
2-6	HONEYWELL Elliott, of New York, and Deborah S. Thompson, of Newport; m. by Rev. Thomas Leaver, Sept. 19, 1841.
218	HOOCKEY Hannah, and Charles Peere, Aug. 6, 1738.
148	" Sarah, and Benjamin Allen, March 24, 1762-3.
58	HOOKEY Stephen, Jr., and Elizabeth Wightman; m. by Job Lawton, Justice, Jan. 16, 1723-4.
131	" Martha, and Isaac Sherman, Sept. 2, 1736.
131	" John, of Newport, and Eliza Greene, of Jamestown; m. by Rev. Nicholas Eyres, April —, 1737.
171	" Daniel Wightman, of Newport, and Lucretia Smith, of Middletown; m. by Rev. Nicholas Eyres, Dec. 16, 1753.
148	" William, and Abigail Burroughs; m. by Rev. Nicholas Eyres, Jan. 17, 1762-3.
190	" Sarah, and Richmond Cranston, July 15, 1765.
190	" Mary, and William Humphrey, —— 4, 1765.
1-16	" Ann, and Samuel C. Carr, Dec. 13, 1789.
209	HOONSLEY Thomas, of Great Britain, and Margaret Wachy, of Newport; m. by Rev. Ezra Stiles, May 22, 1765.
48	HOOPER Dr. Henry, and Mrs. Remembrance Perkins; m. by Nathaniel Coddington, Asst., Dec. 10, 1716.
108	" Elizabeth, and John Mulholland, Sept. —, 1742.
188	HOOPS Ann, and Luke Howell, Jan. 8, 1761.
149	HOPKINS Esek, of Providence, and Desire Burroughs, of Newport; m. by Rev. Nathaniel Eyres, Nov. 29, 1741.
157	" ——— and William Chandler, Nov. —, 1764.
157	" Phebe, and William Fowler, May 12, 1765.
1-74	" Sarah, and John Remington, Dec. 30, 1772.
2-1	" Samuel, and Mary Freeborn; m. by Rev. Isaac Stoddard, Aug. 4, 1839.
2-9	HORSWELL Martha M., and William B. Wilson, Jan. 13, 1842.
2-15	HOUSE Ann A., and Henry Anthony, Aug. 28, 1842.
172	HOVEY Mary, and John Wilbor (also 233) March 24, 1757.
199	" Ann, and Enos Peckham, Nov. 15, 1759.
177	HOWARD Benjamin, and Hannah Lawton, Jan. 23, 1763.
190	" Phebe, and Robinson Kelley, Jan. 30, 1766.
109	" Anne, and Edward Fullerton, —— 21, ——.
145	" Robert, and —— ——; m. by Rev. Nicholas Eyres, Dec. 3, ——.
2-15	" William, of William and Ruth, and Ruth E. Jaques, of Stephen and Renewed; m. by Rev. Joseph Smith, Sept. 22, 1842.
2-34	" Abby S., and Edward Easton, Jan. 4, 1846.

188	HOWELL	Luke, and Ann Hoops; m. by Rev. Ezra Stiles, Jan. 8, 1761.
2-69	"	Henrietta, and James A. Wilson, Sept. 26, 1819.
168	HOWLAND	Elizabeth, and Elisha Gibbs, April 7, 1737.
119	"	Joseph, and Sarah Barker; m. by Rev. Nicholas Eyres, —— 14, 1745.
141	"	Lydia, and Edward Belcher, June 22, 1747.
141	"	Isaac, and Ann Wilbor, ——, 1750.
200	"	Margaret, and Audley Clarke, Feb. 7, 1760.
200	"	Lucy, and Gideon Lawton, —— 16, 1760.
148	"	Job, of Jamestown, and Sarah Bebee, of Newport; m. by Rev. Nicholas Eyres, Sept. 12, 1763.
1-42	"	Mary, and Perry Howland, Sept. 9, 1794.
1-42	"	Perry, and Mary Howland; m. by Christopher Ellery, Justice, Sept. 9, 1794.
240	"	Elizabeth, and Constant Taber, Nov. 3, ——.
1-123	"	Benjamin B., of Henry, and Phebe C. Greene, of Francis; m. by Rev. Daniel Webb, Aug. 3, 1817.
2-7	"	Susan B., and Robert Sherman, July 1, 1839.
2-15	"	Isaac B., of East Greenwich, and Mary B. Johnson, of Newport; m. by Rev. Thomas Leaver, July 24, 1842.
148	HOXSIE	Sarah, and John Smith, May 23, 1764.
1-33	"	Fanny, and Jeremiah Rogers, March 5, 1783.
1-59	"	Mary, and Levi Strong, April 6, 1800.
2-12	"	Freeman M., and Abby E. Davenport; m. by Rev. James A. McKensie, April 12, 1840.
169	HUBBARD	Russell, and Mary Gray, (also 234); m. by Rev. Nicholas Eyres, Jan. 30, 1755.
1-87	"	Mrs. Elizabeth, and Ezra Stiles, (also 188), Feb. 10, 1757.
208	"	James, and Esther Maxon; m. by Rev. John Mason, Nov. 29, 1765.
172	HUBBS	Henry, and Mercy Carr, (also 233); m. by Rev. Nicholas Eyres, May 9, 1756.
177	HUDDY	Martha, and Benjamin Wilbor, Dec. 10, 1760.
1-33	"	Abigail, and Benjamin Fairbanks, Dec. 23, 1784.
132	HUDSON	Joseph, and Ruth Cartwright, (also 139); m. by Rev. John Callender, Jr., July 29, 1742.
199	"	John, and Mary Weaver; m. by Rev. Gardiner Thurston, July 12, 1759.
116	"	Thomas, and Deliverance Greene, (also 1-14); m. by Rev. John Maxon, Jan. 8, 1768.
1-97	"	Rebecca, and Emmanuel Seymour, July 26, 1795.
2-5	"	John, of Newport, and Clarissa Greene, of Coventry; m. by Elder James A. McKensie, Nov. 4, 1839.
2-31	"	Jane F., and William Stevens, 3d, Feb. 11, 1849.
170	HUFFMAN	Margaret, and John Buntin, Feb. 19, 1753.
205	HULING	Alexander, of North Kingstown, and Sarah Freeborn, of Newport; m. by Rev. Gardiner Thurston, May 14, 1761.
17	HULL	Mary, and Henry Stanton, May 22, 1707.
20	"	William, of Jamestown, and Sarah Sands; m. by Matthew Sheffield, Justice, recorded May 28, 1711.
154	"	Patience, and John Han——, Nov. 7, 1751.
118	"	Jonathan, and Abigail Hanson; m. by Rev. Nicholas Eyres, Aug. 10, 1755.
242	"	——, and Conrad Flagg, March —, 1768.
1-129	"	Frances H., and George S. Tilley, Oct. 13, 1833.
2-12	"	Mrs. Susan, and George Hindmarch, April 19, 1840.
190	HUMPHREY	William, and Mary Hookey; m. by Rev. Gardiner Thurston, —— 4, 1765.
190	"	Ann, and William Banon, ——, 1766.
169	HUMPHRIES	Richard, and Ann Edmonds, Nov. 1, 1753.
206	"	Esther, and Thomas Brown, Sept. 16, 1762.
145	HUNTER	Daniel, and Mary Dyer; m. by Rev. Nicholas Eyres, Oct. 9, 1757.
2-43	"	Samuel, and Silena Bliven; m. by Rev. Samuel Robbins, Oct. 20, 1836.
2-28	"	William, of Fall River, and Jane Logan, of Newport; m. by Rev Thatcher Thayer, Jan. 27, 1845.

152	HUNTING	Samuel, and Zerviah Rhodes; m. by Rev. James Searing, May 30, 1746.
240	HUNT	Elizabeth, and Samuel Whitehead, Oct. 15, 1718.
152	"	Mehitable, and —— Thomas, —— —, 1746.
102	"	Content, and Samuel Young, ——, 1751.
102	"	Abigail, and Thomas Tillinghast, Feb. 25, 1753.
102	"	Mary, and William Morris, ——, 1753.
172	"	James, and Elizabeth Newcomb; m. by Rev. Nicholas Eyres (also 233), Feb. 8, 1757.
145	"	John, and Caroline Tyler; m. by Rev. Nicholas Eyres (also 198), Nov. 13, 1757.
177	"	Sarah, and Benjamin Spooner, March 26, 1760.
190	"	Joshua, and Rebecca Sherman; m. by Rev. Gardiner Thurston, —— 7, 1765.
1-33	"	George, and Rebecca Gibbs; m. by Rev. Samuel Hopkins, July 24, 1785.
1-77	"	Jeremiah, of North Kingstown, and Elizabeth Sanford, of Dighton, Mass.; m. by Rev. Frederick Smith, Sept. 22, 1799.
2-21	"	Sarah Ann, and Robert D. Coggeshall, Jan. 4, 1844.
9	HUSK	Thomas, and Eleanor Coleman, both of New York; m. by Nathaniel Coddington, Asst., Nov. 8, 1708.
221	HUXHAM	John, and Elizabeth Dunbar; m. by Ebenezer Richardson, Justice, Nov. 21, 1762.
102	HYER	John, and Frances Simpson; m. by Rev. James Searing, Jan. 11, 1753.

I

2-29	INGHAM	Grace, and Jonathan Barkenshaw, Dec. 14, 1845.
141	INGRAHAM	Elizabeth, and John Lyon, Oct. 4, 1748.
142	"	Mary, and Isaac Rogers, —— 10, 1750.
102	"	Benjamin, and Austress Bennett; m. by Rev. James Searing, ——, 1754.
188	"	Silence, and Stephen Hartshorn, Nov. 20, 1760.
148	"	Lydia, and James Prior, Nov. 3, 1763.
141	INSTANCE	James Woodward, and Deborah Smith, June 25, 1750.
123	IRESON	Elizabeth, and Perkins Chace, —— 9, 1738.
194	IRISH	Lydia, and Jonathan Wood, June 4, 1759.
207	"	Joshua, and Delana Chace; m. by Nicholas Easton, Asst., April 28, 1767.
1-64	"	Jedediah, of Middletown, son of George, and Peace Cornell, of Newport, of William, dec., of Portsmouth; m. by Rev. Michael Eddy, April 12, 1801.
1-125	"	Emily D., and Isaac W. Sherman, March 4, 1832.
222	ISAACKS	Richa, and Isaac Elizer, Feb. 28, 1758.

J

150	JACKSON	Bartholomew, and Mercy Dillingham; m. by Rev. John Callender, Jr., Nov. 29, 1741.
118	"	Mary, and Nathaniel Scudder, Oct. 9, 1755.
157	"	William, and Elizabeth Phillips; m. by Rev. Gardiner Thurston, Nov. 4, 1764.
240	"	William, and —— ——, Aug. 16, ——.
1-116	JACK	Samuel H., and Frances G. Tompkins; m. by Rev. Daniel Webb, Feb. 13, 1825.
2-66	"	Catherine Sherman, and William Fludder, Jan. 26, 1832.
2-29	"	William A., and Mary A. Rodman; m. by Rev. Thatcher Thayer, Aug. 29, 1846.
2-33	"	Stephen C., of Alexander, and Fanny Banks, of Joseph; m. by Rev. B. Othman, Nov. 25, 1849.
1-90	JACOBS	Rev. Bela, of Somerset, and Sally Sprague, of Newport; m. by Rev. John B. Gibson, Feb. 7, 1810.

28	JAMES	William, and Susannah Martin; m. by George Easten, Dec. 10, 1677.
21	"	Content, and Benjamin Bull, Dec. —, 1710.
123	"	Mary, and Thomas Helme, —— —, 1740.
161	"	Peter, and Sarah Harding; m. by Rev. James Honeyman, April 5, 1741.
141	"	Ann, and James Fowler, June 28, 1750.
170	"	Thomas, and Heart Burd; m. by Rev. Nicholas Eyres, June 24, 1753.
172	"	Sarah, and Benjamin Sayer, Oct. 17, 1762.
157	"	Allen, and Elizabeth Pettis; m. by Rev. Gardiner Thurston, March 24, 1765.
209	"	Rebecca, and George Mack, Oct. 28, 1766.
141	JANT	Jemima, and William Byrn, May 11, 1747.
2-15	JAQUES	Ruth E., and William Howard, Sept. 22, 1842.
196	JARSEY	Sarah, and Thomas Stacy, Oct. 22, 1765.
102	JEFFRIES	Jonathan, and Sarah Ayres; m. by Rev. James Searing, Sept. 6, 1751.
102	"	Joseph, and Ann Purchase; m. by Rev. James Searing, —— —, 1752.
203	"	Merebah, and Philip Weeden, Dec. 4, 1755.
204	"	Caleb, and Jerusha Dyer; m. by Rev. Gardiner Thurston, Oct. 17, 1760.
121	"	William, and Hannah Southwick; m. by Rev. John Callender, Jr., —— 22, ——.
154	JENCKS	John, of Providence, and Hannah Corey, of Newport; m. by Nicholas Eyres, Dec. 3, 1751.
191	JENNETT	Sarah, and William Day, Dec. 20, 1766.
153	JENT	Jerusha, and John Wright, Dec. 23, 1750.
206	"	John, and Rachel Cornell; m. by Rev. William Vinall, June 29, 1762.
199	JEPP	John, and Ann Sabin; m. by Rev. Gardiner Thurston, Aug. 9, 1759.
21	JERSEY	Jacob, and Content ——; m. by John Rogers, Justice, Sept. 18, 1707.
2-34	JEWETT	Ann M., and William Goodspeed, Sept. 18, 1848.
119	JOHNSON	John Arthur, and Mary Hayhurst; m. by Rev. Nicholas Eyres, —— —, 1744.
119	"	Benjamin, and Maria Matthews; m. by Rev. Nicholas Eyres, May 8, 1746.
102	"	Mary, and Benjamin Donham, Dec. 15, 1750.
	"	Sylvester, and Mary Ash; m. by William Heffernan, Justice, Nov. 23, 1751.
170	"	Rebecca, and Nehemiah Rogers, May 1, 1753.
170	"	John, and Ann Swan; m. by Martin Howard, Justice, May 15, 1755.
118	"	Ann, and Daniel Johnson, Aug. 17, 1755.
118	"	Daniel, and Ann Johnson; m. by Rev. Nicholas Eyres, Aug. 17, 1755.
177	"	Elizabeth, and Gideon Casey, —— 11, 1764.
208	"	Ann, and Stephen Fry, April 21, 1766.
191	"	Paine, and Mary Winslow; m. by Rev. Gardiner Thurston, Nov. 13, 1766.
121	"	Elisha, and Hannah Seabury; m. by Rev. John Callender, Jr, —— 16, ——.
1-114	"	Ruth, and James Phillips, Oct. 23, 1806.
1-114	"	Benjamin, and Sylvia Bannister; m. by Rev. Samuel Towle, July 14, 1816.
2-59	"	Henry, and Catherine Remington, June 29, 1837.
2-7	"	Eliza, and Stanley Canterbury (Col.), Oct. 14, 1841.
2-15	"	Mary B., and Isaac B. Howland, July 24, 1842.
2-11	"	Levi, of Orange Co., and Amey Fish, of Newport; m. by Rev. Thomas Leaver, Nov. 21, 1842.
152	JONES	Thomas, and Elizabeth Simpson; m. by Rev. James Searing, ——, 1746.
154	"	Agnes, and Abraham Dayton, Sept. 21, 1751.

102	JONES	John, of Rehoboth, Mass., and Jane Grafton, of Newport; m. by Rev. James Searing, ——, 1752.
170	"	Thomas, and M—— Higgins; m. by Rev. Nicholas Eyres, Sept. 9, 1753.
118	"	Sarah, and Peter Lattimore, Jan. 11, 1756.
172	"	John, and Mary Bulfoa; m. by Rev. Nicholas Eyres (also 233), July 8, 1756.
187	"	Hardin, of Newburn, North Carolina, and Mary Whiting, of Middletown; m. by Rev. Ezra Stiles, Oct. 17, 1756.
187	"	Mary, and Benjamin Read, Nov. 21, 1756.
2-10	"	Sarah Fenwick, and Robert Hollowell Gardiner, June 28, 1842.
2-10	"	Sarah Stafford, and Lieut. Peter Turner, Oct. 12, 1842.
171	JOY	Martha, and Gideon Freeborn, April 25, 1754.
204	"	William, and Mary Phillips; m. by Rev. Gardiner Thurston, Nov. 30, 1760.

K

2-69	KAULL	William, and Elizabeth Cox; m. by Rev. Samuel Towle, May 26, 1815.
155	KAY	Mary, and Elijah Knapp, May 28, 1755.
203	KEEN	William, and Hannah Pratt, both of Providence; m. by Rev. William Vinall, May 3, 1756.
171	KELLEY	Patience, and Daniel Hill, Jan. 8, 1755.
172	"	Leah, and Michael Ryan (also 233), Aug. 12, 1756.
190	"	Robinson, and Phebe Howard; m. by Rev. Gardiner Thurston, Jan. 30, 1766.
2-58	"	Kate, and Dennis Cookery, —— ——, 1828.
141	KELSEY	Mary, and William Dawson, —— ——, 1750.
157	"	Ann, and William Taylor, March 31, 1765.
149	KENNEDY	William, and —— ——; m. by Rev. Nicholas Eyres, Sept. 25, 1742.
239	"	Rebecca, and Basten Debey, Nov. 12, 1749.
147	KENNEY	Edward, and Patience Chadwick; m. by Rev. Nicholas Eyres, —— ——, 1762.
148	KENYON	Ann, and John Kenyon, April 24, 1764.
148	"	John, and Ann Kenyon; m. by Rev. Gardiner Thurston, April 24, 1764.
191	"	Esther, and Thomas Coggeshall, Nov. 27, 1766.
1-136	"	George, and Clarrissa R. A. Allen; m. by Elder James A. McKenzie, March 3, 1839.
2-29	"	Mary Ann, of Newport, and —— ——; m. by Rev. Thatcher Thayer, Aug. 23, 1845.
2-26	"	Martin R., of Foster, R. I., and Ann E. Gifford, of Newport; m. by Rev. Thomas Shepherd, Feb. 8, 1848.
148	KILBURN	John, and Katherine Stanton; m. by Rev. Nicholas Eyres, July ——, 1763.
123	KILTON	Dudley, and Elizabeth Potter, Feb. 25, 1738-9.
2-45	KILVEY	John, and Bridget Moran; m. by Rev. Martin Rush, Aug. 22, 1852.
119	KINDLER	Godfrey, and Mary Mashery; m. by Rev. Nicholas Eyres, Nov. 8, 1744.
32	KING	Sarah, and Peter Ares, Feb. 26, 1712-13.
210	"	Abigail, and John Grindall Gardiner, Nov. 27, 1761.
173	"	Martha, and Edward Pinnegar, —— 18, 1770.
240	"	Benjamin, and Mary Magger, July 19, 1772.
2-4	"	James Rivers, and Caroline Florence Little; m. by Rev. Francis Vinton, Sept. 5, 1840.
140	KINNECUT	Daniel, and Mrs. Honora Bennett; m. by Rev. Joseph Gardiner (also 219), Aug. 5 or 25, 1741.
211	KIRBY	Sarah, and Alexander Bonner, Dec. 17, 1741.
119	"	Mary, and Henry Stevenson, July 14, 1745.
171	KIRK	William, and Lucy Pitcher; m. by Rev. Nicholas Eyres June 30, 1754.

13	KITCHEN Richard, and Sarah D——, Jan. 25, 1705.
155	KNAPP Elijah, and Mary Kay; m. by Joseph Silvester, Justice, May 28, 1755.
2	KNIGHT ——, and William Clarke, April 11, 1700.
1-133	" Caleb S., and Penelope Williams; m. by Rev. L. Jansen, June 9, 1836.
1-119	KNOWLES William, of Providence, and Ann Lyon, of Newport; m. by Rev. John B. Gibson, April 30, 1809.
2-18	" Harriet, and Sumner M. Stewart, May 14, 1840.
2-27	" George B., and Sarah B. Westcott; m. by Rev. Thatcher Thayer, Dec. 25, 1842.

L

204	LADD Deborah, and Seth Clarke, —— 10, 1760.
179	" William, and Sarah Gardiner; m. by Rev. Gardiner Thurston (also 210), Dec. 27, 1761.
206	" Mary, and Benjamin Doubleday, March 3, 1763.
2-84	" Uriah, Jr., of Lebanon, Conn., and Mary Catherine Burdick; m. by Rev. Henry Jackson, April 5, 1848.
2-5	LAIRD Eliza, and William Farrens, Nov. 14, 1840.
128	LAKE Hannah, and George ——, Dec. 24, 1739.
1-12	" Sarah, and Alexander Hamilton, Feb. 15, 1784.
1-114	" Mary, and Capt. Teiah Burdick, Feb. 15, 1822.
155	LAMBERT Daniel, and Niobe D——; m. by Joseph Silvester, Justice, June 3, 1753.
151	LAMB Sarah, and George Harris, Jan. 23, 1743-4.
151	" John, and Mary Fairbanks; m. by Rev. James Searing, Aug. 5, 1744.
154	" Robert, and Mary Power; m. by Rev. Nicholas Eyres, Dec. 1, 1751.
2-24	" James W., and Harriet A. or F. Gardiner; m. by Rev. Richard Livesey (also 2-32), Nov. 9, 1846.
145	LANAHAN Joseph, and —— ——; m. by Rev. Nicholas Eyres, —— 12, —.
63	LANCASTER Sarah, and Thomas Coggeshall, Jan. 23, 1717.
156	LANFORD Judith, and John Stoneman, Sept. 17, 1753.
199	LANGLEY Matthew, and Deborah Caswell; m. by Rev. Gardiner Thurston, July 22, 1759.
198	" John, and Catherine Greene, Aug. —, 1762.
190	" William, and Sarah Dunton; m. by Rev. Gardiner Thurston, April 17, 1766.
1-17	" John, and Elizabeth Sinkins; m. by Rev. Gardiner Thurston, April 6, 1769.
1-17	" John, and Lucina Halverson; m. by Rev. Joseph Snow, Jan. 31, 1779.
1-22	" Elizabeth, and Oliver Durfee, Oct. 13, 1782.
1-1	" Lee, and Sarah Veil; m. by Peleg Barker, Justice, Dec. 12, 1782.
1-55	" Peter, and Elizabeth Burden; m. by Rev. Samuel Hopkins, May 17, 1799.
1-61	" John, of Peter, and Mary Nason, of David; m. by Elder William Bliss, Nov. 2, 1800.
2-1	" Capt. William H., of New York city, and Evelyn J. Chaffee, of Newport; M. by Rev. Henry Cha e, March 29, 1839.
2-38	" John S., 2d, and Sarah Peckham Lawton; m. by Rev. Henry Jackson, Jan. 13, 1852.
204	LANGWORTHY Abigail, and Samuel Weeden, July 3, 1760.
157	" Elizabeth, and Zephaniah Heath, Dec. 20, 1764.
242	LARKIN James, of Hopkinton, and Elizabeth Ward, of Thomas, of Newport; m. by Elder John Mason, Sept. 19, 1772.
128	LASHLEY John, and Katherine McCane, June 19, 1740.
142	LATTIMORE Benoni, of Windsor, Conn., and —— ——, May 31, 1753.
118	" Peter, of New London, and Sarah Jones, of Newport; m. by Rev. Nicholas Eyres, Jan. 11, 1756.
2-43	LAWLER Mary, and Thomas Garrick, Nov. 14, 1847.
209	LAWLESS Sarah, and Thomas Underwood, July 24, 1764.
141	" Margaret, and Jonathan Hart, Oct. 29, 1747.

123	LAWRENCE	George, and Mehitable Chace, —— 9, 1738.
190	"	James, and Ann Pearson; m. by Rev. Gardiner Thurston, April 3, 1766.
1-100	LAWSON	William S. and Ann Wry; m. by Rev. John B. Gibson, June 28, 1814.
13	LAWS	Jonathan, of Milford, Conn., and Abigail Arnold, of Jamestown; m. by Nathaniel Coddington, Asst., —— 14, 1704-5.
7	LAWTON	Elizabeth, and Holland Curtis, ——, 1694.
39	"	Elizabeth, and Jonathan Nicolls, 12m., 1706-7.
29	"	Job, and Priscilla Thurston; m. by Walter Clarke, D. Gov., April 16, 1713.
150	"	Jonathan, of Portsmouth, and Freelove Peckham, of Newport; m. by Rev. John Callender, Jr., Dec. 10, 1741.
149	"	George, and Hannah Bidder; m. by Rev. Nicholas Eyres, April 18, 1742.
153	"	Rebecca, and Samuel Rhodes, Sept. 10, 1749.
119	"	Joshua, of Portsmouth, and Martha Manchester, of Newport; m. by Rev. Nicholas Eyres, April 27, 1746.
118	"	Prescilla, and John Walden, March 28, 1756.
111	"	Isaac, Jr., and Hannah Dickinson; m. by Rev. Edward Upham, May 8, 1760.
177	"	Isaac, and Hannah Dickens, May 8, 1760.
200	"	Gideon, and Lucy Howland; m. by Rev. Gardiner Thurston, —— 16, 1760.
187	"	Royal, of Newport, and Phebe Boggs; m. by Rev. Ezra Stiles, (also 188), Sept. 23, 1762.
147	"	Prescilla, and Nathaniel Potter, —— 24, 1762.
177	"	Hannah, and Benjamin Howard, Jan. 23, 1763.
148	"	Elizabeth, and Isreal Brayton, Oct. 29, 1763.
157	"	William, and Rebecca Gibbs; m. by Rev. Gardiner Thurston, Nov. 20, 1764.
206	"	Elizabeth, and James Brattle, Sept. 28, 1766.
158	"	Robert, and Mary Clarke; m. by Rev. Erasmus Kelley, Nov. 14, 1773.
1-16	"	Polly, and William Pratt, Jan. 10, 1785.
1-102	"	Jeremiah, and Mary Coggeshall, Nov. 23, 1788.
1-65	"	Amey, and Abner Hathaway, June 28, 1795.
1-65	"	Capt. Robert, of Portsmouth, and Penelope Brown, of Newport, Dec. 31, 1799.
218	"	Elizabeth, and Benjamin Nichols, ——.
231	"	George, and Hannah ——; m. by Rev. Nicholas Eyres, April ——.
1-89	"	Eliza, and James Coggeshall, Aug. 16, 1810.
1-109	"	Mrs. Ann, and William Williams, March 28, 1819.
1-120	"	Joseph C., and Ruth B. Stanhope; m. by Rev. John O. Choules, May 17, 1829.
1-131	"	Mary H., and Daniel Leach, May 19, 1834.
2-28	"	Thomas H., and Louisa B. Torrey; m. by Rev. Thatcher Thayer, May 1, 1845.
2-22	"	Susan A., and Edward G. Black, Nov. 30, 1845.
2-34	"	George N., and Rosette A. Thompson; m. by Rev. D. H. Lord, Jan. 25, 1846.
2-34	"	William F., and Martha B. Burroughs; m. by Rev. Henry Jackson, May 26, 1847.
2-32	"	Elizabeth, and William Mason, Aug. 18, 1847.
2-32	"	Mary W., and Thomas Barlow, Sept. 26, 1847.
2-34	"	Susan, and James Logan, Dec. 9, 1847.
2-38	"	Sarah Peckham, and John S. Langley, Jan. 13, 1852.
2 54	"	Catherine, and Charles Tierney (also 2-57), Aug. 26, 1855.
148	LA——	John, and —— Church; m. by Rev. Nicholas Eyres, June 24, 1763.
90	LEACH	Thomas, and Sarah Fry; m. by Samuel Cranston, Governor, July 5, 1709.
1-131	"	Daniel, of Quincy, Mass., and Mary H. Lawton, of Newport; m. by Rev. John West, May 19, 1834.
187	LEA	John, and Elizabeth Peckham; m. by Rev. Ezra Stiles, Oct. 31, 1756.

157	LEATHERIN Richard, and Mary Little; m. by Rev. Gardiner Thurston, May 5, 1765.
151	LEATHE ——, and Mercy Clarke; m. by Rev. James Searing, Dec. 25, 1743.
171	LEDBETTER Hannah, and Edward Church, May 5, 1754.
119	LEE Phebe, and John Pritchard, May 14, 1744.
2-28	" Thomas W., and Mary Lewis; m. by Rev. Thatcher Thayer, Jan. 2, 1845.
2-41	LEGALLAIS David, of Marblehead, and Sarah Wanton, of Newport; m. by Rev. Peter Bours, Nov. 18, 1753.
1-26	LEGRAND Elizabeth, and Edward Boss, Oct. 5, 1785.
200	LEONARD Robert, and —— Stonal; m. by Rev. Gardiner Thurston, Feb. 21, 1760.
2-29	LEUSE Frederick, and Hannah Burdick; m. by Rev. Thatcher Thayer, March 1, 1846.
228	LEVY Horam, and Grace ——, July 26, 1768.
147	LEWIS Phebe, and Paul White, ——. 1762.
206	" James, and Sarah Conklin; m. by Rev. William Vinall, July 5, 1763.
2-28	" Frances, and Christopher D. Marble, Nov. 24, 1844.
2-28	" Mary, and Thomas W. Lee, Jan. 2, 1845.
2-36	" George J., of Middletown, and Mrs. Susan Allen, of Newport; m. by Rev. E. B. Bradford, Oct. 24, 1845.
88	LILE Sarah, and James Davis, Oct. 6, 1729.
121	LILLIBRIDGE Edward, and Esther Hill; m. by Rev. Nicholas Eyres, July 19, 1739.
142	" Robert, and Alice Baxter, Jan. 28, 1753.
147	" Jesse, and Margaret ——; m. by Rev. Nicholas Eyres, —— 1762.
148	" Esther, and William Peckham, Sept. 22, 1763.
235	" Patience, and Paul Tew, May 3, ——.
123	LINDSEY David, and Esther Child, —— 11, 1738.
1-31	" Marcy, and Joseph Vickery, July 20, 1756.
1-40	LITTLEFIELD Capt. William, and Elizabeth Brinley; m. by Rev. Moses Badger, March 10, 1785.
2-15	" Deborah M., and James C. Gould, Oct. 16, 1842.
102	LITTLE Hale, and Caleb Blanchard, ——, 1753.
157	" Mary, and Richard Leatherine, May 5, 1765.
122	" Hannah, and Josias Byles, —— 7, ——.
2-47	" Jane, and William Harden, Jan. 25, 1833.
2-4	" Caroline Florence, and James Rivers King, Sept. 5, 1840.
2-28	" —— and David Robertson, Sept. 3, 1844.
148	LOCKE Nathaniel, and Mary Birk; m. by Rev. Gardiner Thurston, July 20, 1764.
2-3	" Betsey M., and George W. Smith, Sept. 29, 1839.
2-8	" Edward C., of Nathaniel and Rebecca, and Mrs. Elizabeth Gilman, dau. of Elijah and Mercy Parker; m. by Rev. Joseph Smith, Dec. 29, 1841.
2-20	" Samuel R., and Rhoda A. Richardson; m. by Rev. Salmon Hall, July 28, 1844.
2-28	LOGAN Jane, and William Hunter, Jan. 27, 1845.
2-34	" James, and Susan Lawton; m. by Rev. Henry Jackson, Dec. 9, 1847.
60	LORD Mrs. Jemima, and Peleg Smith, Nov. 8, 1711.
141	" Rev. Benjamin, of Norwich, Conn., and Elizabeth Tisdale, of Newport, Nov. 21, 1750.
2-48	LOVETT Jane, and Thomas Sullivan, —— —, 1820.
2-48	LOVIE Anna E., and Thomas S. Tilley, July 27, 1842.
2-15	LOWD Julia Mandock, and Lieut. Lewis Golden Arnold, June 27, 1843.
191	LOWDEN Lucretia, and Goodman Halyson, June 11, 1767.
74	LOYAL John, and Sarah Barton, (widow); m. by John Card, Justice. Recorded, Nov. 23, 1727.
123	LUCAS Mary, and John Dunham, —— 29, 1738.
2-31	LUNT James, and Sarah H. Woodside, both of Brunswick, Me.; m. by Rev. Henry Jackson, Oct. 25, 1849.

151	LUTHER Elisha, and Mary Simpson; m. by Rev. James Searing, Dec. 22, 1743.
153	" Elizabeth, and Samuel Corbett, Oct. 14, 1750.
190	" Paris, and Mary Steward; m. by Rev. Gardiner Thurston, Jan. 9, 1766.
109	" Susanna, and Christopher ———; m. by Rev. Nicholas Eyres, Aug. 15, ——.
1-69	LYMAN Daniel, and Mary Wanton, Jan. 20, 1782.
1-69	" Anne Maria, and Richard Kidder Randolph, (also 1-70), July 4, 1802.
7	LYNDON ——uel, of Joshua, and Priscilla Tompkins, of Nathaniel, July —, 1703.
74	" Josias, and Mary Carr; m. by John Coddington, Justice, Oct. 5, 1727.
235	" Samuel, Jr., and Elizabeth Gardiner; m. by Rev. John Callender, Jr., Dec. 22, 1734.
235	" Samuel, and Sarah Minott; m. by Rev. John Callender, Jr., Dec. 25, 1735.
1-5	" Abigail, and William Bliss, Oct. 16, 1783.
1-85	" Abigail, and Benoni Wood, Sept. 1, 1788.
153	LYNG Nicholas, and Mary Brink, (also 173); m. by Rev. Nicholas Eyres, Aug. 11, 1751.
205	" Mary, and Gideon Tanner, July 12, 1761.
152	LYON Abigail, and Benjamin Peabody, Aug. 7, 1745.
141	" John, and Elizabeth Ingraham, Oct. 4, 1748.
169	" Urial, and Patience Heath, Sept. 19, 1754.
192	" Henry, and Sarah Bliss,(also 233); m. by Rev. Nicholas Eyres, Dec. 30, 1756.
199	" Ann, and John Sherman, June 17, 1759.
210	" Mary, and Robert Taylor, Jr., Nov. 10, 1762.
240	" Margaret, and Edward ———, Jan. 8. Recorded 1764.
1-4	" Joseph, and Mary Underwood; m. by Rev. Gardiner Thurston, June 11, 1776.
1-119	" Ann, and William Knowles, April 30, 1809.
206	LY——— Samuel, Jr., and Susanna Rumeril; m. by Rev. Edward Upham, May 20, 1767.

M

118	MACKEE Elizabeth, and Jeremiah Heffernan, Oct. 26, 1755.
131	MACKEY William, and Eliza George; m. by Rev. Nicholas Eyres, Aug. 14, 1737.
153	" Solomon, and Susanna Brown; m. by Rev. Nicholas Eyres, Aug. 16, 1750.
141	MACOMBER Ephraim, of Middletown, and Mary Green, of Newport, Jan. 11, 1749-50.
195	MAGEE John, and Phebe Fairchild; m. by Rev. Thomas Potter, Aug. 3, 1758.
240	MAGGER Mary, and Benjamin King, July 19, ——.
200	MAGRAH Martha, and John Wyatt, Nov. 22, 1759.
121	MAJOR David, and Sarah Castle; m. by Rev. Nicholas Eyres, Aug. 26, 1739.
122	MALLING James, and Mary Burrows; m. by Rev. John Callender, Jr., —— 30, ——.
168	MANCHESTER Thomas, and Jane Cook, Aug. ——, 1737.
149	" Alice, and Stephen Tripp, Sept. ——, 1741.
119	" Martha, and Joshua Lawton, April 27, 1746.
169	" Mary, and Greening Young, Jan. 11, 1754.
171	" Hannah, and Caleb Corey, Aug. 11, 1754.
188	" George, and Rebecca Hannah, Dec. 11, 1760.
2-27	" Mary B., and Solomon Greene, Jan. 15, 1843.
147	MANNING Thomas, and Martha ———; m. by Rev. Nicholas Eyres, Aug. 1, 1762.
33	MAN Mrs. Bathsheba, and Joseph Chaplain, Jan. 22, 1705.

NEWPORT—MARRIAGES.

1-88	**MARBLE** Mary Ann, and John Tripp, Nov. 21, 1808.
2-6	" Sarah C., and Albert Sherman (also 2-9), Sept. 2, 1841.
2-28	" Christopher D., and Frances Lewis; m. by Rev. Thatcher Thayer, Nov. 24, 1844.
8	**MARSHALL** Elizabeth, and —— ——. Recorded Sept. 19, 1704.
123	" Peter, and Rebecca Crandall, Nov. 26, 1738.
283	" Mary, and William Cowdry, Aug. 8, 1756.
190	" Rebecca, and Henry Oman, Sept. 19, 1766.
191	" Peter, and Nancy Bennett; m. by Rev. Gardiner Thurston, June 21, 1767.
2-15	" Mrs. Isabella, and William B. Martin, Feb. 26, 1843.
177	**MARCHANT** Henry, and Rebecca ——; m. by Rev. Marmaduke Brown, Jan. —, 1765.
2-29	**MARCHINGTON** Eliza, and Joseph Barnes, Dec. 25, 1845.
2-29	" Elizabeth, and John Nicoll, Feb. 19, 1846.
209	**MARCOME** Eliphus, and Elizabeth Hendler, Aug. 15, 1764.
206	**MARSH** Gould, and Elizabeth Cahoone; m. by Rev. William Vinall, Nov. 11, 1761.
209	" James, and Martha Carr; m. by Rev. Ezra Stiles, Aug. 8, 1763.
1-128	" Abby, and Joseph B. Weaver, June 9, 1833.
2-5	" William Henry, and Sarah Babcock; m. at Providence by Elder John Tillinghast, June 21, 1840.
2-30	" Benjamin, 3d, and Mary E. Sherman; m. by Rev. Thatcher Thayer, Dec. 13, 1846.
2-33	" Sarah Ann, and Horace F. Underwood, Jan. 9, 1850.
70	**MARTINDALE** ——, and Mrs. Elizabeth Chamberlain, widow of Peter; m. by John Coddington, Justice, July 29, 1725.
155	" Mary, and Benjamin Carr, Sept. 5, 1755.
28	**MARTIN** Susannah, and William James, Dec. 10, 1677.
6	" Mary, and —— Rhodes, Jan. 29, 1701-2.
130	" Joseph, of Joseph and Mary, and Elizabeth Nichols, of Jonathan dec. and Elizabeth; m. by Daniel Gould, Justice, Oct. 14, 1739.
199	" Henry, and —— ——; m. by Rev. Nicholas Eyres, May 26, 1743.
1-39	" Joseph, and Hannah Mumford; m. by Rev. Gardiner Thurston, May 15, 1787.
33	" Miriam, and William Cranston, May 20, ——.
2-66	" Dorcas D., and John W. Goodson, May 26, 1811.
2-15	" William B., U. S. A., and Mrs. Isabella Marshall, of New York; m. by Rev. Thomas Leaver, Feb. 26, 1843.
43	**MARYATT** Samuel, and Margaret Smith; m. by James Brown, Asst., —— 29, 1720.
153	" Samuel, and Ann Hawkins; m. by Rev. Nicholas Eyres (also 154), July 25, 1751.
204	" Samuel, Jr., of Newport, and Michael Fish, of Middletown; m. by Elder John Maxon, Sept. 13, 1761.
116	" Mary, and —— Eldred, Nov. 19, ——.
122	" Samuel, and Elizabeth Sawin; m. by Rev. John Callender, Jr., —— 21, ——.
119	**MASHERY** Mary, and Godfrey Kingler, Nov. 8, 1744.
1-97	**MASON** Elizabeth Champlin, and Oliver Hazard Perry, May, 5, 1811.
1-108	" George, of Dr. Benjamin and Abby Maria Mumford, of Benjamin B.; m. by Thomas Carey, Jr., Justice, Oct. 20, 1818.
2-82	" William, and Elizabeth Lawton, Aug. 18, 1847.
1-37	**MATTESON** Samuel, of Coventry, and Susannah Brown, of Newport; m. by Rev. Timothy Waterhouse, July 4, 1790.
119	**MATTHEWS** Maria, and Benjamin Johnson, May 8, 1746.
199	**MAXON** Jonathan, and Lydia Clarke; m. by Rev. Gardiner Thurston, Nov. 14, 1759.
208	" Esther, and James Hubbard, Nov. 29, 1765.
1-2	" Caleb, of Elder John and Mary Bliss, of William; m. by Elder William Bliss, Oct. 20, 1785.
1-4	" John, of Elder John, and Sarah Shrieve, of Daniel; m. by Elder William Bliss, July 19, 1783.

1-2	MAXON Caleb, of Elder John, and Mary Bliss, of Henry; m. by Elder William Bliss, March 1, 1807.
121	MAXWELL Hannah, and William Salisbury, ——, 29, ——.
141	MAYLEN Frances, and William Gubbins, May 7, 1747.
101	MAYNARD James, and Ann Vroom, Nov. —, 1742.
2-30	" William, of Boston, and Patience Brownell, of Portsmouth; m. by Rev. Thatcher Thayer, Nov. 24, 1846.
114	MAY Elizabeth, and John Davis, —— 23, 1733.
132	M—— John and Sarah Holt; m. by Rev. John Callender, Jr. Sept. 13, 1742.
113	McALPINE Samuel, and Mercy Sturges, Sept. 19, 1763.
123	McCONE Katherine, and John Lashley, June 19, 1740.
190	McCORRIE Andrew, of Geo., and Ann Chace, of Newport; m. by Rev. Gardiner Thurston, Oct. 27, 1765.
188	McDANIEL Alexander, and Nancy Hill; m. by Rev. Ezra Stiles, Feb. 5, 1762.
141	McDONALD Alexander, and Ann Wilson, Nov. 12, 1747.
147	" James, and Lydia ——; m. by Rev. Nicholas Eyres, ——, 1762.
188	McGORON Katherine, and —— Ross, ——, 1758.
141	McGOW —— Daniel, and —— Donnelly, —— 13, 1747.
188	McINTOSH Daniel, and Mary Sabin; m. by Rev. Ezra Stiles, Aug. 6, 1761.
1-70	McMAHON Anne, and Daniel Read, Oct. 27, 1793.
2-31	MEAD James M., of Albany, New York, and Elizabeth W. Heath, of Newport; m. by Rev. B. Othman, June 12, 1849.
2-18	MELVILLE David, and —— Willard, of Rev. Samuel, of Boston, about 1690.
2-18	" David, and Jane Vaughn, before 1730.
2-18	" David, and Elizabeth Vaughn, Jan. 5, 1735.
2-18	" David, and Lydia West, Feb. 11, 1739.
152	" Mary, and Samuel Yates, ——, 1746.
142	" Abigail, and Thomas Vickery, —— 24, 1750.
102	" Thomas, and Elizabeth Yeates; m. by Rev. James Searing, July 19, 1753.
206	" Sarah, and —— Winsor, ——, 1763.
190	" Lettice, and Henry Weeden, Aug. 20, 1766.
2-19	" David, and Elizabeth Thurston, Dec. 1, 1768.
2-19	" David, and Patience S. Sherman, of George, March 4, 1812.
2-17	" David, and Elizabeth Dennis; m. by Rev. Thomas Leaver, Dec. 10, 1843.
2-32	" Margaret W., and George Danville, Jan. 10, 1848.
141	MENSE Jane, and John Donnelly, Aug. 12, 1747.
239	MENHALL Johanna, and Samuel Nichols, May 5, 1747.
154	MEN——ELL, Mary, and William Thurston Gardiner, Sept. 19, 1751.
239	MERRYHEW Sarah, and Edward Carlton, July, 23, 1749.
9	MESSENGER John, and —— ——; m. by Nathaniel Coddington, Justice, —— —, 1704-5.
2-29	METCALF William, of Newport, and Mary Elizabeth Cooke, of Syracuse, N. Y.,; m. by Rev. Thatcher Thayer, Oct. 13, 1845.
46	MEW Mary, and Thomas Coleman, Feb. 12, 1702-3.
2-30	MILBOURNE Mary, and Thomas Armstrong, Feb. 8, 1847.
54	MILLERD Elizabeth, and Jonathan Sabin, March 25, 1718.
123	MILLETT Daniel, and Hannah Clarke, Sept. 27, 1739.
2-28	MILLIKIN Harriet, and D. Cooke, June 23, 1844.
2-25	" Sarah, and Andrew V. Dodge, May 19, 1747.
9	MILLER John, and —— ——; m. by Nathaniel Coddington, Justice, —— 1705. (?)
63	" Margaret, and Henry Osborne, March 5, 1720-1.
83	" Abigail, and Robert Miller, Oct. 19, 1729.
83	" Robert, of Swansey, and Abigail Miller, of Newport; m. by Job Lawton, Justice, Oct. 19, 1729.
119	" Experience, and Alexander Williams, March 14, 1744-5.
141	" Eliza, and George Smith, July 6, 1750.
148	" Henry, and Rachel Cranston; m. by Rev. Nicholas Eyres, Sept. 29, 1763.
1-54	" Rachel, and Joseph Aiken, July 20, 1779.
1-106	" Mary Elizabeth, and John Bernard Gilpin, Nov. 20, 1808.
2-16	" Eliza Ann, and Lowell Brown, Aug. 13, 1842.

199	**MILLWARD** Marian, and Comfert Allen, Aug. 19, 1759.
199	" Ann, and John Fry, Oct. 8, 1760.
147	" Elizabeth, and John Wilson, May 15, 1762.
147	" James, and Phebe Card; m. by Rev. Nicholas Eyres, —— 1762.
235	**MINOTT** Sarah, and Lemuel Lyndon, Jr., Dec. 25, 1735.
99	**MITCHELL** John, of New Shoreham, and Lois Greenman, of Newport; m. by Henry Bull, Justice, June 19, 1720.
1-93	" Mary, and Rouse Taylor, Aug. 2, 1798.
1-94	" Benjamin, and Frances Congdon; m. by Rev. John B. Gibson, Sept. 9, 1810.
2-36	" Abigail, and Harry G. Tompkins, Sept. 9, 1845.
2-30	" Mary G., and Thomas L. Albro (also 2-32), Aug. 19, 1847.
209	**MOCK** George, of Scotland, and Rebecca James, of Newport; m. by Rev. Ezra Stiles, Oct. 28, 1766.
2-4	**MOFFATT** Rachel M., and William Woodroff, April 20, 1840.
121	**MOLTON** John, and Elizabeth Pearce; m. by Rev. Nicholas Eyres, Oct. 23, 1740.
2-29	**MONKHOUSE** James, and Mary Asher; m. by Rev. Thatcher Thayer, Nov. 26, 1845.
239	**MONROE** John, and Abigail Fry, Aug. 16, 1749.
185	" Reville, and Sarah Coggeshall, of Josiah; m. by Daniel Gould, Justice, May 24, 1752.
1-54	" George, and Rachel Aiken; m. by Rev. Gardiner Thurston, March 6, 1785.
142	**MOODY** —— and —— Wilght, March 29, 1751.
2-59	**MOONEY** Bernard, and Bridget Newman; m. by Rev. A. E. O'Connor, May 20, 1869.
142	**MOORE** Peleg, and Sarah Baxter, Nov. 6, 1751.
1-15	" Richard, and Sarah Exan; m. by Rev. Nicholas Eyres, Nov. 12, 1754.
171	" Richard, and Sarah Exceene; m. by Rev. Nicholas Eyres, Nov. 12, 1754.
200	" William, and Peace Borden; m. by Rev. Gardiner Thurston, —— 16, 1760.
206	" David, of Berwick, Mass, and Susanna Moore, of Newport; m. by Rev. William Vinall, Feb. 13, 1765.
206	" Susanna, and David Moore, Feb. 13, 1765.
209	" David, and Elizabeth Gardiner; m. by Rev. Ezra Stiles, Nov. 20, 1765.
1-79	" Elizabeth, and William Coggeshall, Feb. 28, 1771.
1-60	" Henry, and Mary Yeomans; m. by Rev. William Patten, Nov. ——, 1797.
240	" John, and Lydia Yeats, Feb. 17, ——.
1-87	" Sally, and Bernard Hill, Sept. 21, 1806.
2-59	" Andrew L., and Mary A. Walsh; m. by Rev. William O. Reilly, Nov. 4, 1856.
2-45	**MORAN** Bridget, and John Kilvey, Aug. 22, 1852.
172	**MOREY** Anne, and Arthur Tribert (also 233), Oct. 10, 1756.
203	" Robert, and Catherine Guinedo; m. by Rev. William Vinall, March 23, 1758.
205	**MORGAN** William, and Mary Richardson; m. by Rev. Gardiner Thurston, May 10, 1761.
109	**MORRAN** Phebe, and William Cooper, —— 26, ——.
102	**MORRIS** William, and Mary Hunt; m. by Rev. James Searing, ——, 1753.
240	" Sarah, and John Gregory, Oct. 24, ——.
151	**MORSE** Joseph, and Mary Tucker; m. by Rev. James Searing, Dec. 2, 1744.
239	" Edward, and Mary Allen, Sept. 15, 1747.
188	" Philip, and Agnes Topham; m. by Rev. Ezra Stiles, Nov. 28, 1759.
152	**MORTIMER** Benjamin, and Mary Dunham; m. by Rev. James Searing, May 8, 1746.
210	" Mercy, and George Brown, Dec. 13, 1761.
190	" Prudence, and Isaac Cooper, Sept. 18, 1766.
56	**MORTON** Franklin, and Bathsheba Hart; m. by Rev. James Honeyman, June 3, 1717.

56	MORTON	Bathsheba, and Jacob Dehane, Feb. 27, 1721-2.
205	MOSES	Susanna, and Philip Basel, March 15, 1761.
205	"	Ann, and James Clarke, May 18, 1761.
141	MOSHIER	Philip, and Sarah Burgess, Sept. 27, 1750.
142	"	Maxon, and Lydia Burgess, ——, 1750.
171	"	Maxon, and Hannah Clarke; m. by Rev. Nicholas Eyres, Aug. 8, 1754.
2-7	"	Gideon, and Mary Ann Cornell, both of Tiverton; m. by Rev. Thomas Leaver, Sept. 22, 1841.
119	MOSS	Niobe, and Thomas Austin, Aug. 14, 1746.
145	"	——, and Ralph Stanhope, Nov. 19, ——.
1-67	MOTT	Susannah D., and George Wilcox, May 7, 1801.
2-21	MOULTON	Elizabeth H., and Henry Chace, June 26, 1843.
2-32	"	Mary C., and Samuel M. Albro, Nov. 15, 1849.
123	MOYEON	William, and Sarah Driver, Dec. 31, 1738.
142	MUCHNEAR	John, and Phebe Peckham, ——, 1750.
1-54	MULDER	Henry, of Demerara, and Rachel Cranston, of Newport; m. by Rev. Gardiner Thurston, Sept. 29, 1763.
108	MULHOLLAND	John, and Elizabeth Hooper; m. by Charles Bardin, Justice, Sept. —, 1742.
200	MULLEN	Alexander, and Mary Chapman; m. by Rev. Gardiner Thurston, Feb. 14, 1760.
153	MULLONOX	John, and Lydia Sabin; m. by Rev. Nicholas Eyres, Dec. 23, 1750.
26	MUMFORD	Stephen, and Mary ——; m. by Samuel Willard, Justice, Aug. —, 1697.
1	"	——, of Stephen, of Newport, and Peace Perry, of Edward, of Sandwich, Oct. —, 1699.
40	"	Edmund, and Mary Vay; m. by Samuel Cranston, Governor, —— 17, 1718-19.
153	"	Richard, and Mary Nichols; m. by Rev. Nicholas Eyres, Sept. 8, 1751.
199	"	Susanna, and Joseph Peckham, Oct. 14, 1759.
1-1	"	Sarah and Claudius Guillaud, May 18, 1783.
1-39	"	Hannah, and Joseph Martin, May 15, 1787.
1-35	"	Joseph, and Mary Carr; m. by Rev. Gardiner Thurston, May 11, 1788.
1-112	"	Benjamin B., and Hannah Remington; m. by Rev. Gardiner Thurston, April 9, 1797.
1-108	"	Abby Maria, and George Mason, Oct. 20, 1818.
152	MURPHY	James, and Martha Pitman; m. by Rev. James Searing, June 29, 1746.
172	"	Mary, and William Cowdrey, Aug. 8, 1756.
191	"	Amey and Daniel Dennison, Oct. 16, 1766.
2-62	"	Elizabeth, and Eleazer Read, Jr., Sept. 1, 1795.
121	"	Ebenezer, of Newport, and Mercy Reynolds, of North Kingstown; m. by Rev. John Callender, Jr., —— 13, ——.
2-28	"	Nancy, and Silas Albro, Aug. 20, 1844.
2-34	MYERS	John, and Susan M. Burdick; m. by Rev. Henry Jackson, Oct. 14, 1847.

N

141	NAPS	Elizabeth, and Joseph Tulley, May 8, 1747.
1-61	NASON	Mary, and John Langley, Nov. 2, 1800.
2-53	"	Ardelia, and Seth Cleveland, Oct. 9, 1831.
153	NEGRE	Nathaniel, of Newport, and Elizabeth —— of Portsmouth; m. by Rev. Nicholas Eyres, Sept. 1, 1751.
2-41	NEGRI	Leone, and Capt. William H. Dennis, Feb. 18, 1857.
153	NEWCOMB	Elisha, and Elizabeth Oliver; m. by Rev. Nicholas Eyres, Jan. 15, 1750-1.
172	"	Elizabeth, and James Hunt (also 233), Feb. 8, 1757.
240	NEWELL	Timothy, and Margaret ——, Feb. 10, ——.
2-59	NEWMAN	Bridget, and Bernard Mooney, May 20, 1869.

NEWPORT—MARRIAGES.

140	NEWTON Simon, and Mrs. Mary Richardson, Jan. 27, 1740-1.
119	" Daniel, and —— ——; m. by Rev. Nicholas Eyres, Oct. 8, 1745.
188	" Ann, and Sanford Gardiner, Dec. 4, 1760.
209	" John and Abigail Rodgers; m. by Rev. Ezra Stiles, May 30, 1765.
2-27	" Simon, Jr., and Rachel S. Nichols; m. by Rev. Thatcher Thayer, Jan. 9, 1843.
129	NICHOLS Robert, and Alice Coggeshall; m. by Daniel Gould, Justice, Dec. 28, 1738.
130	" Elizabeth, and Joseph Martin, Oct. 14, 1739.
149	" Benjamin, and Frances Bennett; m. by Rev. Nicholas Eyres, ——1743.
152	" Kendall, Jr., of Newport, and Sarah Paine of Jamestown; m. by Rev. James Searing, Mar. 13, 1745-6.
239	" Samuel, and Johanna Mendall, May 5, 1747.
239	" Abagail, and John Pitman, Jr., May 6, 1750.
153	" John, and Katherine Sabin; m. by Rev. Nicholas Eyres, Dec. 23, 1750.
153	" Mary, and Richard Mumford, Sept. 8, 1751.
102	" Robert, and Mary Dykes; m. by Rev. James Searing, ——, 1754.
203	" Frances, and Benjamin Bosworth, Feb. 14, 1757.
205	" David, and Elizabeth Decotay; m. by Rev. Gardiner Thurston, Feb. 15, 1761.
187	" George, and Anna Hammond; m. by Rev. Ezra Stiles (also 188), Sept. 25, 1762.
190	" Mary, and John Goddard, Aug. 8, 1765.
190	" John, and Mary Young; m. by Rev. Gardiner Thurston, —— 1, 1765.
1-6	" Ruth, and Capt. Aaron Sheffield, June 4, 1769.
1-6	" Mary, and Capt. Aaron Sheffield, June 26, 1774.
1-34	" Walter, and Rachel Stoddard, Oct. 5, 1775.
218	" Benjamin, and Elizabeth Lawton, ——.
232	" Richard, and Susanna Bashell, Nov. 16, ——.
2-27	" Rachel S., and Simon Newton, Jr., Jan. 9, 1843.
2-29	NICOLD John, and Elizabeth Marchington; m. by Rev. Thatcher Thayer, Feb. 19, 1846.
18	NICOLLS Robert, and Mary Case; m. by Gov. Samuel Cranston, Feb. ——, 1698.
39	" Jonathan, of Thomas and Hannah, and Elizabeth Lawton, of Robert and Mary, 12th m., 1706-7.
1-60	NICOLL Margaret, and John Tilley, April 20, 1800.
48	NILES Rev. Samuel, of Capt. Nathaniel, of Kings Towne, and Ann Coddington, of Nathaniel, of Newport; m. by Gov. Samuel Cranston, Nov. 22, 1716.
205	NINEGRET Thomas, Indian Sachem, at Charlestown, and Mary Whitfield, of Newport; m. by Rev. Gardiner Thurston, April 23, 1761.
2-30	NOCAKE Charlotte, and Richard Conway, April 6, 1847.
141	NORMAN Moses, and Priscilla Bradford, July 26, 1750.
2-14	" Ruth Rider, and Thomas Sherman, March 8, 1842.
2-34	" William J., and Sarah E. Stacey; m. by Rev. Henry Jackson, Aug. 23, 1848.
170	NORRIS Abigail, and John Yeamans, June 5, 1755.
158	NORTHUP John, of North Kingstown, and Mrs. Margery Telford, of Newport; m. by Rev. Gardiner Thurston, Nov. 24, 1772.
132	" NORTON Martha, of Newport, and ——, of North Kingstown; m. by Rev. John Callender, Jr., ——, 1742.
118	" Sarah, and Thomas White, Oct. 23, 1755.
153	NOYES James, and Robe Carr; m. by Rev. Nicholas Eyres, Aug. 1, 1751.
13	NOYCE ——, of Stonington, Conn., and —— Sanford, of Newport. Recorded Sept. ——, 1705.

O

131	ODLIN Lydia, and Joseph Sanford, Feb. 8, 1721-2.
66	" Mrs Abigail, and Capt. Francis Sanford, Aug. 20, 1724.
182	" Robert and Mary Conner; m. by Rev. John Callender, Jr., Sept. 26, 1742.

153	ODLIN Martha, and William Thurston, Oct. 25, 1750.
170	" Constant, and Job Weeden, June 24, 1753.
155	" Mary, and James Coburn, Feb. 8, 1754.
171	OLDFIELD John, and Anna Clarke; m. by Rev. Nicholas Eyres, Feb. 18, 1754.
187	OLDHAM John, and Mary Scott; m. by Rev. Ezra Stiles (also 188), April 27, 1762.
153	OLIVER Elizabeth, and Elisha Newcomb, Jan. 15, 1750-1.
1-50	OLYPHANT David, of Charleston, S. C., and Ann Vernon, of Newport, dau. of Samuel; m. by Timothy Waterhouse, Justice, Oct. 23, 1785.
2-29	" Robert M., of New York, and Sophia Vernon of Newport; m. by Rev. Thatcher Thayer, Oct. 13, 1846.
190	OMAN Henry, and Rebecca Marshall; m. by Rev. Gardiner Thurston, Sept. 19, 1766.
2-11	" William, and Anna Crabb; m. by Rev. James A. McKensie, Nov. 28, 1839.
2-29	OPENSHAW Joseph, and Mary Booth; m. by Rev. Thatcher Thayer, Dec. 18, 1845.
151	ORNE Elizabeth, and Joseph Dunham, Oct. 21, 1744.
63	OSBORNE, Henry and Margaret Miller, March 5, 1720-1.
239	" John, and Abigail Guy, June 17, 1747.
141	" Edward, and —— ——, —— —, 1747.
1-51	" William W., and Hannah Read; m. by Rev. Gardiner Thurston, Sept. 21, 1783.
206	OSLMAN John Casper, and Ruth Hart; m. by Rev. William Vinall, Sept. 16, 1766.
2-31	OTHMAN Maria, or Mary, Gardiner, and Charles Henry Glover, Aug. 29, 1849.
135	OTIS Jonathan, and Katherine Coggeshall; m. by Rev. James Searing (also 152), Oct. 16, 1745.
209	" Abigail, and William C——, Jan. 15, 1764.
187	OXX Benjamin, of Bristol, and Prescilla Gladding, of Newport; m. by Rev. Ezra Stiles, Nov. 11, 1756.
206	" Prescilla, and William Crapon, Dec. 7, 1761.

P

135	PADDOCK Rebecca, and Thomas Spencer, June 10, 1742.
152	PAINE Sarah, and Kendall Nichols, March 13, 1745-6.
169	" Phillippe, and Seth Chace, Nov. 16, 1752.
209	PANG Elizabeth, and John Stockford, April 29, 1764.
46	PANNEY Christopher, and —— ——; m. by Nathaniel Coddington, Asst. —— 24, 1718.
191	PARKER William, and Deliverance Prior; m. by Rev. Gardiner Thurston, Oct. 16, 1766.
2-12	" Samuel A., of Newport, and Eleanor H. Sisson, of Somerset, Mass., March 16, 1840.
2-36	" Samuel A., and Hannah D. Stevens; m. by Rev. E. B. Bradford, Oct. 15, 1845.
2-36	PARKINSON Joseph W., of Westerly, and Caroline Brown of Middletown; m. by Rev. E. B. Bradford, Sept. 21, 1845.
30	PARROT Elizabeth, and Nathaniel Dyer, Aug. 9, 1688.
171	PARTELOW Richard, and Elaner Sheein; m. by Rev Nicholas Eyres, Oct. 20, 1754.
1-136	PARTLOW Ebenezer, and Abby Solasger; m. by Elder James A. McKinsie, Jan. 31, 1839.
149	PASHLEY Joseph, and Margaret Boyd; m. by Rev. Nicholas Evres, May 27, 1741.
131	PATE Matthew, and Abigail Greenman; m. by Job Lawton, Justice, Dec. 30, 1733.
118	" John, and Sarah Card; m. by Rev. Nicholas Eyres, Nov. 9, 1755.
172	" Abigail, and Edward Dyer, Jan. 27, 1757.
172	" Dorothy, and Joseph Tripp (also 233), April 5, 1757.
233	" Abigail, and Edward Dyer, Jan. 27, 1757.

NEWPORT—MARRIAGES.

205	PATE	Sarah, and William Polack, May 12, 1761.
2-28	PATTERSON	Mary Ann, and Charles Blacklin, May 13, 1844.
2-28	"	Jane, and John Scott, Sept. 2, 1844.
2-27	PATTISON	Jonathan, and Lydia Hathaway; m. by Rev. Thatcher Thayer, Sept. 30, 1842.
120	PAUL	Joshua, and Sarah Sanford; m. by Rev. James Honeyman, March 31, 1726.
153	"	Joshua, and Judeth Pike; m. by Rev. Nicholas Eyres, Nov. 4, 1750.
172, 115	"	Sarah, and Uriah Wilbor, Nov. 11, 1756.
233	"	Sarah, and Uzziah Wilbor, Nov. 11, 1756.
2-11	"	Benjamin C., of Providence, and Sarah R. Carr, of Newport; m. by Rev. Thomas Leaver, Nov. 22, 1842.
57	PEABODY	Joseph, and Sarah Allen, Dec. 27, 1711.
85	"	Hannah, and Joseph Cook, May 23, 1717.
152	"	Benjamin, and Abigail Lyon; m. by Rev. James Searing, Aug. 7, 1745.
122	"	Rachel, and Henry Smith, —— 26, ——.
2-58	"	Edwin, of Newport, and Catherine E. Friend, of Bristol; m. by Rev. E. K. Avery, at Bristol, Oct. 25, 1832.
2-13	"	Jeremiah, Jr., of Newport, and Clarissa Hall, of Middletown; m. by Rev. Thomas Leaver, June 6, 1841.
2-23	"	Caroline H., and Lewis B. Caswell, Jan. 27, 1846.
172	PEACE	Mary, and Robert Stoddard, Oct. 18, 1756.
218	PEACOCK	Henry, and Elizabeth Carr; m. by Charles Bordin, Justice, Nov. 5, 1742.
121	PEARCE	Elizabeth, and John Molton, Oct. 23, 1760.
140	"	Aziekim, of Warwick, and Mrs. Rebecca Burgess, of Newport, Oct. 29, 1741.
148	"	Freelove, and William Godfrey, Nov. 20, 1763.
1-17	"	Isaac, of Swansey, Mass., and Sarah Bliss; m. by Rev. Gardiner Thurston, March 14, 1785.
1-62	"	Giles, of Little Compton, son of Rouse, and Sarah Champlain, of Joseph, of Newport; m. by Rev. Michael Eddy, Dec. 22, 1799.
2-7	"	Sarah, and William Braman, Nov. 14, 1841.
2-29	"	Hannah J., and Daniel Grosvenor, Oct. 21, 1845.
157	PEIRCE	Clothie, and Mary Hill; m. by Rev. Gardiner Thurston, Dec. 26, 1764.
1-83	"	Nancy, and Benning Pickering, Feb. 23, 1806.
152	PEARSON	Samuel, and Ann Cornwell; m. by Rev. James Searing, June 11, 1746.
190	"	Ann, and James Lawrence, April 3, 1766.
2-51	"	James, and Mary Cooper; m. in Chester Co. by Rev. T. Leigh, July 5, 1829.
2-6	"	John, and Hannah Shaw; m. by Rev. Thomas Leaver, Sept. 6, 1841.
233	PEASE	Mary, and Robert Stoddard, Oct. 18, 1756.
206	"	Martha, and John Davis, —— 6, 1763.
68	PECKHAM	William, Jr., —— ——; m. by Gov. Samuel Cranston, June 10, 1703.
62	"	Joseph, of John and Sarah, and Mary Evengs, of Richard and Patience; m. by Edward Smith, Justice, —— 3, 1705.
69	"	Isaac, and Barbara Phillips; m. by John Rogers, Asst., Nov. 8, 1711.
152	"	Hope, and Robert Bridges, Sept. 7, 1729.
88	"	Elizabeth, and John Goodson, May 19, 1731.
92	"	——, and —— Coggeshall, of Thomas; m. by William Dyer, Justice, July ——, 1731.
235	"	William, Jr., and Phebe Barker, Jan. 22, 1735-6.
124	"	Mary, and Hezekiah Babcock, Jan. 3, 1739-0.
150	"	Freelove, and Jonathan Lawton, Dec. 10, 1741.
132	"	Henry, and Hart Sewell; m. by Rev. John Callender, Jr., Sept. 27, 1742.
151	"	Hannah, of Newport, and George ——, of Freetown, Mass.; m. by Rev. James Searing, —— 18, 1744.

152	PECKHAM	Lydia, and Elisha Gibbs, Dec. 19, 1745.
141	"	Mary, and John Williams, Nov. 8, 1750.
142	"	Phebe, and John Mocknear, ——, 1750.
102	"	Elizabeth, and Daniel Bosworth, ——, 1752.
118	"	Elizabeth, and James Clarke, Sept. 11, 1755.
187	"	Elizabeth, and John Lea, Oct. 31, 1756.
187	"	Rebecca, and William Hannah, —— 12, 1756.
188	"	Philip, and Mary Taggart; m. by Rev. Ezra Stiles, June 1, 1757.
199	"	Joseph, and Susanna Mumford; m. by Rev. Gardiner Thurston, Oct. 14, 1759.
199	"	Enos, of Middletown, and Ann Hovey, of Newport; m. by Rev. Gardiner Thurston, Nov. 15, 1759.
148	"	William, of Philadelphia, Pa., and Esther Lillibridge, of Newport; m. by Rev. Nicholas Eyres, Sept. 22, 1763.
209	"	Mary, and John Clarke, Oct. 20, 1766.
206	"	Elizabeth, and George Hall, March 22, 1767.
1-29	"	Lydia, and Clarke Burdick, Jan. 11, 1789.
28	"	——, and Mercy Spooner, ——.
121	"	Sarah, and William Weeden, —— 10, ——.
122	"	Mary, and Joseph Bennett, Sept. 25, ——.
122	"	Joshua, and Ruth Peckham; m. by Rev. John Callender, Jr., Sept. 29, ——.
122	"	Ruth, and Joshua Peckham, Sept. 29, ——.
231	"	Clement, of Newport, and Elizabeth ——, of North Kingstown, —— 3, ——.
1-96	"	Clement, and Mary Pinniger; m. by Rev. Samuel Towle, March 18, 1810.
2-39	"	John A., and Elizabeth Swan, July 18, 1830.
1-125	"	Perry M., of Middletown, and Abby M. Clarke, of Newport; m. by Rev. Michael Eddy, Nov. 27, 1831.
2-12	"	Anna E., and John Gould, March 9, 1840.
2-19	"	Whitman, and Amelia Carr, of Capt. George W.; m. by Rev. Thomas Leaver, June 16, 1844.
2-24	"	Benjamin H., and Catherine B. Anthony; m. by Rev. E. B. Bradford, Dec. 25, 1845.
2-32	"	Greene H., and Catherine R. Slocum, March 6, 1848.
2-39	"	Anna B., and Charles B. Burrington, Dec. 12, 1853.
102	PECK	William Augustus, and Mehitable Treby; m. by Rev. James Searing, (also 177), Oct. 1, 1752.
2-29	PEDRE	Enos, of Providence, and Cornelia E. N. Ray, of Charlestown; m. by Rev. Thatcher Thayer, Aug. 25, 1846.
153	PEET	John, and Ruth Downing; m. by Rev. Nichols Eyres, April 21, 1751.
36	PELHAM	Edward, Jr., and Arabella Williams; m. by Nathaniel Coddington, Asst., March 14, 1717-8.
110	"	Mrs. Arabella, and John Holman, Sept. 24, 1741.
113	"	Mrs. Penelope, and Joseph Cowley, Nov. 15, 1741.
212	PENDLETON	William, and Martha Brown, of John and Ruth, June, 1770.
1-77	PENGELLY	William, of William, and Abigail Crandall, of Philip; m. by Rev. Michael Eddy, June 24, 1819.
43	PERKINS	Mrs. Remembrance, and Dr. Henry Hooper, Dec. 10, 1716.
175	"	Henry, and Phebe Belcher; m. by Joseph Silvester, Justice, Aug. 8, 1755.
70	"	William, and Mary Sherman; m. by John Coddington, Jutsice, Jan. ——.
2-35	"	Elizabeth, and George W. Pitman, April 1, 1850.
	PERRY	Peace, and —— Mumford, Oct. ——, 1699.
154	"	Susanna, and Nathaniel Tiler, Jan. 16, 1752.
170	"	Phineas, and Elizabeth Chapman; m. by Rev. Nicholas Eyres, Aug. 23, 1755.
157	"	George, and Abigail Williams; m. by Rev. Gardiner Thurston, March 25, 1782.
143	"	Stephen, of Hopkinton, and Sarah Whitford, of Newport; m. by Stephen Potter, Justice, Feb. 1, 1789.
1-43	"	Elizabeth, and Jonathan Almy, Jan. 20, 1796.
242	"	Walt, and Anthony Shaw, —— ——, ——.

1-97	PERRY	Oliver Hazard, and Elizabeth Champlin Mason; m. by Rev. Samuel Towle, May. 5, 1811.
1-134	"	C. G., and Fanny Sergeant; m. at Philadelphia, Pa., by Rev. Lewis P. W. Balch, May 31, 1838.
2-14	"	Elizabeth Mason, and Rev. Francis Vinton, March 2, 1841.
2-30	"	Emily, and Henry B., or R., Hill (also 2-32), June 15, 1847.
118	PETERSON	Joseph, and Mary King; m. by Rev. Nicholas Eyres, May 1, 1755.
199	"	Amos, and Katherine Warren; m. by Rev. Gardiner Thurston, Oct. 7, 1759.
1-79	"	Sarah, and James Speare, July 8, 1792.
1-99	"	Alexander, and Sarah Hazard; m. by Rev. Michael Eddy, March 14, 1814.
148	PETTIS	Mary, and Benjamin Baker, Feb. 4, 1764.
157	"	Elizabeth, and Allen James, March 24, 1765.
69	PHILLIPS	Barbara, and Isaac Peckham, Nov. 8, 1711.
230	"	Eleanor, and Zachariah Cohen, June 12, 1735.
149	"	Elizabeth, and Caleb Carr, —— 15, 1741.
132	"	Phebe, and Jonathan Scott, Aug. 12, 1742.
132	"	Rachel Allen, and Richard Swan, Aug. 21, 1742.
105	"	M——y, and Edward Atwood, July 12, 1750.
141	"	Erasmus, and Abigail Cahoone, Oct. 4, 1750.
142	"	——, and —— ——, March 31, 1751.
142	"	Joseph, and —— Chapman, May 7, 1751.
199	"	Joseph, and Hannah Sanford; m. by Rev. Gardiner Thurston, June 28, 1759.
199	"	Elizabeth, and John Dunham, Sept. 20, 1759.
204	"	Mary, and William Joy, Nov. 30, 1760.
204	"	Ruth, and Jonathan Cahoone, Dec. 3, 1760.
205	"	Abigail, and Walter Clarke, April 19, 1761.
205	"	——, and Phebe Purchase; m. by Rev. Gardiner Thurston, ——, 1761.
157	"	Elizabeth, and William Jackson, Nov. 4, 1764.
157	"	Benjamin, and Mary Sheldon; m. by Rev. Gardiner Thurston, March 24, 1765.
191	"	Ruth, and Robert Simms, June 4, 1767.
1-2	"	John, and Phebe Bay; m. by Rev. Gardiner Thurston, May 10, 1782.
236	"	Eleanor, and Zaccheus Cohen, —— —, ——.
1-114	"	James, and Ruth Johnson, both of Providence; m. by Rev. Stephen Gano, Oct. 23, 1806.
1-83	PICKERING	Denning, of Greenland, N. H., and Nancy Pierce, dau. of John M. McIish; m. by Elder William Bliss, Feb. 23, 1808.
153	PIKE	Judith, and Joshua Paul, Nov. 4, 1750.
177	"	Joseph, and Elizabeth Dedwick, March 14, 1762.
2-21	"	Ann Elizabeth, and William W. Caswell, Feb. 15, 1843.
140	PILLSBURY	Mrs. Mary, and Richard Whittemore, Sept. 6, 1741.
151	PINKNEY	Jarvis, and Lydia Caswell; m. by Rev. James Searing, Oct. 19, 1743.
188	"	Lydia, and Thomas Atwood, April 23, 1761.
203	PINNEGAR	William, and Almy Clarke; m. by Rev. John Mason, June 24, 1766.
191	"	Katharine, and Benjamin Hall, Oct. 16, 1766.
173	"	Edward, of William and Martha King, of Joseph and Mary, —— 18, 1770.
1-96	"	Mary, and Clement Peckham, March 18, 1810.
171	PITCHER	Lucy, and William Kirk, June 30, 1754.
38	PITMAN	Mary, and Eleazer Davenport, Feb. 12, 1713.
87	"	Joseph, and Mary Walkman; m. by Nathaniel Coddington, Justice, Dec. 19, 1717.
152	"	Martha, and James Murphy, June 29, 1746.
239	"	John, Jr., and Abigail Nichols, May 6, 1750.
144	"	Martha, and John Corey, (also 203), July 30, 1755.
203	"	Sarah, and William Bentley, Nov. 18, 1756.
188	"	Mary, and Robert Taylor, Jr., Dec. 5, 1759.

188	PITMAN	Sarah, and James Fox, Aug. 6, 1761.
188	"	Mary, and Thomas Brown, Nov. 19, 1761.
1-32	"	Thomas Gilbert, and Abigail Hall, of George; m. by Rev. Benjamin Foster, May 4, 1788.
236	"	James, and Sarah Spooner; m. by Rev. James Searing, —— ——, ——.
240	"	Elizabeth, and Alexander Swan, Nov. 24, ——.
1-109	"	Abby, and Rev. Ebenezer Coleman, Jan. 17, 1819.
2-21	"	Benjamin, and Elizabeth Hall; m. by Rev. Robert M. Hatfield, April 18, 1844.
2-35	"	George W., of Fall River, and Elizabeth Perkins, of New Bedford; m. by Rev. Henry Jackson, April 1, 1850.
157	PLACE	Jerome, and Rebecca Platt; m. by Rev. Gardiner Thurston, Dec. 24, 1764.
118	PLATT	Alice, and Jeremiah Fish, July 7, 1755.
157	"	Rebecca, and Jerome Place, Dec. 24, 1764.
35	POCOCK	Bridget, and James Cary, Dec. 1, 1705.
2-13	POLLARD	Albert, and Elizabeth J. Hurley; m. by Rev. Thomas Leaver, Oct. 25, 1840.
205	POLUCK	William, of South Kingston, and Sarah Pate, of Newport; m. by Rev. Gardiner Thurston, May 12, 1761.
219	"	Hannah, and Isaac Hart, June 1, 1763.
15	POPE	Mrs. Sarah, of Newport, and Capt. William ——, of Barbados; m. by Edward Thurston, Justice, —— 24, 1708.
174	"	Francis, and Freelove Easton; m. by Job Lawton, Sept. 17, 1729.
122	POPPLESTONE	Hannah, and Samuel Wilbour, —— 19, ——.
123	POTTER	Elizabeth, and Dudley Kilton, Feb. 25, 1738-9.
239	"	Susanna, and Constant Taber, ——, 25, 1747..
147	"	Nathaniel, and Priscella Lawton; m. by Rev. Nicholas Eyres, —— 24, 1762.
190	"	Rouse, and Wait Easton; m. by Rev. Gardiner Thurston, Dec. 20, 1765.
133	"	Christopher, and Elizabeth Hazard; m. by William Heffernan, Justice, May 19, 1751.
1-19	"	Robert, Jr., and Rebecca Shaw; m. by Rev. Gardiner Thurston, May 8, 1785.
2-27	"	Capt. Oliver, and Catherine Weaver; m. by Rev. Thatcher Thayer, March 11, 1841.
2-84	"	Deborah Ann, and Thomas Stoddard, Sept. 21, 1848.
2-54	"	Frederic A., and Anne A. Davis; m. by Rev. Luke Walden, Aug. 8, 1851.
154	POWER	Mary, and Robert Lamb, Dec. 1, 1751.
147	"	Ann, and John ——; m. by Rev. Nicholas Eyres, —— 27, 1762.
141	"	Richard, and Margaret Ward, June 13, 1748.
2-49	"	John, and Mary Waters; m. by Rev. Frances M. McAllister, Oct. 17, 1853.
203	PRATT	Hannah, and William Keen, May 3, 1756.
1-16	"	William, and Polly Lawton; m. by Rev. Gardiner Thurston, Jan. 10, 1785.
2-30	"	Caroline, and Samuel Randall, Oct. 25, 1846.
141	PRICE	——, and Mercy Stevens, ——, 1750.
205	"	——, and Mehitable Chace, July ——, 1761.
206	"	Joseph, and Abigail Denham; m. by Rev. William Vinall, April 8, 1762.
1-115	"	Ann, and William Brittain, April 5, 1804.
148	PRIOR	James, and Lydia Ingraham; m. by Rev. Nicholas Eyres, Nov. 3, 1763.
191	"	Deliverance, and William Parker, Oct. 16, 1766.
2-30	"	Elizabeth, and Leander M. Donwell, March 23, 1848.
119	PRITCHARD	John, and Phebe Lee; m. by Rev. Nicholas Eyres, May 14, 1744.
151	PROCTOR	——, and Eunice Thorp; m. by Rev. James Searing, May 19, 1745.
148	PUFFY	John, and Elizabeth Harris; m. by Rev. Nicholas Eyres, Aug. ——, 1763.
102	PURCHASE	Ann, and Joseph Jeffries, ——, 1752.

205		PURCHASE Phebe, and —— Phillips, ——, 1761.
199		PYNE Joseph, of Chilmarth, Mass., and Katharine Hill, of Newport; m. by Rev. Nicholas Eyre, Dec. 18, 1757.

Q R

2-30		RANDALL Samuel, of New York, and Carolina Pratt of Newport; m. by Rev. Thatcher Thayer, Oct. 25, 1846.
1-69		RANDOLPH Richard Kidder, of Peyton and Lucy, of Richmond, Va., and Anne Maria Lyman, of Newport, dau. of Daniel and Mary; m. by Rev. William Patten (also 1-70), July 4, 1802.
148		RATHBUN Martha, and —— Sheffield, May 1, 1763.
1-98		RAWSON Samuel, and Martha Card; m. by Rev. John B. Gibson, April 16, 1813.
2-29		RAY Cornelia E., and Enos Pedre, Aug. 25, 1846.
76		READ William, of Freetown, and Sarah Smith, of Newport; m. by Job Lawton, Justice, —— 26, 1727.
119	"	Eleazer, of Newport, and Hannah Rider, of Middletown; m. by Rev. Nicholas Eyres, June —, 1746.
170	"	Amey, and George Brown, May 17, 1753.
171	"	John, and Mary Corey; m. by Rev. Nicholas Eyres, March 17, 1754.
234	"	Joseph, and Mary Cornell; m. by Rev. Nicholas Eyres, Dec. 5, 1754.
187	"	Benjamin, and Mary Jones; m. by Rev. Ezra Stiles, March 21, 1756.
172	"	Mary, and Gideon Sisson, Feb. 10, 1757.
188	"	Phebe, and Gideon Young, Oct. 1, 1761.
148	"	Eleazer, and Mary Atwood; m. by Rev. Nicholas Eyres, Oct. 11, 1763.
148	"	Lois, and John George Rix, March 25, 1764.
1-47	"	Oliver, and Mary Sherman; m. by Rev. Gardiner Thurston, April 28, 1765.
190	"	John, and Rebecca Rogers; m. by Rev. Gardiner Thurston, Jan. 28, 1766.
1-51	"	Hannah, and William W. Osborne, Sept. 21, 1783.
1-59	"	Rachel, and John Fish, Sept. 5, 1790.
1-70	"	David, and Anne McMahon, Oct. 27, 1793.
2-62	"	Eleazer, Jr., and Elizabeth Murphy, Sept. 1, 1795.
2-63	"	Oliver, and Clarissa Gardiner; m. by Rev. Romeo Elton, Dec. 1, 1822.
2-12	"	Oliver, of Eleazer B., and Catherine Hammett; m. by Rev. A. Henry Dumont, (also 2-63), July 6, 1840.
2-9	"	Oliver, of Eleazer, Jr., and Clarissa Gardiner; m. by Rev. Romeo Elton, Dec. 1, 1842.
2-27	"	Sarah D., and Oliver Cromwell Turner, July 31, 1843.
2-20	"	James B., and Elizabeth Casey; m. by Rev. Robert M. Hatfield, Sept. 4, 1844.
2-30	"	Thomas, and Eliza Allan; m. by Rev. Richard Livsey, (also 2-32), July 6, 1847.
2-64	"	William Gardiner, and Agnes Matilda Clark; m. at New York city Oct. 21, 1847.
2-64	"	William Gardiner, and Kate W. Taylor; m. at New York city by Rev. Dr. Tyng, Nov. 26, 1851.
2-65	"	Edwin Oliver, and Fenny Stow; m. at Brooklyn, N. Y., Oct. 16, 1862.
2-64	"	William Gardiner, and Amelia Gould Taylor, Jan. 4, 1855.
2-65	"	Henry, and Rosa ——; m. at Los Angeles, Cal., ——, 1860.
2-44		REDFIELD Sophia, and Joshua Turner, Feb. 5, 1855.
124		REDWOOD Ann, and John Wanton, June 10, 1718.
73	"	Abraham, and Martha Coggeshall; m. by Rev. Thomas Coggeshall, Justice, March 6, 1726.
128	"	Patience, and John Easton, April 17, 1735.
1-45	"	Mehitable, and Benjamin Ellery, Jan. 22, 1769.

1-30	REDWOOD	Abraham, Jr., of Abraham, and Susanna Honeyman, of James; m. by Henry Ward, Justice, March 8, 1770.
169	REED	Joseph, and Mary Cornell, Dec. 5, 1754.
233	"	Mary, and Gideon Sisson, Feb. 10, 1757.
2-28	"	George S., of Fall River, and Elizabeth Francis, of Newport; m. by Rev. Thatcher Thayer, June 17, 1844.
188	REEVES	Percy, and Robert Hill, Jr., Feb. 1, 1759.
2-27	RELSO	John W., of Pennsylvania, and Dianna L. Hawkins, of Newport; m. by Rev. Thatcher Thayer, Feb. 28, 1843.
220	REMINGTON	——, and William Ellery, Oct. 11, 1750.
205	"	Mary, and Amos Sheffield, March 18, 1761.
147	"	Asa, and Benjamin Barnes, ——, 1762.
1-74	"	John, and Sarah Hopkins; m. by Rev. Gardiner Thurston, Dec. 30, 1772.
1-112	"	Hannah, and Benjamin B. Mumford, April 9, 1797.
2-59	"	Catherine, and Henry Johnson, June 29, 1837.
2-27	"	Henry O., of New Bedford, and Mary Ann C. Rice, of Newport; m. by Rev. Thatcher Thayer, Dec. 1, 1842.
215	REMSON	Abraham, of New York, and Freelove Saunders, of Newport; m. by Rev. John Maxon, July 2, 1765.
151	REM——	James, and Lydia Alden; m. by Rev. James Searing, Aug. 19, 1745.
119	RETSEL	John, and Bathsheba ——; m. by Rev. Nicholas Eyres, Oct. 27, 1745.
118	REYNOLDS	Susannah, and John Thomas, Nov. 18, 1755.
121	"	Mercy, and Ebenezer Murphy, —— 13, ——.
6	RHODES	——, of Walter, and Mary Martin; m. by John Rogers, Justice, Jan. 29, 1701-2.
152	"	Zerviah, and Samuel Hunting, May 30, 1746.
153	"	Lemuel, of Newport, and Rebecca Lawton, of Portsmouth; m. by Rev. Nicholas Eyres, Sept. 10, 1749.
2-27	RICE	Mary Ann C., and Henry O. Remington, Dec. 1, 1842.
2-57	"	Ruth B., and John L. Remend, Feb. 2, 1843.
87	RICHARDSON	Benjamin, and Sarah Coggeshall, of Joshua, dec.; m. by Daniel Gould, Justice, Jan 20, 1730-1.
140	"	Mrs. Mary, and Simon Newton, Jan. 27, 1740-1.
169	"	Sarah, and John Freby, Sept. 5, 1754.
187	"	Ebenezer, and Ruth Hill; m. by Rev. Ezra Stiles, —— 23, 1756.
205	"	Jacob, and Abigail Hammond; m. by Rev. William Vinall, Sept. 13, 1759.
188	"	Keziah, and Nathaniel Greene, Jan. 14, 1761.
205	"	Mary, and William Morgan, May 10, 1761.
242	"	Thomas, and Margaret Walker; m. by Rev. Gardiner Thurston, Feb. 15, 1768.
1-10	"	Valerie, and Hon. William Gibbons, Nov. 7, 1778.
1-11	"	Lydia, and Nicholas Anceaux, March 19, 1781.
1-103	"	Dr. William, of Smithfield, and Mary Almy, of Portsmouth; m. by Rev. John B. Gibson, May 4, 1815.
1-132	"	Jacob Willis, of New York, and Catherine Rodman, of Nathaniel, of Newport; m. by Rev. Robert C. Northam, Sept. 26, 1836.
2-1	"	Abby B., and Philip Simmons, Jan. 17, 1839.
2-6	"	Ann B., and William R. Budlong, June 27, 1841.
2-20	"	Rhoda A., and Samuel R. Locke, July 28, 1844.
2-67	RICHARDS	Sarah A., and William Anderson, Dec. 3, 1834.
42	RICHMOND	Ann, and Harry Tew, Jr., April 6, 1704.
121	"	Eunice, and James Cranston, —— 14, ——.
1-87	"	Mary, and Elisha Rodman, Oct. 2, 1803.
1-89	"	Paris Otis, and Elizabeth Bours; m. at Providence by John T. Spaulding, Justice, May 1, 1809.
149	RIDER	Joseph, and Barbara Williams; m. by Rev. Nicholas Eyres, Nov. 26, 1741.
119	"	Hannah, and Eleazer Read, June —, 1746.
153	"	Mary, and Peleg Hall, May 19, 1751.
205	"	Sarah, and Zebedee Greenhill, May 28, 1761.
147	"	William, and Mary Sherman; m. by Rev. Nicholas Eyres, Oct. 20, 1762.

119	RIGHTON John, and Priscilla ———; m. by Rev. Nicholas Eyres, — 21, 1745.
2-41	RILEY James, and Caroline Stevens; m. by Rev. Robert M. Hatfield, April 17, 1844.
118	RING Mary, and Joseph Peterson, May 1, 1755.
148	RIX John George, and Lois Read; m. by Rev. Gardiner Thurston, March 25, 1764.
2-23	ROBBINS Anna M., and Joseph W. Eddy, May 5, 1822.
2-6	ROBERSON Francis, of Georgetown, D. C., and Harriet Williams, of Newport; m. by Rev. Mr. Stone, Aug. 22, 1841.
2-10	" Rebecca, and Russell Clark Burdick, Nov. 6, 1842.
2-28	ROBERTSON David, and ——— Little, both of Taunton, Mass.; m. by Rev. Thatcher Thayer, Sept. 3, 1844.
212	ROBINSON James, and Mary Challoner; m. by Rev. James Searing, Oct. 15, 1740.
152	" Mary, and ——— Channing, ———, 1746.
153	" Samuel, of Swansey, and Elizabeth Brayton, of Newport; m. by Rev. Nicholas Eyres, Dec. 6, 1750.
102	" Mary, and Edward Simmons, ———, 1753.
148	" Phebe, of Jamestown, and Ebenezer ———, of Newport; m. by Rev. Nicholas Eyres, July 28, 1763.
209	" John, of Ireland, and Mary Cawdry, of Newport; m. by Rev. Ezra Stiles, Nov. 15, 1764.
209	" Elizabeth, and William Tripp, Nov. 21, 1765.
2-28	" Charles T., of Providence, and Sarah Ann Clarke, of Newport; m. by Rev. Thatcher Thayer, Oct. 27, 1844.
49	RODMAN Clarke, and Ann Coggeshall; m. by Gov. Samuel Cranston, Jan. 3, 1717.
186	" Hannah, and Edward Wanton, Sept. 14, 1749.
181	" Thomas, of Clarke, and Catherine Gardiner, of John; m. by Thomas Ward, Justice, July 6, 1750.
114	" William, and Lydia Gardiner, ———.
1-67	" Elisha, of Walter, and Mary Richmond, of Gideon; m. by Rev. Michael Eddy, Oct. 2, 1803.
1-101	" Mary, and Benjamin Taylor, July 13, 1812.
2-69	" Maria, and George Cornell, Nov. 18, 1815.
1-182	" Catherine, and Jacob Willis Richardson, Sept. 26, 1836.
2-29	" Mary A., and William A. Jack, Aug. 29, 1846.
65	ROGERS Jonathan, of Thomas, and Mary Sawdry, of Joseph; m. by John Rogers, Justice, June 18, 1701.
14	" Samuel, of John, and Lydia Holmes, of Capt. Jonathan; m. by Gov. Samuel Cranston, Jan. 31, 1705-6.
92	" Elizabeth, and Edward Smith, Nov. 9, 1732.
125	" James (mariner), and Charity Brayton; m. by William Dyer, Justice, Dec. 1, 1734.
125	" James, and Abigail Arnold; m. by Rev. John Callender, Jr., Sept. 28, 1746.
142	" Isaac, and Mary Ingraham, — 10, 1750.
170	" Nehemiah, and Rebecca Johnson; m. by Rev. Nicholas Eyres, May 1, 1753.
203	" Sarah, and Timothy Balch, Nov. 29, 1757.
199	" Thomas, and Rebecca Sherman; m. by Rev. Gardiner Thurston, June 9, 1759.
199	" Elizabeth, and William Tilley, Oct. 28, 1759.
177	" Thomas, and Elizabeth ———, —ber 2, 1759.
200	" Elizabeth and Josiah Rogers, Dec. 23, 1759.
200	" Josiah, and Elizabeth Rogers; m. by Rev. Gardiner Thurston, Dec. 23, 1759.
200	" Mercy, and Barnett Hill, Feb. 10, 1760.
200	" Mary, and James Clarke, — 13, 1760.
205	" Bathsheba, and Charles Willett, July 12, 1761.
210	" John, and Mary Wolsham; m. by Rev. Gardiner Thurston, Dec. 24, 1761.
147	" James, and Hannah Smith; m. by Rev. Nicholas Eyres, May 26, 1762.

147	ROGERS	Green, and ———; m. by Rev. Nicholas Eyres, ——, 1762.
148	"	Abigail, and Pardon Tillinghast, Feb. 5, 1764.
215	"	Martha, and Joseph Gould, Feb. 5, 1764.
209	"	Abigail, and John Newton, May 30, 1765.
190	"	Rebecca, and John Read, Jan. 28, 1766.
1-83	"	Jeremiah, and Fanny Hoxsie; m. by Rev. Samuel Hopkins, March 5, 1783.
1-87	"	Martin, of Jeremiah, and Sarah Colvin, of Mehitable; m. by Robert Taylor, Justice, July 31, 1790.
121	"	James, and Hannah Smith; m. by Rev. John Callender, Jr., ——.
2-27	ROMAND	John L., of Salem, Mass., and Ruth B. Rice, of Newport; m. by Rev. Thatcher Thayer, Feb. 2, 1843.
2-40	ROMANS	Elizabeth Ann, and Benjamin T. Freebody, Feb. 3, 1826.
141	ROSS	Jeremiah, and Mary Brayton, Nov. 27, 1749.
188	"	——, and Katherine McGown; m. by Rev. Ezra Stiles, ——, 1758.
148	"	William, and Bathsheba Sisson; m. by Rev. Gardiner Thurston, June 3, 1764.
2-18	"	Mary E., and Capt. Erasmus P. Coe, Aug. 11, 1841.
2-6	"	David, and Mary ———; m. by Rev. Thomas Leaver, Sept. 2, 1841.
2-68	ROTCH	Harriet, and George W. Weaver, Sept. 5, 1836.
141	ROUSE	Hannah, and John Galledat, April 5, 1848.
206	RUMERIL	Susanna, and Samuel Ly——, Jr., May 20, 1767.
102	RUNIEL	Mary, and Daniel Russell, Jan. 10, 1754.
102	RUSSELL	Daniel, and Mary Runiel; m. by Rev. James Searing, Jan. 10, 1754.
188	"	Mary, and George Frost, April 9, 1761.
228	"	Caroline, and Stafford Russell, May 6, 1773.
228	"	Stafford, and Caroline Russell; m. by Rev. Gardiner Thurston, May 6, 1773.
172	RYAN	Michael, and Leah Kelley; m. by Rev. Nicholas Eyres, Aug. 12, 1756.
1-107	"	Fanny, and John Brown, Dec. 31, 1809.
2-23	"	John, and Honora Connaughton; m. by B. Howland, Justice, Jan. 16, 1846.
239	RYDER	Joseph, and Mary Seals, Aug. 28, 1747.

S

54	SABIN,	Jonathan, and Elizabeth Mellerd; m. by Gov. Samuel Cranston, March 25, 1718.
153	"	Katherine, and John Nichols, Dec. 23, 1750.
153	"	Lydia, and John Mullonox, Dec. 23, 1750.
199	"	Ann, and John Jepp, Aug. 9, 1759.
200	"	Jane, and Paul Bruidson, Jan. 17, 1760.
200	"	Ann, and Alexander Gillis, Jan. 27, 1760.
205	"	Mary, and John Sheldon, June 7, 1761.
188	"	Mary, and Daniel McIntosh, Aug. 6, 1761.
145	"	Elizabeth, and Nicholas Spencer, —— 17, ——.
235	"	Joseph, and Mary Chapman; m. by Rev. Nicholas Eyres, —— ——, ——.
121	SALISBURY	William, of Swansey, Mass., and Hannah Maxwell, of Newport; m. by Rev. John Callender, Jr., —— 29, ——.
2-17	"	Mary Ann W., and Isaac T. Wilcox, Jan. 21, 1844.
141	SAMMELS	Thomas, and Martha Davis, March 22, 1749-50.
2-17	SAMPSON	Susan, and William Young, Nov. 19, 1843.
20	SANDS	Sarah, and Tiddeman Hull; recorded May 28, 1711.
13	SANFORD	Bridget, and —— Almy, Dec. 6, 1703.
13	"	—— ——, and —— Noyce; recorded Sept. ——, 1705.
47	"	William, and Grizzell Sylvester; m. by Gov. Samuel Cranston, March 1, 1714.
50	"	Eben, and Mary Woodward; m. by Nicholas Long, Justice, Sept. 27, 1716.
87	"	William, and Experience Bull; m. by Nathaniel Coddington, Asst., July 23, 1717.
131	"	Joseph, and Lydia Odlin; m. by Henry Bull, Justice, Feb. 8, 1721-2.

66	SANFORD Capt. Francis, and Mrs. Abigail Odlin; m. by Gov. Samuel Cranston, Aug. 20, 1724.
120	" Sarah, and Joshua Paul, March 31, 1726.
131	" Eliza, and James Gardiner, Jan. 19, 1737-38.
131	" Mary, and Isaac Brayton, Feb. 12, 1737-38.
132	" Elizabeth, and William Burroughs, Sept. 16, 1742.
149	" ———, and Joseph Bailey, May 26, 1743.
141	" Elizabeth, and Barzillai Bailey, July 11, 1748.
154	" Joseph, and Esther Fleet; m. by Rev. Nicholas Eyres, Sept. 18, 1751.
171	" Bathsheba, and Arthur Davis, Oct. 4, 1753.
234	" Lydia, and Nathaniel Sweeting; m. by Rev. Nicholas Eyres, March 20, 1755.
169	" ———, and Nathaniel ———, March 20, 1755.
199	" Hannah, and Joseph Phillips, June 28, 1759.
177	" Mrs. Martha, and Rev. Gardiner Thurston, —— 25, 1760.
148	" Joseph, and Mary Clarke; m. by Rev. Gardiner Thurston, June 13, 1764.
209	" Honora, and Wilkins Treby, Oct. 15, 1766.
1-111	" Mary Ann, and John Tillinghast, May 27, 1791.
1-77	" Elizabeth, and Jeremiah Hunt, Sept. 22, 1799.
215	SAUNDERS Freelove, and Absomhom Remson, July 2, 1765.
1-33	" Mary, and Samuel Thurston, Aug. 7, 1783.
221	" William, and Mary Jane Bones; m. by Rev. Robert M. Hatfield, July 1, 1844.
2-32	" George S., and Mercy B. Stoddard, Sept. 5, 1847.
149	SAVERY William, and Elizabeth Ashbrook; m. by Rev. Nicholas Eyres, ———, 1743.
148	SAWDRY Mary, and Samuel Wetherell, Sept. 29, 1763.
6	SAWDY Mary, and Jonathan Rogers, June 18, 1701.
122	SAWIN Elizabeth, and Samuel Marriott, —— 21, ——.
2-32	" Calvin W., and Margaret R. Conner, Aug. 9, 1846.
172	SAYER Benjamin, and Jane Battey; m. by Rev. Nicholas Eyres, (also 1-8), May 1, 1757.
173	" Benjamin, and Sarah James; m. by John Davis, Jr., Justice, Oct. 17, 1762.
209	" Abigail, and William ———; m. by Rev. Ezra Stiles, Feb. 7, 1764.
2-28	SAYES Mary R., and Thomas Church, Nov. —, 1843.
37	SCOTT Mary, and George Goulding, Aug. 17, 1707.
123	" John, and Ann Chace, July 20, 1740.
132	" Jonathan, and Phebe Phillips; m. by Rev. John Callender, Aug. 12, 1742.
169	" Mary, and John Arnold Hammond, June 6, 1754.
172	" Nathaniel, and Sarah Wyles; m. by Rev. Nicholas Eyres, (also 233), April 3, 1757.
145	" Francis, and Elizabeth ———; m. by Rev. Nicholas Eyres, Sept. 8, 1757.
187	" Mary, and John Oldham, (also 188), April 27, 1762.
148	" Thomas, and Elizabeth ———; m. by Rev. Gardiner Thurston, Aug. 6, 1764.
2-28	" John, and Jane Patterson; m. by Rev. Thatcher Thayer, Sept. 2, 1844.
118	SCRANTON Mehitable, and Edward Chapman, Nov. 25, 1755.
232	" Mercy, and William Hammond, Nov. 19, ——.
118	SCUDDER Nathaniel, and Mary Jackson; m. by Rev. Nicholas Eyres, Oct. 9, 1755.
203	SEABURY Aaron, and Abigail Westgate; m. by Rev. William Vinall, March 18, 1756.
205	" John, and Elizabeth Henshaw; m. by Rev. William Vinall, —— 17, 1758.
121	" Hannah, and Elisha Johnson, —— 16, ——.
239	SEALS Mary, and Joseph Rider, Aug. 28, 1747.
145	SEARING Abigail, and Robert Elliott, (also 209), July 21, 1765.
169	SEARS Martha, and Israel Chapman, Dec. 23, 1754.
177	" George, and Abigail Hall, Jan. 2, 1765.
209	SENTER Ruth, and Benoni Tripp, July 26, 1764.

29	SKREECH	—— of Jamestown, and Mrs. Sarah —— of Newport; m. by Gov. Samuel Cranston, Dec. 4, 1711.
1-134	SERGEANT	Fanny, and C. G. Perry, May 31, 1838.
209	SEVENS	Martha, and Job Bissell, June 26, 1764.
1-97	SEYMOUR	Emanuel, of France, and Rebecca Hudson, of Newport; m. by Rev. Gardiner Thurston, July 26, 1795.
135	SHARP	Elizabeth and Valentine Vaughn, ——, ——.
2-17	"	Sarah C., and Henry H. Young, Jan. 8, 1844.
148	SHAW	John, and Elizabeth Allen; m. by Rev. Gardiner Thurston, June 21, 1764.
190	"	Anthony, and Remembrance Goddard; m. by Rev. Gardiner Thurston, July 25, 1765.
190	"	John, and Elizabeth Strengthfield; m. by Rev. Gardiner Thurston, July 27, 1766.
1-19	"	Rebecca, and Robert Potter, Jr., May 8, 1785.
1-58	"	Benonia M., and Elizabeth Forrester; m. by Rev. Gardiner Thurston, Feb. 3, 1793.
240	"	Mary, and Charles Davenport, Jan. 21, ——.
242	"	Anthony, of Newport, and Wait Perry, of Portsmouth, ——, ——.
1-78	"	William, of Newport, son of Anthony, of Little Compton, and Susannah White, of Noah, of Newport; m. by Rev. Michael Eddy, Dec. 27, 1801.
2-45	"	Elizabeth A., and Nathaniel Fales, July 6, 1839.
2-6	"	Hannah, and John Pearson, Sept. 6, 1841.
2-28	"	Georgianna, and James A. Darling, April 30, 1844.
2-82	"	Ebenezer H., and Susan D. Coombes, both of Middleboro, Mass.; m. by Rev. Henry Jackson, Feb. 15, 1850.
171	SHEEN	Eleanor, and Richard Partelow, Oct. 20, 1754.
55	SHEFFIELD	James, and Katherine Chapman; m. by Gov. Samuel Cranston, May 1, 1714.
154	"	Ruth, and Seth Harvey, Oct. 19, 1746.
171	"	Ruth, and Thomas ——; m. by Rev. Nicholas Eyres, Oct. 11, 1753.
199	"	Joseph, and Elizabeth Claggett; m. by Rev. Gardiner Thurston, June 21, 1759.
205	"	Elizabeth, and Joseph Anthony, March 11, 1761.
205	"	Amos and Mary Burrington; m. by Rev. Gardiner Thurston, March 18, 1761.
148	"	——, of South Kingstown, and Martha Rathbun; m. by Rev. Nicholas Eyres, May 1, 1763.
190	"	Elizabeth, and Joseph Southwick, July 20, 1766.
1-6	"	Capt. Aaron and Ruth Nichols; m. by Rev. Gardiner Thurston, June 4, 1769.
1-6	"	Capt. Aaron, and Mary Nichols; m. by Rev. Gardiner Thurston, June 26, 1774.
122	"	Sarah, and James Tucker, April 5, ——.
205	SHELDON	John, and Mary Sabin; m. by Rev. Gardiner Thurston, June 7, 1761.
157	"	Mary, and Benjamin Phillips, March 24, 1765.
1-33	"	Daniel and Deborah Bailey; m. by Rev. Samuel Hopkins, Nov. 28, 1784.
123	SHELLEY	Ann, and Jonathan Chace, Jr., June —, 1739.
169	SHEPHERD	Wing, and Lydia Yeates, Nov. 15, 1753.
240	SHERBURNE	Benjamin, and Lucy Gardiner, Sept. 5, ——.
18	SHERMAN	Isaac, of Portsmouth, and Mary Godfrey, of Newport; m. by Rev. Edward Thurston, Justice, Nov. —, 1709.
163	"	Robert, and Katherine Taylor; m. by Rev. James Honeyman, Dec. 4, 1729.
129	"	Grizzell, and Benjamin Clarke, Nov. 3, 1734.
131	"	Isaac, and Martha Hookey; m. by Rev. Nicholas Eyres, Sept. 2, 1736.
150	"	William, and Mary Wilbour; m. by Rev. John Callender, Sept. 6, 1741.
176	"	Peleg, and Phebe Thurston, Jan. 6, 1742.

155	SHERMAN	Charles, and Sarah Gibbs; m. by Joseph Sylvester, Justice, Nov. 21, 1755.
155	"	Levi, and Zilpal Cole; m. by Joseph Silvester, Justice, Dec. 24, 1755.
199	"	Rebecca, and Thomas Rogers, June 9, 1759.
199	"	John, and Ann Lyon; m. by Rev. Gardiner Thurston, June 17, 1759.
178	"	Patience, and Peleg Sherman, Sept. 27, 1762.
178	"	Peleg, of Elisha, and Patience Sherman, of Robert; m. by Rev. Gardiner Thurston, Sept. 27, 1762.
147	"	Mary, and William Rider, Oct. 20, 1762.
1-47	"	Mary, and Oliver Read, April 28, 1765.
190	"	Rebecca, and Joshua Hunt, —— 7, 1765.
70	"	Mary, and William Perkins, Jan. ——, ——.
2-19	"	Patience S., and David Melville, March 4, 1812.
2-40	"	Mary, and Samuel Burroughs, Sept. 15, 1822.
2-41	"	Sarah L., and Daniel C. Denham, May 2, 1824.
1-125	"	Isaac W., and Emily D. Irish; m. by Rev. Michael Eddy, March 4, 1832.
2-54	"	Jonathan, and Elizabeth Anthony; m. by Rev. Leland Howard, Nov. 7, 1838.
2-7	"	Robert, 2d, and Susan B. Howland; m. by Rev. Arthur A. Ross, July 1, 1839.
2-6	"	Albert, and Sarah C. Marble; m. by Rev. Thomas Leaver; m. also by Rev. A. Henry Dumont (also 2-9), Sept. 2, 1841.
2-7	"	Eliza B., and Arnold L. Young, Nov. 1, 1841.
2-14	"	Thomas, and Ruth Rider Norman; m. by Rev. Francis Vinton, March 8, 1842.
2-15	"	Jerome, of Providence, and Eliza A. D. Gatewood; m. by Rev. Thomas Leaver, Oct. 12, 1842.
2-30	"	Mary E., and Benjamin Marsh, 3d, Dec. 13, 1846.
2-26	"	Elijah, 3d, son of John W., and Phebe B. Freeborn, of George H.; m. by Rev. Bartholomew Othman (also 2-31), May 7, 1848.
2-27	SHORTBRIDGE	Jane, and Henry Ferguson, March 16, 1842.
2-8	SHORT	Mary, and Joseph B. Freeborn, April 14, 1842.
191	SHOUL	Robert, and Mary Goulder; m. by Rev. Gardiner Thurston, July 5, 1767.
81	SHRIEVE	William, and Elizabeth ——, Nov. ——, 1728.
204	"	Daniel, and Mary Greene; m. by Rev. Gardiner Thurston, Oct. 1, 1760.
209	"	Elizabeth, of Newport, and Thomas ——, of London, Eng.; m. by Rev. Ezra Stiles, Sept. 30, 1764.
190	"	Ann, and John Shrieve, Jan. 30, 1766.
190	"	John, and Ann Shrieve; m. by Rev. Gardiner Thurston, Jan. 30, 1766.
208	"	Hannah, and Richard Bailey, Sept. 7, 1766.
1-4	"	Sarah, and John Maxon, July 19, 1783.
1-82	SILLIMAN	Gold Selleck, and Hepsa Ely; m. at Huntington, Conn., by Rev. David Ely, Sept. 17, 1801.
123	SILVESTER	Joseph, and Mary Whipple, —— 15, 1738.
169	"	Joseph, and Mercy Davenport, June 10, 1754.
187	"	Mary, and Thomas Deering, —— 9, 1756.
2-34	SILVEY	Francis, and Mary Elizabeth Dell; m. by Rev. D. H. Lord, Nov. 20, 1845.
154	SIMMONS	Remembrance, and Sarah Anthony; m. by Rev. Nicholas Eyres, Sept. 20, 1751.
102	"	Edward, and Mary Robinson; m. by Rev. James Searing, ——, 1753.
2-1	"	Philip, and Abby B. Richardson; m. by Rev. Isaac Stoddard, Jan. 17, 1839.
2-9	"	Phebe R., and William Barber, April 24, 1842.
2-32	"	Edward, and Elizabeth Weeden, Aug. 9, 1846.
2-31	"	Harriet, and William B. Pates, April 1, 1849.
2-49	"	Phebe R., and Jeremiah Allen, March 5, 1854.

200	SIMMS Joseph, and Mary Ann Curtis; m. by Rev. Gardiner Thurston, Dec. 19, 1759.	
188	"	William, and Mary Way; m. by Rev. Ezra Stiles, Jan. 1, 1761.
191	"	Robert, and Ruth Phillips; m. by Rev. Gardiner Thurston, June 4, 1767.
171	SIM John, and Susannah Clarke; m. by Rev. Nicholas Eyres, Nov. 18, 1754.	
174	SIMPKINS Mary, and William Chandler, May 8, 1764.	
190	"	George, and Mary Aldridge, Aug. 25, 1765.
151	SIMPSON Mary, and Elisha Luther, Dec. 22, 1743.	
152	"	Elizabeth, and Thomas Jones ——, 1746.
102	"	Frances, and John Hyer, Jan. 11, 1753.
187	"	Richard, and Mary Topham; m. by Rev. Ezra Stiles, Oct. 14, 1756.
188	"	Martha, and Benjamin Baker, Jan. 28, 1759.
1-17	SINKINS Elizabeth, and John Langley, April 6, 1769.	
1-48	SINKINGS Mary, and Thomas Tilley, Sept. 7, 1788.	
149	SISSON James, and Freelove Fish; m. by Rev. Nicholas Eyres, Nov. 12, 1741.	
158	"	Sarah, and John Davis, May 16, 1751.
172	"	Gideon, and Mary Reed (also 233); m. by Rev. Nicholas Eyres, Feb. 10, 1757.
206	"	Ruth, and John Toman, July 21, 1762.
177	"	Gideon, and Mary Hart (also 193), Nov. 14, 1762.
148	"	Bathsheba, and William Ross, June 3, 1764.
1-128	"	Robert C., and Mary Ann Anthony, both of Middletown; m. by Rev. Michael Eddy, Oct. 31, 1830.
2-12	"	Eleanor H., and Samuel A. Parker, March 16, 1840.
2-17	"	William, of Portsmouth, and Phebe A. Esleck, of Newport; m. by Rev. Thomas Leaver, Aug. 14, 1843.
2-24	SITTERLY Eliza, and George W. Gibson, May 24, 1846.	
34	SLOCUM Giles, and Mary Slocum; m. by Joseph Sheffield, Asst., Nov. 23, 1704.	
34	"	Mary, and Giles Slocum, Nov. 23, 1704.
73	"	Joseph, of Giles, dec., of Newport, and Patience Carr, of Caleb, of Jamestown; m. by Jonathan Nichols, Asst., Sept. 27, 1724.
98	"	Ann, and Isaac Gould; recorded Feb. 26, 1732-3.
133	"	Alice, and Job Almy, Jr., Jan. 27, 1742-3.
148	"	Mary, and Oliver Greenbarge, Nov. 13, 1763.
1-33	"	Benjamin, and Elizabeth Coggeshall; m. by Rev. Samuel Hopkins, Aug. 24, 1783.
1-33	"	Peleg, and Hannah Stoddard; m. by Rev. Samuel Hopkins, Aug. 28, 1783.
2-9	"	Laura A., and David Walker, May 15, 1842.
2-32	"	Catherine R., and Greene H. Peckham, March 6, 1848.
2-27	"	Mary J., and John A. Carpenter (also 2-31), Aug. 13, 1848.
60	SMITH Peleg, and Mrs. Jemima Lord; m. by Gov. Samuel Cranston, Nov. 8, 1711.	
63	"	Edward, and Elizabeth Tew, of Major Henry; m. by Nathaniel Sheffield, Asst., Sept. 17, 1713.
43	"	Margaret, and Samuel Maryott, —— 29, 1720.
74	"	Elizabeth, and George Hall, March 25, 1725.
76	"	Sarah, and William Read, —— 26, 1727.
91	"	Sarah, and —— ——, Nov. —, 1730.
92	"	Edward, and Elizabeth Rogers; m. by Peleg Smith, Justice, Nov. 9, 1732.
123	"	Daniel, and Mary Stacy, Jan. 5, 1737-8.
162	"	William, and Ruth Borden; m. by Rev. John Callender, Jr., Nov. 1, 1739.
151	"	Abigail, and Joseph Turner, Aug. 16, 1744.
151	"	Elizabeth, and John Stevens, Sept. 22, 1745.
181	"	George, and Sarah Tulley; m. by Rev. John Callender, Jr., Aug. 23, 1747.
141	"	Deborah, and James Woodward Instance, June 25, 1750.
141	"	George, and Elizabeth Miller, July 6, 1750.

NEWPORT—MARRIAGES.

142	SMITH	Abigail, and Nathaniel ——, June 7, 1751.
154	"	John, of Newport, and Christiana Katherine Cooper, of North Kingstown; m. by Rev Nicholas Eyres, Sept. 18, 1751.
171	"	Lucretia, and Daniel Wightman Hookey, Dec. 16, 1753.
203	"	John, and Eliphal Arnold, m. by Rev. William Vinall, June 30, 1757.
204	"	Hannah, and George Guy, Oct. 23, 1760.
205	"	Sumner, and Merebah Havens; m. by Rev. Gardiner Thurston, May 18, 1761.
210	"	James, and Katherine Edmunds; m. by Rev. Gardiner Thurston, Nov. 15, 1761.
188	"	Joseph, and Abigail Church; m. by Rev. Ezra Stiles, Jan. 24, 1762.
147	"	Hannah, and James Rogers, May 26, 1762.
147	"	Ann, and Samuel Young, —— —, 1762.
148	"	Elizabeth, and John ——; m. by Rev. Nicholas Eyres, July 12, 1763.
148	"	Philip, of Middletown, and Sarah Smith, of Newport; m. by Rev. Nicholas Eyres, Jan. 22, 1764.
148	"	Sarah, and Philip Smith, Jan. 22, 1764.
148	"	John, and Sarah Hoxie; m. by Rev. Gardiner Thurston, May 23, 1764.
192	"	——, and Ann Davis, dau. of Preserved Fish, Jan. 5, 1769.
102	"	Hannah, and Ebenezer Davenport, —— —, 1751.
109	"	Martha, and John Clarke, —— 29, ——.
121	"	Hannah and James Rogers, ——.
121	"	William, and Ann Borden; m. by Rev. John Callender, Jr., —— 1, ——.
122	"	Henry, and Rachel Peabody; m. by Rev. John Callender, Jr., —— 26, ——.
241	"	Hannah, and George Gay, —— 23, ——.
1-124	"	Ann, and James Clarke, Jan. 9, 1831.
2-2	"	George, and Sarah Chappell; m. by Rev. James A. McKensie, Aug. 1, 1839.
2-3	"	George W., of Providence, and Betsey M. Locke, of Newport; m. by Elder James A. McKensie, Sept. 29, 1839.
2-27	"	John, of Pennsylvania, and —— Banks, of Newport; m. by Rev. Thatcher Thayer, Feb. —— 1843.
2-17	"	Pardon, and —— Holt, of John E.; m. by Rev. Thomas Leaver, Dec. 26, 1843.
2-46	"	Philip B., and Patience H. Barker; m. by Rev. S. Adlam, March 29, 1865.
231	SNELL	Job, and Martha Hewattson, by special license, —— —, 1736.
1-33	SNOW	Joseph, of Providence, and Rebecca Downing; m. by Rev. Samuel Hopkins, July 17, 1785.
1-136	SOLASGER	Abby, and Ebenezer Partlow, Jan. 31, 1839.
186	SOULE	Henry, and Barbara Cottrell; m. by Rev. John Callender, May 1, 1743.
148	"	Gideon, and Abigail White; m. by Rev. Gardiner Thurston, July 6, 1764.
142	SOUTHWICK	Ruth, and Henry Brightman, —— 26, 1750.
207	"	Martha, and Joseph Davol, Jr., Aug. 10, 1765.
207	"	Mary, and John Tripp Greve, Oct. 3, 1765.
190	"	Joseph, and Elizabeth Sheffield; m. by Rev. Gardiner Thurston, July 20, 1766.
116	"	Elizabeth, and Peter Wilkey, Oct. ——, 1767.
192	"	Solomon, and Ann Carpenter; m. by Rev. Gardiner Thurston, June 20, 1769.
121	"	Hannah, and William Jeffries, —— 22, ——.
121	"	Mary, and William West, —— 8, ——.
147	SPARKS	John, and Abigail ——; m. by Rev. Nicholas Eyres, ——, 1762.
1-79	SPEARE	James, and Sarah Peterson; m. by William Borden, Justice, July 8, 1792.
17	SPENCER	——, of East Greenwich, and Elizabeth Coggeshall, of Newport; m. by Edward Thurston, Justice, July ——, 1708.
149	"	James, and —— ——; m. by Rev. Nicholas Eyres, March 10, 1742-3.

154	SPENCER Amey, and Peter Bosworth, March 31, 1752.
204	" William, and Sarah Case; m. by Rev. Gardiner Thurston, Sept. 11, 1760.
148	" Waite, and John ——; m. by Rev. Nicholas Eyres, June 20, 1763.
209	" Daniel, and Ann Easton; m. by Rev. Ezra Stiles, Sept. 18, 1764.
145	" Nicholas, and Elizabeth Sabin; m. by Rev. Nicholas Eyres, —— 17, ——.
1-98	" Samuel, of Exeter, and Martha Burdick, of Newport; m. by Rev. John B. Gibson, Nov. 5, 1813.
1-135	" Micah W., and Sarah Ann Eddy; m. by Rev. John West, Sept. 5, 1836.
1-136	" Lydia, and Alexander Williams, April 7, 1839.
2-15	" Mary, and Joshua A. Williams, July 28, 1842.
152	SPINNEY Zebulon, and Mary Eddy; m. by Rev. James Searing, May 11, 1746.
128	SPOONER Elizabeth, and —— ——, 1740.
135	" Thomas, and Rebecca Paddock; m. by Rev. Richard Peirce, at Dartmouth, Mass., June 10, 1742.
..	Benjamin, and Sarah Hunt, March 26, 1760.
205	and Jerusha Barker; m. by Rev. Gardiner Thurston, March 26, 1761.
177	" Elizabeth, and Robert Dunham, Aug. 26, 1762.
147	" Charles, and Mary Gardiner; m. by Rev. Nicholas Eyres, ——, 1762.
206	" Samuel, and Mary Arnold; m. by Rev. William Vinall, —— 6, 1763.
1-36	" Abigail, and Clarke Bliss, Dec. 13, 1789.
28	" Mercy, and —— Peckham, ——, ——.
236	" Sarah, and James Pitman, ——, ——.
2-27	" Caroline, and Benjamin Brown, March ——, 1841.
2-32	" Julia E., and Jeffrey Gardiner (also 2-25), Dec. 13 or 18, 1846.
1-33	SPRAGUE Judah, and James Helme, Dec. 30, 1787.
1-90	" Sally, and Rev. Bela Jacobs, Feb. 7, 1810.
1-103	" Jordan, and Rebecca Durfee; m. by Rev. Samuel Towle, Aug. 14, 1814.
101	SPRINGER Ann, and Peter Vroom, Oct. 12, 1738.
205	SPRING John, and Judith Holden; m. by Rev. Gardiner Thurston, May ——, 1761.
232	SQUIRE Nathan, of Connecticut, and Ann ——, Oct. 3, ——.
123	STACY Mary, and Daniel Smith, Jan. 5, 1737-8.
169	" Eunice, and Isaac Cowdry, Oct. 30, 1754.
188	" Martha, and Jacob Young, Aug. 5, 1759.
196	" Thomas, of Thomas, and Sarah Jarsey, of John; m. by Elder John Mason, Oct. 22, 1765
190	" Joshua, and Mary Gray, m. by Rev. Gardiner Thurston, Oct. 27, 1765.
1-126	" Eliza, and John Whitehouse, Feb. 3, 1833.
1-126	" John J., and Mary Jane Friend; m. by Rev. Michael Eddy, Feb. 3, 1833.
2-34	" Sarah E., and William J. Norman, Aug. 23, 1848.
1-3	STAFFORD Barbara, and Benjamin Butts, May 23, 1782.
141	STAINER George, and Elizabeth Davis, April 20, 1749.
104	STANHOPE Abby, or Abigail, and Edward Erwin (also 188); He of Boston, she of Newport; m. by Rev. Ezra Stiles, Dec. 30, 1759.
145	" Ralph, and —— M——, by Rev. Nicholas Eyres, Nov. 19, ——.
1-120	" Ruth B., and Joseph C. Lawton, May 17, 1829.
153	STANLEY Thomas, and Mary Cooper; m. by Rev. Nicholas Eyres, June 23, 1749.
17	STANTON Henry, of John and Mary, of Newport, and Mary Hull, of Joshua, of Jamestown; m. by Edward Thurston, Justice, May 22, 1707.
112	" Elizabeth, and Robert Taylor (also 165), May 27, 1740.
105	" Elizabeth, and Job Greenman, May 24, 1750.
205	" Marjory, and James Telfoir, April 19, 1761.
148	" Katherine, and John Kilburn, July ——, 1763.

191	STANTON	Lydia, and Daniel Beebe, April 26, 1767.
191	"	John, and Mary Weathers; m. by Rev. Gardiner Thurston, June 4, 1767.
2-7	"	William K., of South Kingstown, and Mary M. Bell of Newport; m. by Rev. Thomas Leaver, Nov. 25, 1841.
154	STAN——	Elizabeth, and Samuel Greene, March 19, 1752.
2-14	STEDMAN	William Marshall, of Boston, Mass., and Elizabeth Bowen Brown, of Newport; m. by Rev. Francis Vinton, April 14, 1841.
39	STEPHENSON	Sarah, and John Gavit, Sept. 13, 1714.
2-28	STERNS	Harriet E., and J. B., Swansey, Jan. 28, 1844.
119	STEVENSON	Henry, and Mary Kirby; m. by Rev. Nicholas Eyres, July 14, 1745.
123	STEVENS	Robert, and Austress Elizabeth Wignel, Sept. 21, 1738.
133	"	William, and Ann ——, —— 1741-2.
152	"	John, and Elizabeth Smith; m. by Rev. James Searing, Sept. 22, 1745.
141	"	Mercy, and —— Price, —— —, 1750.
147	"	Mary, and Peleg Barker, —— 21, 1762.
157	"	——, and Jacob Harman, Nov. 9, 1772.
1-95	"	John, of John, of Newport, and Susanna Brightman, of John, of Portsmouth; m. by Rev. Michael Eddy, April 29, 1807.
2-2	"	Harriet S., and Stephen G. Dodge, Aug. 1, 1839.
2-21	"	——, and James Riley, April 17, 1844.
2-20	"	Ann E., and Henry E. Turner, July 18, 1844.
2-22	"	Susan, and George Burroughs, Oct. 24, 1844.
2-36	"	Benjamin H., and Frances C. Weaver; m. by Rev. E. B. Bradford, Oct. 2, 1845.
2-36	"	Hannah D., and Lemuel A. Parker, Oct. 15, 1845.
2-31	"	William 3d, and Jane F. Hudson; m. by Rev. B. Othman, Feb. 11, 1849.
102	STEWARD	James, and Mary Brattle; m. by Rev. James Searing, —— —, 1753.
190	"	Mary, and Paris Luther, Jan. 9, 1766.
169	STEWART	Gilbert, and Elizabeth Anthony; m. by Martin Howard, Justice, May 23, 1751.
2-13	"	Sumner M., and Harriet Knowles; m. by Rev. Francis Vinton, May 14, 1840.
187	STILES	Rev. Ezra, of Newport, son of Rev. Isaac and Keziah, of New Haven, Conn., and Mrs. Elizabeth Hubbard, of said New Haven; m. by Rev. John Hubbard (also 188), Feb. 10, 1757.
209	STOCKFORD	John, and Elizabeth Pang; m. by Rev. Ezra Stiles, April 29, 1764.
141	STOCKMAN	Jacob, and Ann Wilbour, May 22, 1748.
151	STODDARD	William, and Mary Wanton; m. by Rev. James Searing, June 18, 1745.
172	"	Robert, and Mary Peace; m. by Rev. Nicholas Eyres (also 233), Oct. 18, 1756.
1-34	"	Rachel, and Walter Nichols, Oct. 5, 1775.
1-33	"	Hannah, and Peleg Slocum, Aug. 28, 1783.
2-30	"	Mary, and John Hargreaves (also 2-32), June 6, 1847.
2-32	"	Mercy B., and George S. Saunders, Sept. 5, 1847.
2-34	"	Thomas, and Deborah Ann Potter; m. by Rev. Henry Jackson, Sept. 21, 1848.
200	STONAL	——, and Robert Leonard, Feb. 21, 1760.
156	STONEMAN	John, and Judith Longford; m. by Thomas Ward, Justice, Sept. 17, 1753.
147	STORY	Richard, and Elizabeth Carr; m. by Rev. Nicholas Eyres, —— 28, 1762.
2-9	STOWERS	Harriet S., and Stephen G. Dodge, Aug. 1, 1839.
2-65	STOW	Fanny, and Edwin Oliver Read, Oct. 16, 1862.
170	STRANGE	Jacob, of Newport, and Elizabeth Winslow, of Freetown, Mass.; m. by Martin Howard, Justice, July 9, 1754.
190	STRENGTHFIELD	Elizabeth, and John Shaw, July 27, 1766.
1-59	STRONG	Levi, of Northampton, Mass., son of Simeon, and Mary Hoxsie, of Newport, dau. of Benjamin; m. by Rev. Michael Eddy, April 6, 1800.

113	STURGESS	Mary, and Lemuel McAlpine, Sept. 19, 1763.
121	SULLIVAN	Michael, and Elizabeth High; m. bp Rev. Nicholas Eyres, March 19, 1740.
2-48	"	Thomas, and Jane Lovett; m. by Rev. James Griffin, —— ——, 1820.
2-40	"	John, and Joanna Dunn; m. by Rev. Henry Jackson, June 15, 1851.
36	SWAN	William, and Ann Gifford; m. by Rev. James Honeyman, June 26, 1716.
132	"	Richard, and Rachel Allen Phillips; m. by Rev. John Callender, Jr., Aug. 21, 1742.
170	"	Ann, and John Johnson, May 15, 1755.
240	"	Alexander, and Elizabeth Pitman, Nov. 24, ——.
1-101	"	Richard, of Newport, and Elizabeth Brown, of North Kingstown, Oct. 29, 1803.
2-39	"	Elizabeth, and Job A. Peckham, July 18, 1830.
2-28	SWASEY	J. B., and Harriet E. Stevens; m. by Rev. Thatcher Thayer, Jan. 28, 1844.
234	SWEETING	Nathaniel, and Lydia Sanford, March 20, 1755.
123	SWEET	Sarah, and Joseph Harris, June 15, 1738.
171	"	Bridget, and George Tew, Nov. 17, 1754.
171	"	Sarah, and John Gill, Dec. 12, 1754.
1-104	"	Mercy, and Thomas R. Tilley, Nov. 30, 1817.
2-4	"	Peleg G., and Catherine E. Briggs; m. by Elder James A. McKensie, Jan. 5, 1840.
2-26	"	Almira, and George M. Hazard, Feb. 1, 1847.
47	SYLVESTER	Grizzell, and William Sanford, March 1, 1714.
191	"	Christopher, and Abigail Holt; m. by Rev. Gardiner Thurston, Nov. 6, 1766.

T

239	TABER	Benedick, and Rebecca Gladding, Aug. 5, 1747.
239	"	Constant, and Susanna Potter, ——, 25, 1747.
240	"	Constant, and Elizabeth Howland, Nov. 3, ——.
1-61	"	Phebe, and Simeon Coggeshall, Jan. 23, 1800.
171	TAGGERT	William, and Mary Clarke; m. by Rev. Nicholas Eyres, Jan. 26, 1755.
188	"	Mary, and Philip Peckham, June 1, 1757.
1-52	"	Mary, and Joseph Allen, Jan. 21, 1780.
169	"	Talley, and Nicholas Nerrier, May 27, 1753.
102	TALLID	Abigail, and Amos Griffith, June —, 1751.
13	TALLMAN	Nathaniel, of Bristol, and —— ——; m. by Nathaniel Coddington, Justice, Oct. 9, 1705.
141	TALLY	Joseph, and Elizabeth Naps, May 8, 1747.
181	"	Sarah, and George Smith, Aug. 23, 1747.
205	TANNER	Gideon, and Mary Lyng; m. by Rev. Gardiner Thurston, July 12, 1761.
215	"	James, Jr., and Hannah Hazard; m. by Rev. Ezra Stiles, July 7, 1771.
40	TAYLOR	Robert, and Patience Chapman, widow of John (also 165); m. by Edward Thurston, Justice, Aug. 9, 1711.
73	"	John, and Mary Easton; m. by Peleg Smith, Justice, May 10, 1724.
163	"	Katherine, and Robert Sherman, Dec. 4, 1729.
112	"	Robert, and Elizabeth Stanton, (also 165); m. by Gov. John Wanton, May 27, 1740.
165	"	Robert, and Rebecca Coggeshall; m. by Peter Bours, Justice, Dec. 30, 1742.
102	"	Nathaniel, and Elizabeth Arnold; m. by Rev. James Searing, June 7, 1750.
142	"	Deborah, and Job Townsend, May 31, 1753.
234	"	Benjamin, and Jane Battey; m. by Rev. Nicholas Eyres, May 1, 1757.
208	"	Rebecca, and George Buckmaster, June 19, 1759.

NEWPORT—MARRIAGES.

188	TAYLOR	Robert, Jr., and Mary Pitman; m. by Rev. Ezra Stiles, Dec. 5, 1759.
204	"	Katherine and Benjamin Congdon, Aug. 9, 1760.
210	"	Robert, Jr., Mary Lyon; m. by Rev. Gardiner Thurston, Nov. 10, 1762.
148	"	Sarah, and George Hazard, —— 17, 1762-3.
157	"	Mary, and Charles Wigneren, Nov. 7, 1764.
157	"	James, and Mary Wigneren; m. by Rev. Gardiner Thurston, Nov. 21, 1764.
157	"	William, and Ann Kelsey; m. by Rev. Gardiner Thurston, March 31, 1765.
1-68	"	Catherine, and Nicholas Paris Tillinghast, Aug. 17, 1766.
190	"	Sarah, and Joseph Warren, ——, 1766.
1-93	"	Rouse, of Peter, and Hannah, and Mary Mitchel, of James, Jr., and Rhoda, both dec., 8m, 2d, 1798.
1-67	"	Humphrey, of Peter and Sarah Crandall, of Azariah; m. by Rev. Michael Eddy, May 3. 1801.
1-101	"	Benjamin, of James, of Salem, Mass., and Mary Rodman, dau. of Gideon, Richmond, of Newport; m. by Rev. Michael Eddy, July 13, 1812.
1-100	"	Edward Easten, and Rebecca Chapman; m. by Rev. Samuel Towle, April 14, 1814.
1-121	"	Eliza, and John Clarke, Sept. 7, 1830.
2-2	"	Martha S., and Caleb, J. Atbro, June 27, 1839.
2-64	"	Kate W., and William Gardiner Read, Nov. 26, 1851.
2-64	"	Emeline Gould, and William Gardiner Read, Jan. 4, 1855.
57	TAYS	Jacob, and Sarah Weeden; m. by Peleg Slocum, Justice, July 14, 1722.
2-57	TEARNEY	Charles, and Catherine Lawton; m. by Rev. William O'Reilley, Aug. 26, 1855.
205	TELFAIR	James, and Margary Stanton; m. by Rev. Gardiner Thurston, April 19, 1761.
158	"	Mrs. Margery, and John Northup, Nov. 24, 1772.
123	TELLFORTE	Mary, and Richard Hargest, —— 30, 1738.
50	TERRY	Bathsheba, and Peter Hallock, July 13, 1719.
1-35	TESTINGS	Samuel, Vernon, and Elizabeth Almy; m. by Rev. Timothy Waterhouse, Dec. 31, 1784.
132	TEWELL	Hart, and Henry Peckham, Sept. 27, 1742.
118	"	Katherine, and Sherman Clarke, Jan. 22, 1756.
1-33	"	Benjamin, and Elizabeth Gibbs; m. by Rev. Samuel Hopkins, Nov. 6, 1787.
236	"	Content, of Newport, and John ——, of Boston; m. by Rev. James Searing, ——.
5	TEW	Henry, Jr., and Ann Richmond; m. by Gov. Samuel Cranston, April 6, 1704.
63	"	Elizabeth, and Edward Smith, Sept. 17, 1713.
79	"	Henry, and Margaret Easton; m. by John Coddington, Justice, Oct. 2, 1728.
171	"	George, and Bridget Sweet; m. by Rev. Nicholas Eyres, Nov. 17, 1754.
188	"	Elizabeth, and James Drew, March 30, 1759.
200	"	Thomas, and Ann Clarke; m. by Rev. Gardiner Thurston, Dec. 6, 1759.
1-60	"	Ruth, and Abraham D. Tilley, Sept. 3, 1799.
235	"	Paul, and Patience Lillibridge; m. by Rev. Nicholas Eyres, May 3, ——.
1-84	"	William, of William, of Newport, and Ann Tilley, of Newport, dau. of William, of Portsmouth; m. by Rev. Michael Eddy, June 1, 1806.
2-13	"	Sarah A., and Silas D. Deblois, April 2, 1841.
2-14	"	Catherine S., and Robert Goff, Dec. 5, 1841.
2-28	"	Thomas H., of Newport, and Laura E. Willing, of New Shoreham; m. by Rev. Thatcher Thayer, Jan. 1, 1844.
2-29	"	He____ M., and John S. Deblois, Oct. 2, 1845.

2-32	THATCHER	Eliza T., and Horatio W. Wood, Nov. 11, 1849.
2-29	THEOBALD	George, and Jane Bell; m. by Rev. Thatcher Thayer, Sept. 25, 1846.
2-21	THIDDY	Ann, and William Bryer, Oct. 13, 1844.
152	THOMAS	Sarah, and —— ——; m. by Rev. James Searing, ——, 1746.
152	"	——, and Mehitable Hunt; m. by Rev. James Searing, ——, 1746.
153	"	Abigail, and John Armstrong, July 13, 1749.
153	"	Burgess, and Desire Baker; m. by Rev. Nicholas Eyres, Aug. 10, 1749.
154	"	Lydia, and James Bordin, Dec. 29, 1751.
171	"	Esther, and John Gassin, Nov. 25, 1753.
171	"	Mary, and Robert Hudson, Sept. 10, 1754.
118	"	John, and Susannah Reynolds; m. by Rev. Nicholas Eyres, Nov. 18, 1755.
191	"	Mrs. Sarah, and Samuel Carr, Dec. 6, 1767.
145	"	Mary, and Robert Grant, Oct. 8, ——.
139	THOMPSON	John, and Elizabeth Arnold; m. by Charles Bardin, Justice, March 26, 1742.
155	"	Moses, and Susannah Blake; m. by Joseph Silvester, Justice, March 23, 1755.
204	"	Ann, and John Hicks, Oct. 9, 1760.
190	"	James, and Elizabeth Greene; m. by Rev. Gardiner Thurston, Oct. 2, 1765.
2-6	"	Deborah S., and Elliott Honeywell, Sept. 19, 1841.
2-34	"	Rosetta A., and George N. Lawton, Jan. 25, 1846.
2-33	"	Ellen G., and Henry P. Williams, Sept. 9, 1847.
2-33	"	Jane, and David Wells, Oct. 17, 1849.
151	THORP	Eunice, and —— Proctor, May 19, 1745.
2-31	"	Jane R., and William Allen, June 14, 1849.
150	THREADKILL	John, and Hannah Claggett; m. by Rev. John Callender, Jr., Nov. 29, 1741.
21	THURSTON	Mary, and John Tompkins, Sept. 7, 1710.
29	"	Priscilla, and Job Lawton, April 16, 1713.
126	"	Edward, and Elizabeth ——, May 9, 1723.
176	"	Phebe, and Peleg Sherman, Jan. 6, 1742.
153	"	William, and Martha Odlin; m. by Rev. Nicholas Eyres, Oct. 25, 1750.
142	"	Sarah, and —— Turner, —— ——, 1750.
170	"	Edward, and Elizabeth Crocum; m. by Rev. Nicholas Eyres, April 8, 1753.
169	"	William, and Dorothy Carter, Sept. 4, 1754.
204	"	Mehitable, and John Calvert, Aug. 14, 1760.
177	"	Rev. Gardiner, and Mrs. Martha Sanford, —— 25, 1760.
205	"	Katherine, and William Wilson, March 19, 1761.
177	"	Edward and Mary Fountain, June 17, 1764.
191	"	Sarah, and William Bell, Dec. 15, 1766.
2-19	"	Elizabeth, and David Melville, Dec. 1, 1768.
1-33	"	Lemuel, and Mary Saunders; m. by Rev. Samuel Hopkins, Aug. 7, 1783.
1-88	"	Sarah Casey and Thomas Ward Bliss, Nov. 13, 1788.
1-38	"	Paul, of John and Sally Hall, of Benjamin; m. by Rev. Michael Eddy, Jan. 2, 1791.
1-58	"	John W., and Elizabeth Anthony; m. by G. Allen, Justice, Mar. 24, 1800.
2-30	"	Carolina M., and Daniel Atkins, March 19, 1848.
191	TIBBETTS	Elizabeth, and Robert Babcock, Feb. 5, 1767.
2-54	TIERNEY	Charles, and Catherine Lawton; m. by Rev. William O'Reilley, Aug. 26, 1855.
123	TIFFANY	Sarah, and Ebenezer Emmons, —— 6, 1738.
154	TILER	Nathaniel, and Susanna Perry; m. by Rev. Nicholas Eyres, Jan. 16, 1752.
160	TILLEY	Ann, and George Chaffin, Jan. 16, 1742-3.
199	"	William, and Elizabeth Rogers; m. by Rev. Gardiner Thurston, Oct. 28, 1759.

NEWPORT—MARRIAGES.

1-46	TILLEY	Thomas, and Mary Sinkings; m. by Rev. Gardiner Thurston, Sept. 7, 1788.
1-53	"	Dorcas, and Clarke Cooke, Dec. 11, 1791.
1-60	"	Abraham D., of William, and Ruth Tew, of William; m. by Rev. W. Collier, Sept. 3, 1799.
1-60	"	John, of William, and Margaret Nicoll, of John; m. by Rev. W. Collier, April 20, 1800.
1-84	"	Ann, and William Tew, June 1, 1806.
1-104	"	Thomas R., of Thomas, of Newport, and Mercy Sweet, of Lemuel, of Warwick; m. by Rev. Pardon Tillinghast, Nov. 30, 1817.
1-124	"	Charles N., and Abby H. Chappell; m. by Rev. Michael Eddy, Nov. 3, 1830.
1-129	"	George S., and Frances H. Hull; m. by Rev. Michael Eddy, Oct. 13, 1833.
2-48	"	Thomas S., and Anna E. Lavir; m. by Rev. Asa Bronson, July 27, 1842.
2-85	"	Elizabeth R., and James H. Hammett, Oct. 31, 1849.
21	TILLINGHAST	Mary, and Richard Ward, Nov. 2, 1709.
21	"	Charles, and Elizabeth Cranston; m. by Gov. Samuel Cranston, May 17, 1711.
92	"	Mary, and John Tweedy, July 10, 1732.
105	"	Mercy, and John Tweedy, Sept. 10, 1732.
1-68	"	Patience Taylor, and Capt. John Vilett, Sept. ——, 1795.
153	"	Mary, and Elias Bryer, Dec. 6, 1750.
102	"	Thomas, and Abigail Hunt; by Rev. James Searing, Feb. 25, 1753.
171	"	Elizabeth, and Matthew Cozzens, Oct. 17, 1754.
172	"	Martha, and James Hawdon (also 233), Aug. 19, 1756.
199	"	Amey, and Thomas Eyres, July 12, 1759.
204	"	Avis, and James Carpenter, Sept. 15, 1760.
204	"	Joseph, and Mary Cranston; m. by Rev. Gardiner Thurston, Oct. 9, 1760.
147	"	Lydia, and William Grinnell, June 17, 1762.
148	"	Pardon, and Abigail Rogers; m. by Rev. Nicholas Eyres, Feb. 5, 1764.
148	"	Henry and Rebecca ——; m. by Rev. Gardiner Thurston, Aug. 13, 1764.
1-68	"	Nicholas Paris, and Catherine Taylor, Aug. 17, 1766.
1-68	"	William Edward, and Sarah Almy, May 30, 1782.
1-111	"	John, of Newport, son of Pardon and Mary Ann Sanford, of Joseph; m. by Rev. Michael Eddy, May 27, 1791.
109	"	Sarah, and —— ——; m. by Rev. Nicholas Eyres, ——.
141	TISDALE	Elizabeth, and Benjamin Lord, Nov. 21, 1750.
147	TOMALIN	Eunice, and Benjamin, Trowbridge, —— ——, 1762.
206	TOMAN	John, and Ruth Sisson; m. by Rev. William Vinall, July 21, 1762.
205	TOMLIN	Gideon, and Mary Grant; m. by Rev. Gardiner Thurston, Feb. 3, 1761.
7	TOMPKINS	Priscilla, and —uel Lyndon, July ——, 1703.
21	"	John, and Mary Thurston; m. by Edward Thurston, Justice, Sept. 7, 1710.
1-116	"	Frances G., and Samuel H. Jack, Feb. 13, 1825.
2-36	"	Henry G., and Abigail Mitchell; m. by Rev. E. B. Bradford, Sept. 9, 1845.
102	TOPHAM	Margaret, and William Finch, Nov. 1, 1753.
187	"	Mary, and Richard Simpson, Oct. 14, 1756.
188	"	Agnes, and Philip Morse, Nov. 28, 1759.
2-21	"	Mary F., and Lewis B. Caswell, June 27, 1843.
2-28	TORREY	Louisa B., and Thomas H. Lawton, May 1, 1845.
48	TOSH	Daniel, and Margaret Acors, both of Block Island; m. by Rev. Morgen Jones, Oct. 19, 1686.
123	TOWNMAN	Mary, and Thomas Child, May 17, 1738.
72	TOWNSEND	Mary, and John Wignel, June 20, 1722.
134	"	Christopher, and Patience Easton; m. by Daniel Updike, Justice, Dec. 26, 1723.

151	TOWNSEND	Nathan, and Mary Davenport; m. by Rev. James Searing, July 1, 1745.
185	"	Hannah, and John Goddard, Aug. 7, 1746.
237	"	Susanna, and James Goddard, Jan. 17, 1750.
142	"	Job and Deborah Taylor of Peter, and Thankful, May 31, 1753.
190	"	Thomas, and Mary Dyer; m. by Rev. Gardiner Thurston, Dec. 20, 1765.
1-83	"	Sarah, and George Cornell, Dec. 9, 1784.
2-24	TOWN	Calvin H., and Margaret T. B. Conner; m. by Rev. R. Livesey, Aug. 9, 1846.
153	TREBY	Solomon, and Elizabeth Bennett; m. by Rev. Nicholas Eyres, Sept. 2, 1750.
102	"	Mehitable, and John Wilkinson —— 1752.
102	"	Mehitable, and William Augustus Peck (also 177), Oct. 1, 1752.
169	"	John, and Sarah Richardson, Sept. 5, 1754.
209	"	Wilkins, and Honora Sanford; m. by Rev. Ezra Stiles, Oct. 15, 1766.
102	TREVITT	Eleazer, and Mary Channing; m. by Rev. James Searing, ———— —, 1752.
240	"	Eleazer, and Mary Church, Oct. 18, ——.
172	TRIBUT	Arthur, of Newport, and Ann Mosey, of North Kingstown; m. by Rev. Nicholas Eyres (also 233), Oct. 10, 1756.
149	TRIPP	Stephen, and Alice Manchester; m. by Rev. Nichols Eyres, Sept. —, 1741.
149	"	Sarah, and Zebulon Greene, April 1, 1742.
211	"	Othniel, and —— Coggeshall, m. by Jonathan Nichols, D. Gov. July 9, 1751.
172	"	Joseph, and Dorothy Pate; m. by Rev. Nicholas Eyres (also 233), April 5, 1757.
204	"	Othniel, and Sarah Crapon; m. by Rev. Gardiner Thurston, Sept. 29, 1760.
148	"	Martha, and Richard Card, May 12, 1764.
209	"	Benoni, and Ruth Senter; m. by Rev. Ezra Stiles, July 26, 1764.
209	"	William, and Elizabeth Robinson; m. by Rev. Ezra Stiles, Nov. 21, 1765.
191	"	Mary, and Thomas Earl, May 14, 1767.
1-88	"	John, and Mary Ann Marble; m. by Rev. John B. Gibson, Nov. 21, 1808.
2-3	"	Joshua W., of Providence, and Anna S. Goodson, of Newport; m. by Rev. Leland Howard, Dec. 9, 1839.
2-27	"	Harriet C., and William Eddy, Aug. 8, 1843.
140	TROWBRIDGE	Ebenezer, and Mrs. Abigail Wilson, Nov. 13, 1740.
147	"	Benjamin, and Eunice Tomalin; m. by Rev. Nicholas Eyres, July 11, 1762.
47	TUBBS	Mary, and Joseph Dill, Dec. 12, 1715.
151	TUCKER	Mary, and Joseph Morse, Dec. 2, 1744.
122	"	James, and Sarah Sheffield; m. by Rev. John Callender, Jr., April 5, ——.
153	TUEL	Jerusha, and Paul Coffin, Nov. 15, 1750.
190	"	Benjamin, and Dorcas Downer; m. by Rev. Gardiner Thurston, ——, 1766.
68	TURNER	Phebe, and James Coggeshall, Nov. 24, 1723.
151	"	Joseph, and Abigail Smith; m. by Rev. James Searing, Aug. 16, 1744.
142	"	——, and Sarah Thurston, ——, 1750.
2-10	"	Lieut. Peter, U. S. N., and Sarah Stafford Jones; m. by Rev. N. B. Crocker, Oct. 12, 1842.
2-27	"	Oliver Cromwell, and Sarah D. Read; m. by Rev. Thatcher Thayer, July 31, 1843.
2-20	"	Henry E., and Ann E. Stevens; m. by Rev. Thomas Leaver, July 18, 1844.
2-44	"	Joshua, and Sophia Redfield; m. by Rev. Henry John Stewart, Feb. 5, 1855.
2-37	TUTTLE	Caroline M., and Alphonso Barnes, Aug. 5, 1851.

92	TWEEDY John, and Mary Tillinghast; m. by John Gardiner, Asst., July 10, 1732.
105	" John, and Mercy Tillinghast, July 10, 1732.
95	" Elizabeth, and John Cook, Sept. 16, 1734.
105	" John, and Freelove Crawford, July 28, 1735.
145	TYLER Caroline, and John Hunt, (also 198), Nov. 13, 1757.

U

1-77	UDALL Adino, of Oliver, of Vermont, and Olive Clarke, of Thomas, of Newport; m. by Elder William Bliss, Oct. 13, 1805.
148	UNDERWOOD Amey, and William Weeden, —— 17, 1762-3.
209	" Thomas, and Sarah Lawless; m. by Ezra Stiles, Justice, July 24, 1764.
1-4	" Mary, and Joseph Lyon, June 11, 1776.
1-113	" Almy, and Otis Chaffee, April 5, 1801.
2-14	" Benjamin Ward, and Abby Packard Helme; m. by Rev. Francis Vinton, Nov. 2, 1841.
2-33	" Horace F., of Middletown, and Sarah Ann Marsh, of Newport; m. by Rev. B. Othman, Jan. 9, 1850.
206	UPHAM Sarah, and Benedict Bliss, Dec. 24, 1766.

V

2-18	VAUGHN Jane, and David Melville, before 1730.
93	" Rebecca, and Gideon Cornell, Feb. 22, 1732.
2-18	" Elizabeth, and David Melville, Jan. 5, 1735.
111	" Sarah, and Joseph Cahoone, —— 5, 1740.
132	" Samuel, and Anna Bailey; m. by Rev. John Callender, Jr., June 27, 1742.
121	" Sarah, and Joseph ——; m. by Rev. John Callendar, Jr., —— 5, ——.
135	" Valentine, and Elizabeth Sharpe, ——.
40	VAY Mary, and Edmund Mumford, —— 17, 1718-19.
1-1	VEIL Sarah, and Lee Langley, Dec. 12, 1782.
66	VERNON Samuel, and Elizabeth Fleet; m. by Nathaniel Coddington, Asst., April 10, 1707.
123	" Samuel, and Almy ——, Dec. 29, 1736.
188	" Mary, and Christopher Ellery, Nov. 26, 1760.
1-50	" Ann, and David Olyphant, Oct. 23, 1785.
2-29	" George F., and Ann A. Bradford; m. by Rev. Thatcher Thayer, June 25, 1845.
2-29	" Sophia, and Robert M. Olyphant, Oct. 13, 1846.
169	VERRIER Nicholas, and Mary Talley; m. by Martin Howard, Justice, May 27, 1753.
123	VIAL Hezekiah, and —— ——, Oct. 14, 1736.
132	" Judith, and James Cooley, Feb. 4, 1741-2.
141	" John, and Elizabeth Donnelly, May 5, 1747.
242	VICKERY Hannah, and Thomas Ash, —— 1749.
142	" Thomas, and Abigail Melville, —— 24, 1750.
1-31	" Joseph, and Marcy Lindsey, of Capt. David, July 20, 1756.
1-68	VILETT Capt. John, and Patience Taylor Tillinghast, Sept. —, 1795.
205	VINSON Elizabeth, and Samuel Little Billings, April 21, 1761.
148	" Ann, and Abraham Hardin, June 26, 1764.
2-14	VINTON Rev. Francis, and Elizabeth Mason Perry, of Com. Oliver H.; m. by Rev. Alexander H. Vinton, March 2, 1841.
188	VOSE Mary, and John Holmes, Dec. 4, 1757.
147	" Benjamin, and Sarah Clarke; m. by Rev. Nicholas Eyres, —— 1762.
101	VROOM Peter (mariner), and Ann Springer; m. by William Dyer, Justice, Oct. 12, 1738.
101	" Ann, and James Maynard, Nov. —, 1742.

W

74	WADSWORTH	John W., and ——, ——, ——.
100	WADY	James, and Mary Claggett; m. by Rev. John Callender, Jr., May 27, 1736.
171	"	James, and Elizabeth Bink; m. by Rev. Nicholas Eyres, Jan. 1, 1755.
204	"	Elizabeth, and Edmund Bell, Jan. 4, 1761.
209	"	Margaret, and Thomas Hoonsley, May 22, 1765.
118	WALDEN	John, and Prescilla Lawton; m. by Rev. Nicholas Eyres, March 28, 1756.
200	WALKER	——beth, and Thomas ——; m. by Rev. Gardiner, Thurston, ——, 1760.
157	"	Elizabeth, and Thomas ——; m. by Rev. Gardiner Thurston, ——, 1764.
242	"	Margaret, and Thomas Richardson, Feb. 15, 1768.
2-9	"	David, of New London, Conn., and Laura A. Slocum, of Newport; m. by Rev. Thomas Leaver, May 15, 1842.
87	WALKMAN	Mary, and Joseph Pitman, Dec. 19, 1717.
2-28	WALLACE	Catherine, and Michael Cottrell, May 16, 1845.
132	WALLEN	Elizabeth, and John Easton, Nov. 25, 1742.
153	WALSHAM	James, and Mary Wilks; m. by Rev. Nicholas Eyres, July 14, 1751.
210	"	Mary, and John Rogers, Dec. 24, 1761.
2-59	"	Mary A., and Andrew L. Moore, Nov. 4, 1856.
206	WAMPSEE	Silvia, and Michael Grice, May 1, 1763.
89	WANTON	Gideon, of Tiverton, and Mary Cadman, of Newport; m. by Gov. Samuel Cranston, Feb. 26, 1717.
124	"	John, of John, and Ann Redwood, of Abraham, of Antigua, W. I.; m. by Gov. Samuel Cranston, June 10, 1718.
151	"	Mary, and William Stoddard, June 18, 1745.
152	"	Martha, and George Hazard, Nov. 24, 1745.
186	"	Edward, of George and Hannah Rodman, of Clarke; m. by Daniel Coggeshall, Asst., Sept. 14, 1749.
2-41	"	Sarah, and David Legallais, Nov. 18, 1753.
203	"	Abigail, and Nathaniel Coggeshall, May 12, 1756.
206	"	Ruth, and George Champlain, July 26, 1763.
1-69	"	Mary, and Daniel Lyman, Jan. 20, 1782.
27	WARD	Amey, (widow,) and ——; m. by Benedict Arnold, Asst., March —1691-2.
40	"	Mary, and Sion Arnold, Feb. 7, 1700.
21	"	Richard, and Mary Tillinghast; m. by Rev. James Honeyman, Nov. 2, 1709.
141	"	Margaret, and Richard Power, June 13, 1748.
142	"	Olive, and John Goddard, June 19, 1753.
190	"	Mary, and Valentine Wightman, —— —, 1765.
242	"	Elizabeth, and James Larkin, Sept. 19, 1772.
1-85	"	Benoni, and Abigail Lynden; m. by Rev. Benjamin Foster, Sept. 1, 1788.
122	"	Mary, and Ebenezer Flagg, —— 8, ——.
154	WARNER	Oliver, and Elizabeth Wyatt; m. by Rev. Nicholas Eyres, June 23, 1752.
1-33	"	Amos, of Providence, and Hannah Hacker, of Newport; m. by Rev. Samuel Hopkins, Dec. 9, 1787.
109	"	Mary, and Benjamin Gibson, —— 31, ——.
119	WARREN	——, and Michael Bryn, April 9, 1746.
199	"	Katherine, and Amos Paterson, Oct. 7, 1759.
190	"	Joseph, and Sarah Taylor; m. by Rev. Gardiner Thurston, ——, 1766.
188	WASHBURN	Ebenezer, and Joanna Child; m. by Rev. Ezra Stiles, ——, 1761.
2-27	"	WATERMAN Lydia, and Joseph Ashley, Oct. 24, 1843.
2-49	WATERS	Mary, and John Power, Oct. 17, 1853.
140	WATMAUGH	Eliza, and Benjamin Wickham, Sept. 1, 1733.

2-28	WATSON Charles H., of Westfield, Mass., and Jane E., of West Williamstown, Mass.; m. by Rev. Thatcher Thayer, Oct. 20. 1844.
188	WAY Mary, and William Simmons, Jan. 1, 1761.
119	WEATHERDON Sarah, and John Downer, —— 1, 1744.
149	WEATHERD Robert, and ——; m. by Rev. Nicholas Eyres, March 13, 1742-3.
191	WEATHERS Mary, and John Stanton, June 4, 1767.
44	WEAVER John, of Newport, and Alice Berry, of East Greenwich, by John Spencer, Justice, March 15, 1710.
95	" Thomas, of John, and Sarah Davis; m. by Daniel Gould, Justice, May 1, 1735.
199	" Mary, and John Hudson, July 12, 1759.
157	" Thomas, and Elizabeth Beardin; m. by Rev. Gardiner Thurston, Jan. 27, 1765.
206	" Hannah, and John Cary, July 4, 1765.
1-25	" Thomas, Jr., of Newport, and Jane Holmes; m. by Rev. Gardiner Thurston, June 30, 1783.
1-117	" Sarah, and William W. Freeborn, Oct. 19, 1806.
1-128	" Joseph B., and Abby Marsh; m. by Rev. Michael Eddy, June 9, 1833.
2-68	" George W., of Newport, and Harriet Rotch, of South Kingstown; m. by Rev. Charles P. Grosvenor, Sept. 5, 1836.
2-27	" Catherine, and Capt Oliver Potter, March 11, 1841.
2-15	" John, and Eliza Downing; m. by Rev. Thomas Leaver, Aug. 16, 1842.
2-36	" Frances C., and Benjamin H. Stevens, Oct. 2, 1845.
2-25	" James L., and Johanna Holt; m. by Rev. Richard Livesey (also 2-32), Dec. 17, 1846.
57	WEEDEN Sarah, and Jacob Lays, July 14, 1722.
131	" Mary, and Joseph Card, Aug. 7, 1736.
121	" Phebe, and William Whitehead, Sept. 25, 1740.
119	" Jonathan, of Newport, and —— ——, of Middletown; m. by Rev. Nicholas Eyres, Aug. 21, 1746.
170	" Job, and Constant Odlin; m. by Rev. Nicholas Eyres, June 24, 1753.
203	" Job, and Ann Heath; m. by Rev. William Vinal, Nov. 20, 1755.
203	" Phillip, and Merebah Jeffers; m. by Rev. William Vinal, Dec. 4, 1755.
203	" Sarah, and Henry Brickley, Aug. 17, 1756.
203	" Mary, and Henry Davis, Sept. 9, 1756.
204	" Samuel, and Abigail Langworthy; m. by Rev. Gardiner Thurston, July 3, 1760.
206	" Jonathan, and Katherine Chandler; m. by Rev. William Vinall, Dec. 30, 1762.
148	" William, and Amey Underwood; m. by Rev. Nicholas Eyres, —— 17, 1762-3.
215	" Rebecca, and Samuel Albro, Sept. 13, 1764.
190	" Amey, and Charles Wright, Aug. 27, 1765.
190	" Henry, and Lettice Melville; m. by Rev. Gardiner Thurston, Aug. 20, 1766.
121	" William, and Sarah Peckham; m. by Rev. John Callender, Jr., —— 10, ——.
2-16	" Clarissa, and James W. Cary, Nov. 21, 1843.
2-29	" Charles, and Eliza Weeden; m. by Rev. Thatcher Thayer, Nov. 3, 1845.
2-29	" Eliza, and Charles Weeden, Nov. 3, 1845.
2-32	" Elizabeth, and Edward Simmons, Aug. 9, 1846.
147	WELFORD John, and Ann ——; m. by Rev. Nicholas Eyres, June 6, 1762.
188	WELLS Gideon, of Weathersfield, Conn., and Welthia Whiting, of Middletown; m. by Rev. Ezra Stiles, June 24, 1757.
2-33	" David, and Jane Thompson; m. by Rev. B. Ottoman, Oct. 17, 1849.
1-118	WENCH Henry, and Ann Coggeshall; m. by Rev. Samuel Towle, Jan. 18, 1812.

2-27	WESTCOTT	Sarah B., and George B. Knowles, Dec. 25, 1842.
203	WESTGATE	Abigail, and Aaron Seabury, March 18, 1756.
1-33	"	Abigail, and William Lemuel Newton Allen, June 27, 1784.
100	WEST	Ichabod, and Rebecca Holt; m. by Rev. John Callender, Jr., Aug. 12, 1736.
2-18	"	Lydia, and David Melville, Feb. 11, 1739.
154	"	Thomas, and Elizabeth Gladding; m. by Rev. Nicholas Eyres, Feb. 28, 1752.
200	"	Ebenezer, and Wait Carr; m. by Rev. Gardiner Thurston, Feb. 23, 1760.
210	"	Hannah, and John Caswell, Dec. 31, 1761.
121	"	William, and Mary Southwick; m. by Rev. John Callender, Jr., —— 8, ——.
1-129	"	Hannah, and Daniel Wilbour, June 24, 1834.
148	WETHERELL	Samuel, and Mary Sawdry; m. by Rev. Nicholas Eyres, Sept. 29, 1763.
1-83	WHEATON	Dr. Levi, and Martha Burrell; m. by Rev. Samuel Hopkins, Dec. 20, 1784.
1-132	WHEELER	Cyrel C., of Warren, R. I., and Hannah Mary Hazard, of Newport; m. by Rev. William Gammell, May 9, 1827.
2-33	WHILEY	Sarah M., and David G. Baker, July 11, 1839.
19	WHIPPLE	Joseph, of Joseph and Ann Almy; m. by Gov. Samuel Cranston, about 1708 (?).
123	"	Mary, and Joseph Silvester, —— 15, 1738.
240	WHITEHEAD	Samuel, of New Jersey, and Elizabeth Hunt, of Newport; m. by James Brown, Justice, Oct. 15, 1718.
121	"	William, and Phebe Weeden; m. by Rev. Nicholas Eyres, Sept. 25, 1740.
1-126	WHITEHOUSE	John, of New Hampshire, and Eliza Stacy, of Newport; m. by Rev. Michael Eddy, Feb. 3, 1833.
112	WHITE	Thomas, and Sarah Norton; m. by Rev. Nicholas Eyres, (also 118), Oct 23 or 25, 1755.
147	"	Paul, and Phebe Lewis; m. by Rev. Nicholas Eyres, —— ——, 1762.
148	"	Abigail, and Gideon Soule, July 6, 1764.
1-78	"	Susanah, and William Shaw, Dec. 27, 1801.
205	WHITFIELD	Mary, and Thomas Nenegret, April 23, 1761.
1-43	"	Sarah, and Stephen Perry, Feb. 1, 1789.
70	WHITING	William, and Ann ——; m, by Rev. James Honeyman, Jan. 31, 1725-6.
187	"	Mary, and Hardin Jones, Oct. 17, 1756.
188	"	Wealthian, and Gideon Wells, June 24, 1757.
205	"	Eleanor, and James Bourk, June 25, 1761.
21	WHITMAN	Sarah, and William Collins, April —, 1697.
74	"	Vemorias, and Palgrave ——; m. by Job Lawton, Justice, July 18, 1720.
2-29	"	Lucretia A., and Edwin W. Harren, Oct. 14, 1845.
140	WHITTEMORE	Richard, and Mrs. Mary Pillsbury, Sept. 6, 1741.
58	WIGHTMAN	Elizabeth and Stephen Hookey, Jr., Jan. 16, 1723-4.
131	"	Valentine, of South Kingston, and —— ——, of Newport; m. by Rev. Nicholas Eyres, March 18, 1737-8.
153	"	Irathonne, and Benjamin Boss, Sept. 23, 1750.
169	"	John, and Elizabeth Wilbour, Aug. 15, 1754.
190	"	Valentine, and Mary Ward; m. by Rev. Gardiner Thurston, ——, 1765.
235	"	Daniel, and Katherine ——; m. by Rev. Nicholas Eyres, ——.
190	WIGHT	Charles, and Amey Weeden; m. by Rev. Gardiner Thurston, Aug. 27, 1765.
72	WIGNELL	John, and Mary Townsend; m. by Rev. James Honeyman, June 20, 1722.
84	"	Mary, and Elnathan Hammond, Dec. 27, 1728.
123	"	Anstress Elizabeth, and Robert Stevens, Sept. 21, 1738.
157	WIGNERON	Charles, and Mary Taylor; m. by Rev. Gardiner Thurston, Nov. 7, 1764.
157	"	Mary, and James Taylor, Nov. 21, 1764.
150	WILBOUR	Mary, and William Sherman, Sept. 6, 1741.

NEWPORT—MARRIAGES.

152	WILBOUR William, and Sarah Hammett; m. by Rev. James Searing, May 29, 1746.
152	" Deborah, and —— ——; m. by Rev. James Searing, ——, 1746.
141	" Ann, and Jacob Stockman, May 22, 1748.
141	" Hannah, and Isaac Candry, Dec. 28, 1749.
141	" Ann, and Isaac Howland, ——, 1750.
170	" Joseph, and Susannah Dewick; m. by Iev. Nicholas Eyres, Sept. 2, 1753.
169	" Elizabeth, and John Wightman, Aug. 15, 1754.
115	" Uriah, and Sarah Paul; m. by Rev. Nicholas Eyres (also 172), Nov. 11, 1756.
233	" Uzziah, and Sarah Paul; m. by Rev. Nicholas Eyres, Nov. 11, 1756.
172	" John, and Mary Hovey; m. by Rev. Nicholas Eyres (also 233), March 24, 1757.
177	" Benjamin, and Martha Huddy, Dec. 10, 1760.
205	" Mary, and —— Hill, ——, 1761.
147	" Ann, and William ——; m. by Rev. Nicholas Eyres, ——, 1762.
190	" Anthony, and Martha Greene; m. by Rev. Gardiner Thurston, April 3, 1766.
1-132	" Phebe, and Michael Eddy, Sept. 27, 1787.
122	" Samuel, and Hannah Popplestone; m. by Rev. John Callender, Justice, —— 19, ——.
1-120	" Job B., and Amey R. Williams; m. by Benjamin Anthony, Justice, at Fall River, Mass., July 24, 1827.
1-129	" Daniel, of Newport, son of William, and Hannah West, of Gloucester, dau. of Stephen; m. by Rev. James Wilson, June 24, 1834.
140	WICKHAM Benjamin, and Eliza Watmaugh, both of London, Eng., Sept. 1, 1733.
113	" Benjamin, and Mary Gardiner; m. by Rev. Nicholas Eyres (also 149), Dec. 25, 1743.
149	WILCOX Daniel, and Eunice Cranston; m. by Rev. John Callender, June 16, 1743.
204	" Daniel, and Sarah Clarke; m. by Rev. Gardiner Thurston, Oct. 27, 1760.
209	" Phebe, and James Cahoone, —— 28, 1763.
190	" Rhoda, and Edward Greene, Oct. 1, 1766.
116	" ——, and Peleg Barker, April 5, 1768.
1-67	" George, of Robert, of Washington, D. C., and Susannah D. Motte, of Louis D., of French Co.; m. by Rev. Michael Eddy, May 7, 1801.
2-17	" Isaac T., of Fall River, Mass., and Mary Ann W. Salisbury, of Newport; m. by Rev. Thomas Leaver, Jan. 21, 1844.
172	WILES Sarah, and Nathaniel Scott, April 3, 1757.
2-2	WILEY Sarah M., and David G. Barker, July 11, 1839.
2-33	" Jane, and Richard Frederic Bell, March 17, 1850.
191	WILKEY Jannah, and James Hamblin, Dec. 7, 1766.
116	" Peter, and Elizabeth Southwick; m. by Elder John Maxson, Oct. —, 1767.
1-74	" Samuel, and Huldah Collins, both of Dartmouth, Mass.; m. by Rev. Daniel Hix, June 2, 1796.
102	WILKINSON John, and Mehitable Treby, m. by Rev. James Searing, ——, 1752.
153	WILKS Mary, and James Walsham, July 14, 1751.
2-18	WILLARD ——, and David Melville, about 1690.
209	WILLEKEY Thomas, and Mary Hill; m. by Rev. Ezra Stiles, June 20, 1764.
78	WILLETT Mary, and Weston Clarke, June 20, 1728.
205	" Charles, and Bathsheba Rogers; m. by Rev. Gardiner Thurston, July 12, 1761.
8	WILLIAMS ——, and ——, Sept. 9, 1703.
38	" Arabella, and Edward Pelham, Jr., March 14, 1717-8.
149	" Barbara, and Joseph Rider, Nov. 26, 1741.
119	" Alexander, and Experience Miller; m. by Rev. Nicholas Eyres, March 14, 1744-5.

141	WILLIAMS	John, and Mary Peckham, Nov. 8, 1750.
153	"	Hannah, and Thomas Andrews, Aug. 18, 1751.
171	"	John, and Patience Barker; m. by Rev. Nicholas Eyres, Oct. 20, 1754.
1-57	"	Abigail, and George Perry, March 25, 1782.
1-80	"	John, and Sally Chadwick, Sept. 25, 1785.
1-109	"	William, and Mrs. Ann Lawton; m. by Rev. George G. Miller, March 28, 1819.
1-120	"	Amey R., and Job B. Wilbour, July 24, 1827.
1-133	"	Penelope, and Caleb S. Knight, June 9, 1836.
1-136	"	Alexander, and Lydia Spencer; m. by Elder James A. McKensie, April 7, 1839.
2-6	"	Harriet, and Francis Roberson, Aug. 22, 1841.
2-15	"	Joshua A., and Mary Spencer; m. by Rev. Thomas Leaver, July 28, 1842.
2-28	"	Charles A., and Ann Cottrell; m. by Rev. Thatcher Thayer, March 10, 1844.
2-33	"	Henry P., of Taunton, Mass., and Ellen G. Thompson, of Newport; m. by Rev. B. Othman, Sept. 9, 1849.
2-32	"	Catherine Jane, and Lewis Coburn, Dec. 11, 1849.
2-28	WILLING	Laura E., and Thomas H. Tew, Jan. 1, 1844.
188	WILLS	John, and Elizabeth Fry; m. by Rev. Ezra Stiles, Nov. 8, 1759.
169	WILLIS	Henry, and Elmira Cahoone; m. by Martin Howard, Justice, Aug. 26, 1749.
41	WILSON	Benjamin, and Ann Greenman, Jan. 9, 1719-20.
211	"	Benjamin, and Elizabeth Coggeshall; m. by Samuel Vernon, Justice, March 4, 1729.
140	"	Mrs. Abigail, and Ebenezer Trowbridge, Nov. 13, 1740.
151	"	Hester, and Timothy Egan, Sept. 1, 1745.
141	"	Ann, and Alixander McDonald, Nov. 12, 1747.
239	"	Elizabeth, and Michael Braston, July 4, 1749.
203	"	Benjamin, and Elizabeth Brown; m. by Rev. William Vinall, Feb. 5, 1756.
205	"	William, and Katherine Thurston; m. by Rev. Gardiner Thurston, March 19, 1761.
147	"	John, and Elizabeth Millward; m. by Rev. Nicholas Eyres, May 15, 1762.
209	"	Benjamin, and Mary Baxter; m. by Rev. Ezra Stiles, Jan. 4, 1763.
122	"	Sarah, and William Benson, —— 5, ——.
1-81	"	Sarah W., and Sylvester Brownell, Oct. 14, 1804.
2-69	"	James A., and Henrietta Horswell; m. by Rev. Romeo Elton, Sept. 26, 1819.
2-9	"	William B., and Martha M. Horswell; m. by Rev. Thomas Leaver, Jan. 13, 1842.
2-29	"	Samuel, and Margaret ——, m. by Rev. Thatcher Thayer, July 13, 1845.
157	WIL——	Patience, and Woodman ——; m. by Rev. Gardiner Thurston, Feb. 5, 1765.
200	WING	Obed, and Sarah Greene; m. by Rev. Gardiner Thurston, Jan. 17, 1760.
170	WINSLOW	Elizabeth, and Jacob Strange, July 9, 1754.
191	"	Mary, and Paine Johnson, Nov. 13, 1766.
206	WINSOR	——, and Sarah Melville; m. by Rev. William Vinall, ——, 1763.
123	WITHERELL	Timothy, and Sarah Caswell, Oct. 5, 1738.
45	WOODARD	Ezekiel, and —— Clarke; m. by Nathaniel Coddington, Asst., June 8, 1716.
1-76	WOODMANSEE	John, of Swansey, and Merebah Downing, of Newport; m. by Rev. William Patten, Oct. 18, 1803.
142	WOODONS	John, and Abigail Brown, March 19, 1753.
2-4	WOODROFF	William, of Philadelphia, Pa., and Rachel M. Moffatt, of Connecticut; m. by Rev. Isaac Stoddard, April 20, 1840.
2-31	WOODSIDE	Sarah H., and James Lunt, Oct. 25, 1849.
50	WOODWARD	Mary, and Eben Sanford, Sept. 27, 1716.
11	WOOD	Rebecca, and —— ——; m. by Gov. Samuel Cranston, March 25, 1708.

197	WOOD	Mary, and Robert Carr, May 18, 1749.
194	"	Jonathan and Lydia Irish; m. by Rev. Gardiner Thurston, June 4, 1759.
206	"	Mary, and Isaac Hull, ——, 1763.
1-64	"	Elizabeth, and Joseph Freeborn, July 12, 1776.
2-32	"	Horatio W., and Eliza I. Thatcher, both of Middleboro, Mass.; m. by Rev. Henry Jackson, Nov. 11, 1849.
2-17	WOOLLEY	Sarah, and John Hamilton, Jan. 28, 1844.
1-39	WRIGHTINGTON	Margaret, and Thomas Bailey, Jan. 20, 1719-20.
1-39	"	Thomas, and Sarah Dennis, Jan. 7, 1728-9.
153	WRIGHT	John, and Jerusha Jent; m. by Rev. Nicholas Eyres, Dec. 23, 1750.
142	"	——, and —— Moody, March 29, 1751.
241	"	Benjamin, and Ann ——; m. by Rev. Mr. Brown, July 13, 1771.
1-21	"	Sabrina, and Samuel Fisk, Aug. 13, 1785.
1-100	WRY	Ann, and William S. Lawson, June 28, 1814.
154	WYATT	Elizabeth, and Oliver Warner, Jan. 23, 1752.
200	"	John and Martha Magrah; m. by Rev. Gardiner Thurston, Nov. 22, 1759.
203	"	Eliphal and Thomas Arnold, Sept. 16, 1757.
1-24	"	Alice and Martin Cobellee, Aug. 5, 1781.
153	WYLES	Amey, and Jeremiah Greenman, Aug. 13, 1749.
233	"	Sarah, and Nathaniel Scott, April 3, 1757.

X Y Z

152	YATES	Samuel, and Mary Melville; m. by Rev. James Searing, —— ——, 1746.
1-33	"	Lydia, and Ezekiel Burr, July 9, 1786.
141	YEATES	Mary, and James Cahoone, Dec. 20, 1747.
102	"	Elizabeth, and Thomas Melville, July 19, 1753.
169	"	Lydia, and Wing Shepherd, Nov. 15, 1753.
240	YEATS	Lydia, and John Moore, Feb. 17, ——.
170	YEOMANS	John, and Abigail Norris; m. by Martin Howard, Justice, June 5, 1755.
1-60	"	Mary, and Henry Moore, Nov. ——, 1797.
239	YOULDRIDGE	John, and Dorothy Fox, March 9, 1748-9.
141	YOUNG	James, and Mary Dawley, Sept. 7, 1749.
102	"	Samuel, and Content Hunt; m. by Rev. James Searing, —— ——, 1751.
170	"	Greening, and Mary Manchester; m. by Martin Howard, Justice, Jan. 11, 1754.
188	"	Jacob, and Martha Stacy; m. by Rev. Ezra Stiles, Aug. 5, 1759.
188	"	Gideon, of Providence, and Phebe Read, of Newport; m. by Rev. Ezra Stiles, Oct. 1, 1761.
210	"	Charles, and Patience Brayton; m. by Rev. Gardiner Thurston, Nov. 20, 1761.
147	"	Samuel, and Ann Smith; m. by Rev. Nicholas Eyres, —— ——, 1762.
190	"	Mary, and John Nichols, —— 1, 1765.
2-1	"	Samuel, and Frances Dennis; m. by Rev. James A. McKenzie (also 35), Aug. 6, 1839.
2-7	"	Arnold L., and Eliza B. Sherman; m. by Rev. Thomas Leaver, Nov. 1, 1841.
2-17	"	William, and Susan Sampson; m. by Rev. Thomas Leaver, Nov. 19, 1843.
2-17	"	Henry H., and Sarah C. Sharpe; m. by Rev. Thomas Leaver, Jan. 8, 1844.

NEWPORT.

BIRTHS AND DEATHS.

A

8	ADLIM ——, son of John and Lydia,	July
1-76	ALBRO George Waite, of Benjamin and Abigail, (b. North King. July 12, 1779.	
58	ALLEN Rowland, of Rowland and Marian,	Oct. 9, 1723.
1-68	" Abigail, of Wm. S. N., Jr. and Mehitable,	June 20, 1807.
170	ALMY Sarah, of Christopher and Mary,	Jan. 26, 1707-8.
170	" Sarah,	d. Nov. 14, 1711.
170	" Christopher,	June 10, 1711.
170	" Christopher,	d. Sept. 23, ——.
68	" John, of John and Anstice,	July 9, 1718.
68	" Anstice,	Aug. 7, 1720.
68	" Mary,	Feb. 3, 1721-2.
68	" Benjamin,	Dec. 16, 1724.
88	" Deborah, of Job and Bridget,	March 21, 1723-4.
130	" John, of John and Mary,	July 24, 1741.
130	" Elisha,	April 15, 1743.
103	" Joshua, of Joshua and Mary,	Nov. 1, 1746.
103	" dau,,	March 17, ——.
1-42	" Jonathan, of William and Mary,	Feb. 18, 1746.
1-42	" Elizabeth (Hammond, of Joseph and Elizabeth), wife of Jonathan, April 17, 1751.	d. Feb. 18, 1783.
1-13	" John Coggeshall, of Benjamin and Anstress,	March 2, 1752.
1-13	" Sarah,	May 26, 1754.
1-13	" Sarah,	d. April 17, 1755.
1-13	" Sarah, 2d,	Feb. 22, 1756.
1-13	" Anstress, wife of Benjamin,	d. Feb. 22, 1756.
	Note—On page 117 this wife is given Sarah with all dates as above given.	
184	" Elizabeth, of Benjamin and Martha,	Jan. 14, 1758.
1-43	" Elizabeth, wife of Jonathan, April 29, 1763; d. Feb. 4, 1801.	
1-43	" William Terry, of Jonathan and Elizabeth,	Nov. 19, 1796.
1-43	" Frances,	Dec. 16, 1798.
1-43	" Hope, wife of Jonathan, died in her 40th year,	Sept. 24, 1804.
1-13	" Benjamin, of Benjamin and Almy,	Aug. 31, 1763.
1-13	" Susanna,	Jan. 2, 1765.
1-13	" Samuel,	Dec. 9, 1766.
1-13	" Walter,	Dec. 9, 1766.
1-13	" Anstrus Ellery,	Oct. 21, 1769.
1-13	" Katherine,	April 7, 177—.
1-13	" James,	March 14, 1772.
1-13	" William Barnett,	May 30, 1776.
1-133	" Benjamin, Jr., died	Sept. 12, 1781.
1-133	" Walter, died	Sept. 28, 1782.
1-43	" William, of Jonathan and Elizabeth,	May 9, 1771.
1-43	" Mary,	June 7, 1774.
1-43	" Elizabeth,	June 7, 1774.
1-43	" Elizabeth,	d. Sept. 4, 1776.

1-43	ALMY Ann, of Jonathan and Elizabeth,	March 6, 1780.
1-43	" Jonathan Thurston,	Jan. 20, 1782.
1-43	" William, drowned at sea,	Feb. 16, 1794.
1-12	ANCEAUX, Nicholas, of Nicholas and Lydia, Dec. 17, 1781.	
1-12	" Lydia,	Sept. 19, 1783.
2-67	ANDERSON William, b. Quakertown, Penn., May 15, 1827.	
2-67	" Sarah A. (Richards), his wife; b. Baltimore, Md., Dec. 3, 1832.	
230	ANTHONY Elizabeth, of Albro and Susanna,	April 27, 1728.
230	" Sarah,	Nov. 23, 1730.
230	" John,	Oct. 2, 1732.
230	" William,	Sept. 14, 1734.
230	" Samuel,	July 23, 1736.
230	" Joseph,	Dec. 18, 1738.
230	" Mary,	June 30, 1743.
158	" James, of James and Elizabeth,	Oct. 28, 1770.
158	" Elizabeth,	—— 17, 1773.
1-70	" William, of William and Alice,	Jan. 10, 1773.
1-70	" Albro,	Aug. 17, 1775.
1-70	" Elizabeth,	Dec. 17, 1777.
1-70	" Alice,	March 15, 1781.
1-70	" Hannah,	July 4, 1783.
1-70	" James,	Nov. 6, 1785.
1-58	" Coggeshall, of James and Elizabeth,	June 12, 1779.
1-58	" Welcome,	Aug. 23, 1782.
1-58	" James,	June 18, 1787.
	Note.—1st b. Rehoboth, the others Newport.	
1	ARNOLD Benedict, of —— and Mary,	May 9, 1670-1.
1	" Godsgift,	May 19, 1672.
1	" Sion,	Sept. 12, 1674.
1	" Mary,	——, 1678.
1	" Content,	——, 1680.
1	" Benedict,	Aug. 8, 1683.
1	" Caleb,	—— 5, 16—.
88	" Oliver, of Oliver and Elizabeth,	May 26, 1719.
88	" Abigail,	Dec. 21, 1721.
88	" William,	Feb. 4, 1723.
88	" Elizabeth,	Feb. 9, 172—.
242	ASH Susan, of Thomas and Hannah,	June 23, 1754.
242	" Mary,	Nov. 23, 1757.
105	ATTWOOD Elizabeth, of Charles and Mary,	Dec. 20, 1709.
1-90	AUBOYNEACE Francis Malbone, of Julius and Catherine, Sept. 27, 1807.	
26	AYRAULT Anthony, of Daniel and Mary,	Jan. 15, 1711-2.
30	" Son of,	—— 14, 1713-4.
38	" Judeth,	Sept. 8, 1716.
38	" Dau. of,	Sept. 22, 1718.
54	" Francis,	Sept. 22, 1718.
54	" Samuel,	March 22, 1720-1.
54	" Susannah,	June 29, 1723.

B

1-56	BACHOLER Leonard Rostal, of James G. A. and Martha M., Sept. 2, 1793.	
1-56	" Katherine Matilda,	Sept. 29, 1795.
1-56	" Katherine Matilda,	d. Nov. 9, 1796.
1-56	" James Gould, Jr.,	July 2, 1798.
1-56	" Martha Matilda, wife of James G. A.,	d. May 9, 1799.
213	BALLARD William Hudson, of William Samuel and Hannah, Jan. 23, 173—.	
213	" John,	Sept. 14, 1741.
11	BARBAT William, of William and Esther,	March ——, 1705-6.
28	BARKER Robert, of Caleb, and Ann,	March 27, 1712.
228	" Jerusha, of Peleg and Ruamy,	April 12, 1747.
228	" Richard Rennals,	July 7, 1746.
228	" Peleg,	Feb. 11, 1748.

228	BARKER	Benjamin, of Peleg and Ruamy,	Nov. 23, 1749.
228	"	Charles,	Jan. 1, 1752.
228	"	Esther,	Feb. 26, 1753.
228	"	Eunice,	May 22, 1754.
228	"	Deborah,	June 24, 1756.

Note.—Also read 1-28.

1-41	"	Robertson, of Peleg, Jr., and Mary,	March 18, 1766.
1-41	"	Robertson,	d. Feb. 6, 1779.
1-41	"	Mary,	March 18, 1766.
1-41	"	Mary,	d. Oct. 20, 1767.
1-41	"	Peleg,	(sic.) Jan. 28, 1769.
1-41	"	Charles,	(sic.) Dec. 28, 1769.
1-41	"	Daniel,	Dec. 22, 1771.
1-41	"	Daniel,	d. Jan. 30, 1772.
1-41	"	Daniel Wilcox,	(sic.) Feb. 11, 1776.
1-41	"	Ruamy,	(sic.) March 20, 1776.
1-41	"	Sally,	Dec. 25, 1778.
1-41	"	William,	May 7, 1781.
1-62	"	Daniel, of Daniel W. and Elizabeth,	May 8, 1802.
1-62	"	Mary Ann,	Nov. 12, 1804.
1-62	"	Elizabeth Almy,	Jan. 27, 1807.
1-62	"	Peleg,	May 18, 1808.
1-86	"	William F., of Abraham and Ruth,	March 14, 1803.
1-86	"		July 13, 1806.
2-30	"	Alexander, died in his 62d year,	June 11, 1848.
2-53	"	Alexander, of Alexander and Francis R.,	June 16, 1848.
2-27	"	Alexander,	d. Jan. 11, 1848.
1-98	BARLOW	Anson, of Levi and Rachel; b. Falmouth, Mass.	March 5, 1773.
5	BARNEY,	son of Jonathan and Sarah	April 2, 1704.
94	"	John, of Israel,	recorded Dec. 9, 1734.
103	BASSETT	Mary, of William and Mary,	Aug. 31, 1737.
1-39	BAYLEY	Elizabeth, of Thomas and Margaret,	Jan. 17, 1721-2.
1-39	"	Susannah,	July 26, 1727.
1-39	"	Richard,	June 25, 1732.
1-39	"	Rebecca,	Aug. 26, 1740.
167	BEEBE	——, wife of Samuel,	d. Oct. 8, 1737.
162	"	Daniel, of Daniel and Hannah	——, 1741-2.
162	"	Sarah,	——, 1743-4.
218	BEERE	Sarah, of Charles and Hannah,	April 16, 1740.
218	"	Henry,	April, ——.
218	"	Mary,	May 10, 1743-4.
23	BELCHER	Benjamin, of Benjamin and Phebe,	Nov. 7, 1704.
23	"	Phebe,	June 11, 1708.
23	"	Edward,	Aug. 24, 1711.
226	BELL	Jennett, of John and Mary,	Nov. 24, 1765.
226	"	dau.,	May —, 1767
226	"	Tonga,	March —, 1769.
226	"	son,	Sept. —, 1770.
226	"	dau.,	May 29, 1772.
36	BENNETT,	son of Joseph and Mary,	Feb. 6, 1713.
36	"	son,	——, 1716.
160	"	Batchelor, of Cornelius and Ruth,	April 10, 1742.
160	"	Philip,	April 10, 1745.
1-36	BENSON	Martin, of William and Sarah,	Oct. 2, 1741.
136	"	William Collins,	Jan. 30, 1742.
136	"	John,	June 20, 1744.
136	"	Gardiner, of William and Frances,	Aug. 15, 1747.
136	"	George,	Aug. 20, 1751.
91	BERKELEY	Henry, of Rev. George, and Ann,	May 6, 1729.
124	BINGHAM,	son of Thomas and Elizabeth,	Feb. 8, 1696-7.
15	BISSEL,	son of Harry and Sarah,	March —, 1708.
241	"	Hannah, of Job,	——
241	"	Sarah,	——, 1730.
241	"	Isaac,	Sept. 18, 1732.
241	"	Job,	July 14, 1736.

241	BISSEL	Susannah, of Job,	Sept. ——.
2-41	"	William,	Jan. 24, 1741.
87	"	dau. of Job and Anne,	March 2, 1728-9.
87	"	dau.,	Nov. 30, 1736.
24	BLACKWELL	Sarah, of Nathaniel and Johanna,	June 26, 1712.
226	BLISS	Marcy,	Oct. 25, 16—.
226	"	George,	Oct. 25, 16—.
226	"	John, of George and Sarah,	March 17, 1720.
226	"	George,	d. Aug. 31, 1767.
1-88	"	Elizabeth Eyres, of Thomas Ward and Sarah C.,	Oct. 2, 1784.
1-88	"	Barbara Phillips,	March 14, 1786.
1-88	"	Benjamin Thurston,	March 20, 1788.
1-88	"	Sarah Thurston,	Sept. 11, 1790.
1-88	"	Thomas Ward,	Nov. 13, 1792.
1-88	"	Ebenezer David,	Dec. 29, 1796.
1-36	"	Henry, of Clarke and Abigail,	Feb. 13, 1791.
1-36	"	Charles Spooner,	Oct. 13, 1792.
1-36	"	Mary,	July 30, 1795.
1-36	"	Abigail,	March 31, 1797.
1-36	"	Peggy,	Nov. 18, 1798.
1-36	"	Peggy,	d. March 7, 1799.
1-36	"	Clarke,	Feb. 7, 1800.
1-36	"	Margaret,	April 22, 1802.
1-36	"	Susannah,	April 25, 1804.
1-36	"	Susannah, 2d,	Oct. 7, 1805.
1-36	"	Hannah,	Oct. 4, 1807.
1-73	BLIVEN	Joseph Southwick, of Henry,	Sept. 1, 1793.
1-73	"	Sally,	Dec. 13, 1796.
211	BONNER	John, of Alexander and Sarah, bap.	Sept. 4, 1742.
211	"	Alexander, bap.	Aug. —, 1743.
211	"	Elizabeth, bap.	March 20, 1745.
211	"	George, bap.	July 20, 1746.
93	BORDIN	Charles, of Charles and Ann, b. —— 18, ——; died —— —, 1736.	
236	"	Amey,	—— —, 1737-8.
236	"	William,	May —, ——.
236	"	Ann,	Sept 30, ——.
236	"	Winchels,	March 7, 1742-3.
236	"	Mary,	Nov. 27, 1744.
236	"	Stephen,	—— 15, 1748.
236	"	Charles,	Oct. 26, 1749.
236	"	Charles d.	Sept. 18, 1750.
236	"	Freelove,	April 25, 1751.
236	"	Barbara,	June 12, 1752, d. next day.
236	"	Peleg,	July 12, 1753.
236	"	Richard,	March 8, 1757.
236	"	Elizabeth,	Nov. —, 1759.
115	"	Elizabeth, of Abraham and Martha,	Aug. 20, 1742.
115	"	Joseph,	Nov. 15, 1744.
115	"	Joseph, d.	Dec. 10, ——.
115	"	Sarah,	Dec. —, 1748.
115	"	Abraham,	Dec. —, ——.
115	"	Abraham, d.	June 9, 1753.
115	"	dau.	June 2, 1753.
115	"	Martha, wife of Abraham, d.	—— 27, 1753.
133	"	Thomas, of Thomas and Mary,	Sept. 17, 1749.
228	"	Mason, of Benjamin,	Feb. 10, 1770.
228	"	Haile,	April 24, 1772.
228	"	William,	May 4, 1774.
32	BOURSE	Peter, of Peter and Bathsheba,	Sept. 27, 1707.
82	BOWCOTT	Mary, of Thomas and Mercy,	April 2, 1729.
164	BRADFORD	John, of Theophilus and Ruth,	Nov. 27, 1732.
164	"	Mary,	Sept. 5, 1786.
70	BRAYTON	Bathsheba, of Israel,	Sept. 7, 1722.
70	"	son,	March 11, 1723-4.
180	"	Content, of Benjamin and Hannah,	June 8, 1744.

180	BRAYTON	Patience, of Benjamin and Hannah,	Feb. 2, 1745-6.
180	"	James Wheaton,	Oct. 7, 1757.

Note.—First two born Tiverton.

27	BRENTON	Benjamin, of Benjamin and Sarah,	Oct. 16, 1710.
128	"	——, of Jahleel and Frances,	Aug. —, 1716.
128	"	Mary,	Nov. 24, 1719.
128	"	Mercy,	July 10, 1721.
128	"	Heart,	Feb. 26, 1723.
128	"	Martha,	Jan. 12, 1726.
128	"	Elizabeth,	Feb. 3, 1727.
128	"	Jahleel,	Oct. 22, 1729.
128	"	——,	Dec. 3, 1730.
128	"	——,	Nov. 10, 1733.
128	"	——,	April 18, 1735.
128	"	——,	Nov. 2, 1736.
128	"	Benjamin,	Feb. 7, 1737.
92	"	Ja——, died Nov. 9, 1732.	
1-92	BRETTAIN	William, of William and Elizabeth,	March 6, 1786.
1-92	"	Margaretta,	April 15, 1787.
1-92	"	Eliza,	March 9, 1790.
1-92	"	Eliza,	d. Aug. 23, 1791.
1-92	"	Eliza, 2d,	Sept. 17, 1793.
1-92	"	Eliza, 2d,	d. Sept. 16, 1794.
1-92	"	Nathaniel Mumford,	May 22, 1795.
1-92	"	Eliza, 3d,	Aug. 21, 1798.
1-92	"	John Henry,	Jan. 15, 1803.
1-92	"	John Henry,	d. July 16, 1803.
1-92	"	John Henry, 2d,	Sept. 15, 1805.
1-92	"	John Henry, 2d,	d. Sept. 19, 1805.
1-115	"	Mary Ann, of William and Ann,	Sept. 26, 1805.
1-115	"	William Audley,	April 8, 1811.
1-115	"	John Price,	May 16, 1818.
73	BREWER	Hannah, of John and Ann,	Aug. 19, 1706.
73	"	John,	March 22, 1708.
73	"	Rebecca,	July, 11, 1710.
73	"	Ann,	July 6, 1712.
73	"	Thomas,	Jan. 28, ——.
73	"	Mary,	May —, ——.
73	"	Sarah,	—— —, ——.
152	BRIDGES	John, of Robert and Hope,	Aug. 1, 1739.
152	"	James,	March 24, 1747-8.
229	BROOKS	Thomas, of Thomas and Mary,	Feb. 11, 1733-4.
1-81	BROWNELL	Harriet, of Sylvester and Sarah W.,	Aug. 1, 1805.
1-81	"	William,	Jan. 2, 1807.
1-81	"	Henry Mumford,	June 19, 1808.
1-81	"	Jonathan Wilson,	May 2, 1810.
1-81	"	Henry Mumford, 2d,	April 28, 1812.
1-81	"	Hannah Wilson,	March 2, 1815.
1-81	"	Sarah Wilson,	Oct. 2, 1818.
62	BROWN	Mary, of John, of Swansey, Mass.,	Nov. 21, 1697.
170	"	Son of John and Mary,	—— 11, ——.
212	"	Samuel, of Samuel and Sarah,	Oct. 8, 1738.
212	"	Penelope,	Dec. ——.
212	"	Sarah,	April 1, 1744.
212	"	Daniel,	——, ——.
212	"	William,	April 23, 1748.
1-107	"	Sarah Ann, of John and Fanny,	Sept. 29, 1810.
1-107	"	Jane,	Jan. 5, 1812.
1-107	"	Louisa,	May 5, 1814.
1-107	"	Frances,	May 12, 1816.
1-107	"	Rebecca,	July 7, 1818.
1-107	"	Eleanor,	Dec. 14, 1820.
1-107	"	George,	Aug. 14, 1823.
173	BRUFF	Mary, of William and Mary,	Aug. 24, 17——.

100	BRYER	Joseph, of John and Elizabeth,	Nov. 14, 1730.
100	"	Jonathan,	Dec. 5, 1732.
114	BUCKMASTER	Abiah, of William, and Hannah,	June 29, 1753.
144	"	Elizabeth Olive,	Sept. 26, 1755.
2-4	BUDLONG	Syria, of Rhodes A. and Bettey,	Dec. 25, 1838.
2-6	"	Edward Forrester,	June 11, 1841.
16	BULL	Jirah, of Jirah and Godsgift,	——— —, 1682.
16	"	son,	Sept. 5, 1685.
16	"	son,	———, 1688.
42	"	Nathan, of Ezekiel, and Elizabeth,	Nov. 30, 1711.
95	"	Jirah, of Henry and Martha,	Jan. 23, 1720.
95	"	Martha, wife of Henry, died,	Feb. 11, 1720.
95	"	Joseph, of Henry, and Phebe,	Sept. 29, 1722.
95	"	Ann,	———, 25, 1723.
100	"	son,	Dec. 10, 1725.
100	"	Mary,	April 18, 1728.
100	"	Peleg,	Nov. 6, 1730.
100	"	Henry,	Dec. 18, 1732.
100	"	John,	Sept. 18, 1734.
100	"	William,	Oct. ——, 1740.
100	"	Godsgift, of Benjamin Content,	Aug. ——, 1729.
17	"	Phebe, of Henry, and Phebe,	Sept. 22, 1738.
233	"	Joseph, of Joseph and Sarah,	Sept. 21, 1747.
233	"	Joseph,	d. Oct. 11, 17—.
233	"	Sarah,	April 19, 1750.
233	"	Sarah,	d. Sept. 3, 1750.
233	"	Peleg,	Aug. 1, 1752.
233	"	Peleg,	d. Sept.—, 1752.
233	"	Daniel,	Sept. 16, 1753.
233	"	Daniel,	d. Nov. 13, 1753.
15	"	Elizabeth, of Ezekiel, ——, ——.	
1-114	BURDICK	Benjamin Lake, of Capt. Isaiah and Mary,	Oct. 9, 1822.
1-114	"	Amey Elizabeth,	Jan. 25, 1824.
2-52	"	Rhoda, of Stephen, and Mary A.,	Oct. 13, 1854.
92	BURGESS	Aaron, of Abraham and Sarah,	April 23, 1684.
3	"	son,	May 7, 1689.
29	"	son of James and Rebecca,	May 30, 1713.
106	BURROUGHS	William, of Samuel and Mary,	Jan. 1, 1742.
106	"	Samuel, and Mary, 2w.,	Nov. 6, 1746.
106	"	Peleg,	June 5, 1748.
106	"	John,	April 16, 1750.
106	"	Mary,	Feb. 3, 1752.
243	"	Abigail, of William and Elizabeth,	July 11, 1743.
243	"	son,	July 4, 1745.
243	"	dau.,	May 6, 1747.
243	"	dau.,	Jan. 6, 1749.
243	"	dau.,	July 3, 1750.
243	"	dau.,	June 11, 1752.
147	"	Ezekiel, of James and Martha,	Sept. 30, 1753.
147	"	Mary,	Sept. 25, 1756.
147	"	Martha,	Sept. 25, 1758.

C

1-24	CABELLEE	George, of Martin and Alice,	March 24, 1782.
1-24	"	Alice,	Oct. 1, 1784.
1-24	"	Martin,	Feb. 11, 1787.
1-24	"	Adelaide,	June 6, 1793.
1-24	"	Alice Ann,	Aug. 11, 1795.
111	CAHOONE	John, of Joseph and Sarah,	May 1, 1743.
168	CALLENDER	Elizabeth, of John and Elizabeth,	July —, 1730.
168	"	Mary,	Dec. 10, 1731.
168	"	John,	Jan. 12, 1733-4.
168	"	John,	d. Oct. 22, 1734.

168	CALLENDER	John, 2d, of John and Elizabeth,	Sept. —, 1735.
168	"	Elias,	Dec. 27, 1737.
168	"	Elisha,	July 17, 1738.
168	"	Sarah,	Feb. 7, 1739-40.
168	"	Abigail,	April —, 1741.
168	"	John,	d. Jan. 26, 1747-8.
237	CAMPBELL	Arnold, of John and Mary,	Dec. 11, 1734.
237	"	John,	Aug. 30, 1737.
106	"	Thomas, of Thomas and Sarah,	June 25, 1750.
106	"	Sarah,	Jan. 22, 1751.
106	"	James,	Dec. 23, 1753.
32	CARD	Joseph, of Joseph and Hope,	Oct. 5, 1712.
32	"	Phebe,	May 6, 1714.
32	"	Joseph,	—, 1716.
32	"	Hope,	—, 1716.
144	CAREY	Alice Pitman, of John and Martha,	May 27, —.
144	"	Moses Clarke Pitman,	Oct. 21, 1757.
163	CARPENTER	John, of Nathan, and Mary,	May 3, 1744.
163	"	Jerusha,	Dec. 27, 1745.
163	"	Benjamin,	Aug. 16, 1752.
174	"	Richard, of Richard and Ruth,	Oct. 3, 1757.
174	"	Elizabeth,	June 7, 1759.
174	"	Mary,	June 8, 1761.
174	"	Andrew,	July 24, 1762.
174	"	Andrew,	d. Sept. 28, 1765.
174	"	Jabez,	April 17, 1764.
174	"	Samuel,	Aug. 25, d. Sept. 17, 1765.
128	CARR	Samuel, of Samuel and Mary,	July 28, 1722.
128	"	Ebenezer,	Oct. 2, 1735.
128	"	John,	Oct. 6, 1738.
164	"	Samuel, of Caleb and Elizabeth,	— 13, —.
164	"	Caleb,	—, —.
164	"	William,	Jan. 27, 1745-6.
164	"	Wait,	June 20, —.
164	"	John,	—, —.
164	"	Walter Clarke,	—, —.
164	"	Philip,	—, —.
180	"	William,	d. — 12, —.
180	"	Walter Clarke,	d. Aug. —.
180	"	Philip,	d. June 30, —.
180	"	Nicholas,	d. Oct. 17, —.
180	"	Patience,	July 20, 1755
180	"	Patience,	d. Aug. 4, 1755.
180	"	Bailey,	Oct. 4, 1756.
180	"	Bailey,	d. Nov. 2, 1756.
180	"	Ebenezer,	Jan. —, 1758.
180	"	Peter Greene,	Feb. 27, 1759.
180	"	Peter Greene,	d. Aug. 16, 1759.
180	"	Ann,	Nov. 5, 1760.
180	"	Ann,	d. March 13, 1761.
180	"	Deliverance,	March 19, 1762.
180	"	Deliverance,	d. Sept. 7, 1762.
180	"	Greene Easton,	Sept. 24, 1763.
180	"	William Pitt,	July 7, 1766.
197	"	Mary, of Robert and Mary,	Feb. 11, 1749-50.
197	"	Mehitable,	Oct. 24, 1750.
197	"	Abigail,	Jan. 16, 1756.
197	"	Robert,	Nov. 30, 1757.
197	"	Job,	May 15, 1762.
120	"	Mary, of Samuel and Danaries	Nov. 25, 17—.
120	"	Hannah,	Nov. 26, 1751.
120	"	Comfort,	Jan. 18, 1754.
120	"	Samuel,	Sept. 26, 1756.
120	"	Ebenezer,	Sept. 26, 1760.
120	"	Abigail,	Aug. 22, 1766.

227	CARR	John, of John and Mary,	April 12, 1762.
227	"	Mary,	June 13, 1763.
227	"	Sarah,	May 29, 1765.
227	"	Samuel,	Sept. 24, 1766.
227	"	Caleb Arnold,	——, 1768.
227	"	Abigail,	Sept. 4, 1771.
227	"	Comfort,	July 15, 1773.
216	"	Robert Robinson, of Ebenezer and Phebe,	Jan. 12, 1767.
216	"	Samuel,	Jan. 15, 1769.
216	"	Abigail,	Dec. 2, 1771.
1-16	"	Caleb, 3d, of Samuel C. and Sarah,	Dec. 7, 1768.
1-16	"	Mary,	Dec. 17, 1771.
1-16	"	Sarah,	July 13, 1776.
1-16	"	Elizabeth,	Nov. 18, 1778.
1-16	"	John,	Jan. 29, 1781.
1-16	"	John, 2d,	Sept. 11, 1782.
1-16	"	Wait,	Sept. 16, 1784.
1-16	"	Sarah, his wife, died Sept. 30, 1784.	
1-16	"	William Phillips, of Samuel C. and Ann, 2d wife,	Oct. 11, 1793.
124	"	Patience, of John and Mary, ——,	
2-57	"	Phebe Bull, of David King Carr, died aged 42 years,	July 30, 1848.
59	CARTWRIGHT	Bryant, of Edward and Ruth,	Sept. 30, 1711.
59	"	Asher,	Sept. 10, 1713.
59	"	Cyrus,	June 1, 1715.
59	"	Samuel,	Feb. 24, 1717-8.
59	"	Gideon,	Jan. 19, 1719-20.
59	"	Ruth,	Feb. 3, 1721-2.
59	"	Eliza,	Sept. 12, 1723.

Note.—Last 3 born in Nantucket, Mass.

35	CARY	Rebecca, of James and Bridget,	— 17, 1707.
35	"	Seth,	Sept. 5, 1708.
35	"	Peleg,	March 6, 1710.
35	"	Bridget,	Feb. 4, 1711-2.
35	"	Eliz,	Sept. 4, 17—.
35	"	James,	Oct. 7, 17—.
161	CASEY	Mary, of John and Elizabeth,	12m. —, 1719-20.
161	"	Elizabeth,	4m. —, ——.
161	"	John,	9m. 30, 1729.
161	"	John,	d. 2m. 28, 1730.
161	"	Rebecca,	1m. 2, 173—.
161	"	Rebecca	d. 3m. 12, 173-.
161	"	Sarah,	10m. 4, 1732.
161	"	Hannah,	11m. 29, 1733.
161	"	Amey,	8m. 3, 1735.
161	"	John,	1m. 9, 1738-9.
14	"	Thomas, of Adam and Mary,	——.
14	"	Silas,	——.
1-61	CASTOFF	Catherine, of Henry and Mehitable,	June 24, 1800.
2-60	CASWELL	Mercy, first wife of William, died aged 49 years,	July 20, 1816.
2-60	"	Mary, second wife of William, died aged 77 years,	Jan. 5, 1849.
2-60	"	William, died aged 87 years, 1 month, 29 days,	Aug. 11, 1852.
2-60	"	Elizabeth, of William and Mercy, died, aged 62 y. 6m.,	Jan. 22, 1869.
2-60	"	William, of William and Mercy, died, aged 75 y. 5 m.,	July 16, 1869.
49	CHACE	Rachel, of James and Rachel,	Aug. 30, 1712.
49	"	James,	July 31, 1715.
49	"	Brown,	March 13, 1717-8.
81	"	Sarah, of John and Ann,	Sept. 29, 1718.
81	"	Elizabeth,	March 10, 1719-20.
81	"	Samuel,	July 30, 1722.
81	"	John,	Nov. 1, 1726.
81	"	William,	Jan. 1, 1732-3.
158	"	Constant, of Constant and Ruth,	July 26, 1769.
1-121	"	Lewis, of Benjamin and Abby,	Dec. 4, 1804.
1-121	"	Abby,	Jan. 14, 1807.

1-121	CHACE	Vienna, of Benjamin and Abby,	Dec. 9, 1810.
1-121	"	Amelia,	July 18, 1812.
1-121	"	Angelina,	March 30, 1814.
1-121	"	Elizabeth Smith,	Jan. 19, 1819.
1-121	"	Benjamin Homer,	April 8, 1822.
30	CHADWICK,	son of John and Mary,	Sept. 4, 1713.
45	"	Elizabeth,	Dec. 13, 171—.
54	"	Sarah,	March 11, 1721-2.
175	CHAFFEE	John, of John and Ruth,	Sept. 30, 1762.
175	"	Ezra,	Dec. 15, 1764.
175	"	Ruth,	April 22, 1768.
1-113	"	Sally Monroe, of Otis and Almy,	April 17, 1802.
1-113	"	Nicholas Underwood,	Oct. 14, 1803.
1-113	"	Otis Hollyburton,	Jan. 19, 1805.
1-113	"	Amey Underwood,	Sept. 24, 1806.
1-113	"	Edward Otis,	May 7, 1808.
1-113	"	Mary Ann,	Dec. 31, 1809.
1-113	"	Eveline Jane,	Aug. 21, 1811.
1-113	"	Elizabeth Webb,	May 27, 1813.
1-113	"	Otis Jacob,	Jan. 13, 1815.
1-113	"	Nathan Munroe,	June 6, 1816.
1-113	"	Henry Worthington,	March 1, 1818.
1-113	"	Caroline Matilda,	Sept. 24, 1819.
1-113	"	Laura Sophia,	April 15, 1821.
1-113	"	Hannah Mary,	Aug. 9, 1822.
1-113	"	Charles Henry,	April 4, 1824.
2-20	"	Louisa Sophia, of Nathan L. and Harriet,	Jan. 5, 1840.
2-20	"	Mary Elizabeth,	Dec. 25, 1841.
2-20	"	Amey,	Dec. 30, 1843.
2-25	"	Charles Henry,	May 16, 1847.
160	CHAFFIN	Elizabeth, of George, and Anna,	Feb. 10, 1743-4.
167	CHOLONER	John, of Monton,	—— ——, ——.
167	"	William,	—— 18, 1731.
167	"	Sarah,	Nov. 21, 1733.
219	"	Mynion of Mynion, dec. and Phebe,	April 22, 1749.
136	"	John, of John, and Martha,	bap. March 7, 1748.
136	"	William,	bap. July 17, 1749.
136	"	Brenton,	Nov. 30, 175—.
136	"	Francis,	Nov. 5, 1754.
136	"	Francis,	d. Nov. 22, 1754.
136	"	James,	July 17, 1756.
136	"	James,	d. Nov. 26, 1756.
118	CHAMPLAIN	Hannah, of Jabez, and Hannah,	Aug. 24, 1751.
118	"	George Stiles,	April 5, 1753.
232	"	Margaret, of Christopher and Margaret,	Sept. 11, 1764
232	"	Christopher, Jr.,	April 12, 1768.
232	"	Elizabeth,	Nov. 21, 1769.
	Note., Also recorded 1-48,		
174	CHANDLER	John Simpkins, of William, and Mary,	March 16, 1766.
227	CHANTAT	John, of Port au Prince,, W. I.	d. Nov. 17, 1771.
33	CHAPLAIN	William, of Joseph, and Bathsheba,	March —, 1707.
33	"	Moses,	June ——, ——.
33	"	Joseph,	—— ——, ——.
200	CHAPMAN	Elizabeth, of Handley and Jane,	Feb. 19, ——.
200	"	John,	July 21, 1742.
200	"	Margaret,	July 17, 1743.
200	"	John,	Dec. —, 1744.
200	"	Katherine,	Nov. 11, 1746.
200	"	Handley,	Oct. 9, 1748.
200	"	Rebecca,	Nov. 25, 1750.
200	"	Thomas Handley	Jan. 17, 1752.
200	"	William Allen,	Nov. 8, 1757.
138	CHILD	Timothy, of Jeremiah and Susanna,	Feb. 2, 1753.
138	"	Nathan,	Nov. 11, 1764.
1-96	CHURCH	Benjamin B., of Benjamin and Elizabeth,	Oct. 25, 1775.

10, 61	CLARKE	Joseph of Cary and Ann,	Oct. 20, 1694.
10, 61	"	Cary,	Sept. 20, 1696.
10, 61	"	Ann,	Sept. 8, 1698.
10, 61	"	Mary,	Aug. 8, 1700.
10, 61	"	Caleb,	May 22, 1703.
61	"	Jonathan,	Aug. 12, 1705.
61	"	William,	Jan. 15, 1707.
61	"	Elisha,	May 6, 1709.
61	"	Samuel,	Oct. 1, ——.
61	"	Margaret,	Oct. 24, ——.
61	"	Hutchinson,	May 1, ——.
61	"	James,	Feb. ——, ——.
4	"	Jonathan, of Richard and Hannah,	Sept. 15, 1695.
4	"	Hannah,	July ——, 1697.
92	"	Thomas, of Thomas and Elizabeth,	Nov. 23, 1695.
5	"	——, of Thomas and Elizabeth,	March 5, 1701-2.
6	"	Martha, of William,	Feb. 18, 1702.
11	"	Francis, of James and Mary,	Feb. 7, 1744.
11	"	John, of James and Mary,	July ——, 1707.
11	"	Son,	July 14, 1711.
33	"	James (of Portsmouth),	Dec. 14, 1714.
75	"	Abigail, of John and Abigail,	Aug. 1, 1725.
75	"	Samuel,	Oct. 5, 1727.
95	"	Sarah, of John and Mary,	Jan. 25, 173—.
95	"	John,	Aug. 4, 1733.
95	"	Joseph,	Dec. 20, 1735.
129	"	Mary, of Benjamin and Grizzell,	Sept. 17, 1735.
129	"	Peleg,	May 26, 1738.
129	"	Elizabeth,	May 31, 1739.
176	"	Hart, of Sherman and Katherine,	March 6, 1757.
176	"	Katherine,	Dec. 4, 1759.
176	"	Sherman,	Oct. 4, 1761.
176	"	Dau.,	Aug. 2, 1763.
176	"	Ruth,	Jan. 6, 1765.
197	"	Rebecca Redwood, of Joseph and Rebecca,	Aug. 3, 1762.
99	"	——, of John and Ruth,	May 25, ——.
99	"	dau.,	Feb. 20, ——.
99	"	son,	May ——, ——.
99	"	dau.,	——— ——, ——.
99	"	William,	March ——, ——.
1-38	"	Samuel Ward, of Ethan and Anne, b. Westerly,	Oct. 17, 1778.
1-38	"	Ray,	Feb. 13, 1782.
1-38	"	Anna,	Nov. 8, 1783.
1-46	"	Joseph, died aged 73y. 1m. 5d.,	Oct. 8, 1792.
1-102	"	Desire, of George and Desire,	March 13, 1801.
1-102	"	Desire, of George and Desire,	d. Aug. 19, 1803.
1-102	"	Desire Ann,	Feb. 25, 1804.
1-102	"	John Bliven,	July 8, 1806.
1-102	"	William Alfred,	Nov. 25, 1807.
1-102	"	James Madison,	Aug. 2, 1809.
1-102	"	Almira Elizabeth,	May 22, 1811.
1-102	"	Emeline Frances,	Oct. 3, 1813.
1-102	"	George Washington,	April 5, 1816.
92	CODDINGTON	William, of Thomas and Priscilla,	Nov. 2, 1684.
16	"	——, March ——, 1708 (?),	
16	"	Susanna, of William and Content,	May 30, 1708.
16	"	William,	Oct. 8, 1710.
16	"	Edward,	July 30, 1712
16	"	Thomas,	Dec. 4, 1715.
16	"	Nathaniel,	June 22, 1717.
16	"	Arnold,	July 4, 1718.
16	"	Content,	July 4, 1718.
85	"	Nathaniel, of William,	——, 1717.
88	"	Arnold, of William and Content,	July 4, 1718.
84	"	**Ann, of Nathaniel, Jr., and Hope,**	Feb. 19, 1720-1.

84	CODDINGTON	John, of Nathaniel, Jr., and Hope,	Dec. 28, 1724.
84	"	Catherine,	Aug. 27, 1726.
84	"	Mary,	Dec. 21, 1728.
65	"	Content, of Col. William and Jane,	April 12, 1724.
65	"	Content,	bap. April 19, 1724.
65	"	Esther,	Jan. 21, 1726-7.
65	"	John,	Oct. 28, 1728.
65	"	Jane,	March 29, 1730.
65	"	Francis,	Feb. 2, 1731-2.
65	"	Ann,	May 30, 1734.
139	"	Hope, of Nathaniel,	June 18, 1733.
139	"	James,	Jan. 19, 1735-6.
139	"	Susanna,	Jan. 12, 1736-7.
139	"	Edward,	April 12, ——.
139	"	Elizabeth,	April 23, 1739.
137	"	Mary, of William and Penelope,	Oct. 21, 1740.
137	"	Mary,	d. Dec. 16, 1740.
137	"	Roger Goulding,	Feb. 17, 1744-5.
137	"	Roger Goulding,	d. May 23, 1745.
137	"	Nathaniel,	——.
137	"	William,	June 16, 1750.
137	"	William,	d. Aug. 12, 1750.
137	"	Elizabeth,	July 12, 1751.
138	"	Edward,	Aug. 19, 1752.
138	"	Edward,	d. May 25, 1753.
111	"	Penelope, wife of William, died,	Sept. 6, 1777.
23	"	William, of William and Content,	Oct. 8, ——.
101	CODNER	Ann, of William,	May 25, 17—.
89	COGGESHALL	Thomas, of Joshua and Sarah,	April 25, 1688.
19	"	Patience, of —— and Sarah,	Aug. 7, 1710.
19	"	Alce,	Aug. ——, 1717.
19	"	James,	——.
229	"	James, of Benjamin, and Sarah,	Feb. 5, 1712.
229	"	Hannah, wife of James,	June ——, 1721.
229	"	Sarah, of James and Hanna	Dec. 4, 1737.
229	"	Mary,	Aug. 15, ——.
229	"	Patience,	April 24, ——.
229	"	Benjamin,	March 2, ——.
229	"	Rebecca,	July 29, 1745.
229	"	Hannah,	Aug. 3, 1747.
229	"	Katherine,	Sept. 1, 1749.
229	"	Alice,	Aug. 20, 1752.
229	"	Ruth,	Sept. 29, 1753.
229	"	Susannah,	April 27, 1755.
229	"	Content,	Nov. 14, 1756.
19	"	Rebecca, of Benjamin and Sarah,	Dec. 14, 1721.
19	"	Ruth,	——.
63	"	John, of Thomas and Sarah,	Oct. 20, 1718.
63	"	John,	d. May 27, 1736.
63	"	Sarah,	Jan. ——, 1720-1.
63	"	Samuel,	Feb. 23, 172—.
77	"	Bathsheba,	June 18, 1723.
53	"	Alice, of Benjamin and Sarah,	July 17, 1719.
83	"	Nathaniel, of Nathaniel and Sarah,	Jan. 27, 1728-9.
88	"	Edward, of Peter and Elizabeth,	March 8, 1728-9.
117	"	John, of Thomas and Austress,	Oct. 27, 1736.
117	"	John,	d. Jan. 10, 1736-7.
1-77	"	William,	Nov. 27, 1746.
1-77	"	Elizabeth Moore, his wife,	June 7, 1748.
1-77	"	Elizabeth,	d. July 5, 1799.
1-77	"	David Moore,	Feb. 26, 1772.
1-77	"	Mary Tripp,	Dec. 15, 1773.
1-77	"	William,	May 24, 1775.
1-77	"	Rebecca Chapman,	June 20, 1777.
1-77	"	Susanna Moore,	Feb. 28, 1779.

1-77	COGGESHALL	Sarah Billings, of Thomas and Austress,	Dec. 26, 1780.
1-77	"	Mary Tripp,	April 26, 1783.
1-77	"	Ann Cranston,	Sept. 21, 1784.
201	"	John Jepson, of Nathaniel, Jr., and Elizabeth,	Sept. 28, 1753.
201	"	Benjamin Wilson, of Nathaniel, Jr., and Elizabeth, 3d wife, Oct. 27, 1756.	
201	"	Nathaniel,	July 21, 1759.
201	"	Elizabeth Jepson,	Feb. 28, 1763.
201	"	Sarah,	Feb. 24, 1765.
201	"	Thomas Cranston,	Jan. 25, 1766.
201	"	Freegift,	July 26, 1768.
198	"	Mary, of Caleb and Phebe,	Aug. 31, 1763.
198	"	Abigail,	April 20, 1767.
198	"	Joseph,	Aug. —, 1770.
1-109	"	James Monroe, of James and Eliza,	April 17, 1819.
1-109	"	Benjamin Lawton,	July 5, 1821.
1-109	"	Eliza Hannah,	June 30, 1826.
230	COHEN	Charles, of Zachariah and Eleanor,	April 10, 1786.
230	"	William,	March 17, 1742.
230	"	Abigail,	Aug. 13, 1745.
1-96	COIT	Richard Mumford, of John and Mary,	March 11, 1785.
1-109	COLEMAN	Abby Pitman, of Rev. Ebenezer and Abby,	Oct. 14, 1819.
1-109	"	Susan,	Nov. 29, 1820.
1-109	"	Emily,	May 30, 1823.
1-109	"	Elizabeth,	June 14, 1824.
27	COLLINS	Sylvester, of Arnold and Sarah,	Oct. 27, 1688.
27	"	Sarah,	Aug. 13, 1690.
27	"	Arnold,	Feb. 2, 1692-3.
27	"	Elizabeth,	June 28, 1695.
27	"	Henry,	March 25, 1699.
21	"	Anna, of William and Sarah,	Jan. 29, 1698.
21	"	Sarah,	Feb. 27, 1700.
21	"	William,	—— 16, 1701.
21	"	Elizabeth,	Dec. 28, 1709.
207	"	Mary, of John and Mary,	Jan. 6, 1763.
207	"	John Avery,	Nov. 5, 1764.
1-43	"	Mary, (colored servants.)	
1-43	"	Cuff,	May 6, 1773.
1-43	"	Thomas,	July 22, 1775.
1-43	"	Hannibal,	May 1, 1781.
1-43	"	Lucinda,	Oct. 9, 1784.
1-43	"	Sambo,	April 12, 1787.
1-43	"	Jenny,	March 4, 1795.
71	COMER	John, of John and Sarah,	Feb. 2, 1726-7.
34	COOK	John, of Peleg and Sarah,	Sept. 30, 1711.
34	"	dau.,	May 1, 1713.
34	"	Jane,	Dec. 21, 1714.
85	"	Mary, of Joseph and Hannah,	June 5, 1718.
85	"	Joseph,	Feb. 7, 1719-20.
85	"	Rebecca,	March 21, 1721-2.
85	"	Constant,	July 16, ——.
85	"	Paul,	Oct. 19, ——.
85	"	Paul, d.	Nov. 6, 1726.
85	"	Joseph, Sr., died	Oct. 29, 1726.
1-53	"	David Godfrey, of Clarke and Dorcas,	Sept. 6, 1792.
1-53	"	dau.	Dec. 24, 1793.
1-53	"	dau. d.	Dec. 26, 1793.
1-53	"	George Irish,	Dec. 14, 1794.
1-53	"	Elizabeth,	Dec. 7, 1796.
1-53	"	Charles Clarke,	Aug. 21, 1798.
1-53	"	Hannah,	Aug. 3, 1801.
1-53	"	William Tilley,	June 19, 1802.
1-53	"	Henry Hudson,	May 20, 1804.
166	COREY	William, of Caleb and Hannah,	July 21, 1750.
1-86	"	Mary Brown, of Caleb and Hannah,	March 5, 1806.

1-86	COREY	Sally, of Caleb and Hannah,	Sept. 19, 1803.
1-86	"	Lydia Tillinghast,	July 18, 1811.
1-86	"	Hannah Amanda,	July 10, 1814.
119	CORNELL	Sarah, of Thomas and Rachel,	July 19, 1747.
119	"	Elizabeth,	Nov. 21, 1749.
1-83	"	Stephen, of Oliver and Hannah,	June 21, 1797.
2-21	"	Stephen Northam, of Stephen and Harriet,	Sept. 22, 1826.
2-21	"	Hannah Elizabeth,	June 30, 1829.
2-21	"	Oliver (b. New London, Conn.),	March 10, 1832.
2-21	"	Sarah Harwood,	April 12, 1837.
2-21	"	Sarah Harwood,	d. June 25, 1844.
2-21	"	Ellen Grinnell,	March 29, 1839.
2-21	"	Harriet Earl (b. at New London, Conn.),	Nov. 2, 1842.
1-43	COWING	James, of William and Abigail,	Nov. 27, 1767.
213	COWLEY	Penelope Pelham, of Joseph and Penelope,	Nov. 15, 1742.
213	"	Penelope,	bap. Nov. 21, 1742.
201	COZZENS	Margaret, of Gregory and Mary,	May 22, 1760.
1-92	"	John Henry Brittain, of John and Margaretta,	Jan. 13, 1805.
14	CRANSTON,	dau. of Benjamin and Sarah,	March 7, 1701.
14	"	son,	April ——.
14	"	dau.,	April 19, 1705.
14	"	son,	Feb. 27, 1706-7.
17	"	Samuel, of Samuel and Elizabeth,	Jan. 17, 1707-8.
34	"	Thomas, of Samuel, Jr.,	Oct. 30, 1710.
34	"	Mary,	Jan. 29, 1712-3.
34	"	Elizabeth,	Jan. 17, 1714-5.
80	"	Ann, of William and Marian,	Dec. 4, 1715.
80	"	Alice,	Sept. 26, 1717.
80	"	Sarah,	Feb. 5, 1719.
80	"	William,	March 19, 1721-2.
80	"	Elizabeth,	Feb. 7, 1723-4.
80	"	John,	Jan. 6, 1725-6.
80	"	Martin,	Dec. 14, 1727.
175	"	Mary, of Thomas and Mary,	Aug. 18, 1730.
175	"	Rhoda,	Dec. 22, 1741.
175	"	Thomas,	June, ——.
164	"	Thomas Coggeshall, of Benjamin and Bathsheba,	Feb. 13, 1744-5.
234	"	John, of William and Frances,	May 6, 1752.
202	"	Thomas, of Peleg and Sarah,	Dec. 13, 175—.
202	"	Samuel,	April 12, 1752.
202	"	Patience,	Aug. 29, 1753.
202	"	Hannah,	Nov. 1, 1754.
202	"	John,	Nov. 3, 1755.
202	"	Peleg,	April 22, 1757.
202	"	Elizabeth,	April 19, 1759.
202	"	Rhoda,	May 20, 1761.
202	"	James,	June 1, 1764.
202	"	Nicholas,	Nov. 11, 1766.
1-83	"	James, of Samuel and Rachel,	March 19, 1787.
1-83	"	Mary,	Jan. 19, 1789.
104	CRANDALL	Joseph, of Samuel and Margaret,	Nov. 24, 1731.
104	"	Thomas,	Jan. 10, 1734.
104	"	Mary,	—— 16, 1735.
104	"	Simeon,	——.
104	"	Rebecca,	——.
104	"	Ezekiel,	——.
104	"	Hannah,	——.
106	CROSSMAN	Hannah, of Seth and Hannah,	April 6, 1748.
106	"	Abigail,	June 23, 1751.
106	"	Seth,	Jan. 31, 1753.
106	"	Peleg,	Oct. 31, 1754.
214	CROSSWALL	George, of George and Mary,	Jan. 5, 1756.
8	CURTIS	Nancy, of Holland and Elizabeth,	Nov. 15, 1696.
8	"	Elizabeth,	July 23, 1698.
8	"	Obedience Holland,	June 30, 1700.

D

1-47	DEVALLON, Children of Luis Rene Adrien Dagas Devallon, and Mary Francoise Pauline Dagas Davallon, his wife.		
1-47	"	Adrienne Dagas,	May 8, 1794.
1-47	"	Amelia Dagas,	April 1, 1796.
179	DARRELL William, of Thomas and Sarah,		Dec. 4, 1765.
38	DAVENPORT Mary, of Eleazer and Mary,		Dec. 25, 1714.
38	"	Charles,	April 24, 1720.
38	"	dau.,	—— 7, 1724-5.
75	"	Ebenezer, of Ebenezer and Mary,	May 3, 1727.
75	"	son,	Aug. 25, ———.
75	"	Elizabeth,	Nov. 27, 172—.
75	"	son,	—— 4, 1734.
46	DAVIS John, of John and Mary,		Aug. 12, 1711.
46	"	son,	Aug. 30, 1715.
46	"	son,	d. Sept. 18, 1716.
46	"	dau.,	April 24, 1717.
88	"	John, of James and Sarah,	Sept. 19, 1730.
114	"	Elizabeth, of John and Elizabeth,	Jan. 31, 1734.
114	"	Elizabeth,	d. —— 3, 1744.
114	"	Mary,	June 6, 1736.
114	"	Mary,	June 6, 1738.
114	"	Mary,	d. Sept. 19, 1743.
114	"	John,	March 17, 1740-1.
114	"	James,	May 28, 1743.
114	"	Anne,	May 13, 1745.
114	"	Edward,	March 17, 1746.
114	"	William,	April 8, 1749.
114	"	William,	d. Nov. 10, 1753.
114	"	Mary,	Sept. 3, 1751.
114	"	Mary,	d. Oct. 1, 1751.
114	"	Peter,	Oct. 22, 1752.
114	"	Peter,	d. Sept. 29, 1757.
114	"	William,	March 12, 1756.
114	"	Elizabeth,	Feb. 25, ——.
146	"	John, of Mary and Ann,	Nov. 9, 1763.
146	"	John, of Mary and Ann,	d. June 14, 1764.
146	"	John, 2d,	March 14, 1765.
146	"	Preserved Fish,	March 9, 1766.
146	"	Preserved Fish,	d. Aug. 4, 1766.
146	"	May,	d. June 30, 1776.
1-111	"	Phebe, of John Warner and Elizabeth,	May 7, 1799.
1-111	"	Eliza,	May 23, 1802.
1-111	"	John Warner,	April 21, 1804.
1-111	"	Ann Maria,	Feb. 12, 1806.
1-111	"	Henry Moore,	Dec. 6, 1809.
57	DEHANE Bathsheba, wife of Jacob,		d. Jan. —, 1722-3.
133	DENNIS Marcy, of Abraham and Rebecca		Aug. 10, 1739.
133	"	Abraham,	Aug. 12, 1751.
155	DILLINGHAM Hannah, of Cornelius and Sarah,		Dec. 2, 1748.
155	"	Edward,	Jan. 2, 1750.
156	"	William,	Oct. 14, 1751.
156	"	Samuel,	May. 29, 1753.
156	"	Sarah,	Oct, 21, 1755.
156	"	Remembrance,	Nov. 23, 1758.
47	DILL Joseph, of Joseph and Mary,		May 6, 1713.
2-26	DOLBEAR Amos Emerson, of Samuel and Eliza G.,		Nov. 10, 1837.
2-26	"	Samuel,	Sept. 3, 1839.
2-25	"	Eliza Godfrey, wife of Samuel,	d. Dec. 1, 1847.
219	DOUBLEDAY Elijah, of Benjamin and Mary,		Dec. 27, 1763.
219	"	Dorcas,	Oct. 25, 1765.
219	"	Lydia,	Aug. 5, 1767.
219	"	Benjamin,	Feb. 2, 1769.

219	DOUBLEDAY Benjamin, of Benjamin and Mary,	d. Nov. 28, 1771.
219	" Deborah,	June 5, 177--
1-76	DOWNING Rachel, of William and Merebah,	March 29, 1794.
1-76	" Mary Ann,	April 2, 1796.
1-55	" Mary, wife of Henry,	d. -- --, ----,
1-104	" John Wheeler, of Benjamin and Sarah,	Sept. 22, 1810.
1-104	" George Albro,	Dec. 6, 1812.
1-104	" George Albro,	d. Aug. 24, 1816.
1-104	" Mary Ann Fenney,	Nov. 18, 1814.
1-104	" Elizabeth, Albro,	Dec. 24, 1816.
1-104	" Susan Louisa,	Dec. 17, 1818.
1-104	" George, Albro,	Dec. 30, 1820.
1-104	" Benjamin,	Dec. 28, 1822.
1-104	" Benjamin,	drowned Sept. 1, 1827.
1-104	" Sarah Jane,	Jan. 7, 1825.
1-104	" William Henry,	Dec. 2, 1826.
1-104	" Benjamin,	Jan. 14, 1829.
1-104	" Benjamin,	d. June 25, 1833.
1-104	" Caroline Matilda,	May 4, 1831.
1-104	" Caroline Matilda,	d. June 9, 1835.
1-104	" Benjamin Franklin,	Feb. 24, 1834.
1-110	" William Henry, of Benjamin, killed by explosion of a steam boiler at Stamford, Conn.,	Aug. 30, 1847.
	Note—Left a wife, Mary E., and one child, Sarah Elizabeth, aged then about 2 years.	
57	DRINKWATER Warren, of Thomas and Elizabeth,	Aug. 8, 1700.
25	DUNBAR Thankful, of ---- and Mercy,	Jan. 31, ----.
25	" Mercy,	May 30, 1712.
183	DUNHAM Daniel, of Daniel and Abigail,	June ----, 1738.
183	" John Duckworth,	---- 15, 1740.
183	" Robert,	July 16, 1742.
44	DUNN, son of Samuel and Ann,	May ----, 1720.
44	" ----,	Feb. 11, 1723-4.
70	" Clarke,	Feb. 26, 1725-6.
70	" Gideon,	March 26, 1730.
127	" Gideon, 2d,	March ----, 1736.
127	" Felix,	Nov. 19, 1739.
195	" Samuel, of Richard and Mary,	July 14, 1746.
195	" Mary,	Jan. 4, 1747-8.
214	DURFEE Robert, of Joseph, and Ann,	Sept. 2, 1758.
214	" Hannah,	July 13, 1760.
214	" Mary.	July 15, 1762.
214	" Ann,	----, 1764.
214	" Ann,	April 9, 1766.
214	" Elizabeth,	March 15, 1768.
1-22	" Oliver, of Oliver and Elizabeth,	Aug. 7, 1783.
30	DYER Elizabeth, of Nathaniel and Elizabeth,	Sept. 15, 1689.
30	" Mary,	Dec. 1, 1691.
30	" Phebe,	Dec. 26, 169--.
30	" Ann,	Jan. 10, 1700-1.
23	" William, of William and Hannah,	May 15, 1705.
23	" Charles,	March 2, 1707.
23	" Mary,	Nov. 5, 1709.
22	" Son,	May 4, 1712.

E

35	EADY Parker, of John and Elizabeth,	Feb. 24, 1716-7.
213	EASTMAN Thomas James, of Thomas and Mary,	Nov. 3, 1773.
128	EASTON Mary, of John and Patience,	April 17, 1739.
128	" John,	July 21, 1741.
128	" Rebecca,	March 10, ----.
228	" Samuel, of Job and Susanna,	Feb. 28, 1750-1.
207	EARL Dorcas, of John and Dorcas,	April 14, 1767.

193	ECKSTEIN	Jacob, of Gottlieb and Katherine,	June 3, 1761.
193	"	Renererias (b. Providence),	July 5, 1765.
171	ECKSTONE	Katherine Bonnoway Gottlieb,	Aug. 19, 1754.
2-23	EDDY	Joseph Wilbour, of Michael and Phebe, March 18, 1791, d. March 20, 1889.	
2-23	"	Anna M. (Robbins of Asher), his wife,	Dec. 14, 1795.
2-23	"	Asher Robbins, of Joseph W. and Anna M.,	Nov. 1, 1823.
2-23	"	Abby Maria,	Oct. 13, 1825.
2-23	"	Anna Louisa,	Feb. 22, 1828.
2-23	"	Anna Louisa,	d. March 23, 1828.
2-23	"	Ellery Wilbour,	Aug. 9, 1832.
2-23	"	Sarah Ann,	June 28, 1834.
2-23	"	John Middletown Clayton,	Jan. 5, 1837.
1-132	"	Joseph Wilbour, of Rev. Michael and Phebe,	March 18, 1791.
1-132	"	Pamelia,	Oct. 7, 1796.
1-132	"	Michael,	Jan. 24, 1799.
1-132	"	Sarah Ann,	March 23, 1803.
109	ELDRED	Phebe, of Thomas and Phebe,	Sept. 13, 1748.
109	"	John,	June 22, 1748.
222	ELIZER	Eleazer, of Isaac and Richa,	Oct. 7, 1761.
222	"	Hannah,	May 21, ——.
222	"	Pitah,	Jan. 17, 1765.
222	"	Priscilla,	——.
222	"	Moses,	Aug. 27, 1772.
222	"	Frances,	Nov. 11, 1774.
59	ELLERY	Abigail, of William and Elizabeth, Dec. 14, 1723-4.	
59	"	Benjamin,	Feb. —, 1725.
59	"	William,	Dec. —, 172—.
220	"	Ann,	May 6, 1732.
59	"	Christopher,	April 22, 1736.
220	"	Elizabeth, of William, Jr.,	Aug. 13, 1751.
220	"	Lucy,	Sept. 21, 1752.
220	"	Ann,	April 16, 1755.
220	"	William,	March 2, 1757.
220	"	Almy,	Feb. —, ——.
220	"	William,	Oct. 9, ——.
220	"	Edmund Trowbridge,	Nov. 2, 1763.
1-46	"	Martha Redwood, of Benjamin and Mehitable,	March 13, 1772.
1-46	"	Abraham Redwood,	May 24, 1773.
1-46	"	Mehitable, wife of Benjamin, d. in 64th year,	Dec. 4, 1794.
1-71	"	Franklin, of Christopher and Clarrissa,	Aug. 19, 1793.
1-71	"	Frank,	July 23, 1794.
1-71	"	Alfred,	Oct. 29, 1795.
1-71	"	Charles,	Sept. 1, 1797.
1-71	"	Clarrissa,	June 6, 1799.
1-71	"	Cornelia,	Jan. 27, 1801.
1-71	"	Eugene,	May 24, 1802.
1-71	"	Christopher,	July 31, 1803.
1-71	"	Emmeline,	Jan. 7, 1805.
1-52	"	Benjamin, d. aged 73 years,	Dec. 12, 1797.
146	ELLIOTT	Elizabeth, of Robert and Abigail,	March 29, 1766.
146	"	Hannah Vincent,	Oct. 28, 1769.

F

2-37	FAISNEAN	George E., of George and Julia Ann,	July 4, 1829.
2-37	"	Julia E.,	May 17, 1831.
2-37	"	Hannah E., of George and Amelia,	July 29, 1842.
2-37	"	Charles T.,	Aug. 5, 1843.
2-37	"	Mary A.,	Aug. 29, 1844.
2-37	"	John D.,	Nov. 13, 1845.
2-37	"	Charles T. 2d,	Jan. 19, 1847.
2-37	"	Henrietta D.,	April 11, 1848.
2-37	"	Theresa E.,	June 26, 1849.
2-37	"	David B.,	Oct. 19, 1850.

2-46	FALES	Theodore C., of Nathaniel and Elizabeth,	May 1, 1840.
2-46	"	Sarah E.,	April 27, 1842.
2-46	"	Melvina S.,	Feb. 3, 1846.
2-46	"	Nathaniel E.,	May 22, 1849.
2-46	"	Hattie S.,	Sept. 8, 1851.
242	FANNIT	John Coggeshall, of John and Amey,	Oct. 8, 1770.
1-102	FIELD	Richard, b. Dublin, Ireland,	July 20, 1769.
151	FLAGG	Henry Collins, of Ebenezer,	Aug. 21, ——.
151	"	Lydia,	Nov. 19, 1744.
151	"	Elizabeth,	———
151	"	Elizabeth,	d. Feb. —, 1746.
151	"	Ebenezer,	April 13, ——.
151	"	Mary,	March 6, ——.
151	"	Mary,	d. Aug. 28, 1749.
151	"	Margaret,	——.
151	"	Margaret,	d. Nov. ——.
151	"	Elizabeth,	Sept. —, 1751.
151	"	Richard,	——— 10, 1754.
151	"	Arnold,	Sept. 14, ——.
2-66	FLUDDER	William, of John and Jane, b. England,	May 2, 1804.
2-66	"	Catherine Sherman (Jack, of Alexander and Sarah (Hudson), his wife), Oct. 8, 1808.	
2-66	"	William Henry	Oct. 26, 1832.
2-66	"	George Madison,	May 24, 1834.
2-66	"	Alexander Jack,	May 2, 1836.
2-67	"	Stephen Stephenson,	April 12, 1838.
2-67	"	John,	Jan. 27, 1841.
2-67	"	Edward Vose,	Dec. 20, 1843.
2-67	"	Sarah Jane Bignall,	April 2, 1845.
2-67	"	James,	July 18, 1847.
2-67	"	Rebecca Jack,	April 8, 1849.
4	FOSTER	Hannah, of George and Mary, Nov. 29, 1700,	d. March 30, 1701.
15	FOWLER,	dau. of Cornelius and Mary,	Aug. 10, 1709.
19	"	——, 3d son of James and Mary,	May 18, 1708.
19, 25	"	Samuel,	April 13, 1710.
106, 25	FRANKLIN,	dau. of John and Elizabeth,	Feb. —, 1754.
2-67	FRANK	Philip, of Ludwig and Maria L.,	July 13, 1859.
2-67	"	Richard,	Aug. 15, 1861.
2-67	"	William,	Oct. 26, 1863.
2-67	"	Ludwig,	March 25, 1865.
2-67	"	Erbin,	May 10, 1869.
184	FREEBORN,	son of Joseph and Dorcas,	Nov. —, 174—.
238	"	Henry, of Henry and Sarah,	Nov. 11, 1750.
238	"	Ann,	Jan. 28, 1752.
238	"	Mary,	Feb. 16, 1754.
1-48	"	Henry,	June 18, 1755.
1-48	"	Mary Simpson, his wife, May 4, 1763.	
1-48	"	Sarah, of Henry and Mary S.,	Aug. 27, 1781.
1-48	"	John Topham,	Sept. 4, 1783.
1-48	"	Benjamin,	Dec. 22, 1785.
1-48	"	Mary,	April 4, 1788.
1-48	"	Theophilus,	Oct. 14, 1790.
1-48	"	Henry,	Oct. 1, 1792.
1-48	"	Richard,	Feb. 12, 1795.
1-64	"	William Wood, of Joseph and Elizabeth,	Feb. 4, 1780.
1-64	"	George,	Aug. 5, 1783.
1-64	"	Michael,	Aug. 30, 1785.
1-117	"	Joseph, of William W. and Sarah,	March 3, 1807.
1-117	"	Catherine,	Dec. 27, 1808.
1-117	"	Catherine,	d. Oct. 15, 1809.
1-117	"	Perry Weaver,	Aug. 29, 1810.
1-117	"	William,	Dec. 19, 1812.
1-117	"	Sarah,	May 21, 1820.
1-95	"	Elizabeth Wood, of George and Mary M.,	Sept. 13, 1808.
1-95	"	Joseph Barker,	March 9, 1810.

1-95	FREEBORN Abigail Barker, of George and Mary M.,	Oct. 16, 1812.
1-95	" Mary Mitchell,	Jan. 19, 1821.
1-95	" Michael,	May 7, 1824.
1-95	" Phebe Barker,	Feb. 1, 1826.
1-95	" Caroline Amelia,	Dec. 28, 1828.

G

127	GARDINER Samuel, of Samuel and Elizabeth,	Oct. 28, 1685.
22	" John, of Joseph and Catherine,	Sept. 17, 1697.
22	" Robert,	Aug. 16, 1699.
22	" Frances,	Sept. 7, 1701.
22	" Joseph,	April 17, 1703.
22	" George,	Feb. 4, 1704.
22	" dau.,	Feb. 1, 1707.
22	" Lydia,	March 2, 1709.
29	" dau. of Jeremiah and Sarah,	Sept. 22, 1712.
74	" Freelove, of Robert and Ann,	Oct. 24, 1727.
214	" Amey, of William and Mary,	Jan. 23, 1762.
214	" John,	June 10, 1766.
1-11	" Joseph, of James and Dorcas (Mason), of North Carolina, Sept. 26, 1768.	
1-11	" Peleg,	Sept. 21, 1771.
1-11	" James,	July 4, 1779.
1-108	" Charles Cazenove, of William C. and Eliza F.,	April 17, 1817.
26	GAVITT Elizabeth, of John and Elizabeth,	Sept. 14, 1699.
26	" John,	Dec. 21, 1701.
26	" son,	May 29, 1705.
39	" Thomas, of John and Sarah,	July 8, 1715.
57	GEY Naoma, of Abraham and Abigail,	April 25, 1722.
57	" Peace,	Oct. 25, 1723.
1-10	GIBBONS William, of Joseph and Hannah, of Georgia, born in South Carolina, Dec. 6, 1750.	
1-10	" Valerie (Richardson, of Thomas and Elizabeth), his wife, born in Newport Jan. 25, 1756.	
138	GIBBS Hannah, of George and Hannah,	— —, ——.
138	" George,	May —, 1735.
138	" Sarah,	Jan. 4, 173—.
138	" John,	April 11, 173—.
138	" Mary,	Nov. 25, 173—.
138	" Elizabeth,	Sept. —, 17—.
138	" Ruth,	March —, 17—.
1-91	" Susannah, of George and Mary,	April 15, 1770.
1-91	" Susannah, d.	Sept. 10, 1790.
1-91	" Mary,	May 3, 1772.
1-91	" Mary, d.	May 27, 1772.
1-91	" Mary, 2d,	Sept. 23, 1773.
1-91	" G o ge, (b. for s	Jan. 7, 1776.
1-91	" Ruth,	Nov. 7, 1778.
1-91	" John,	Oct. 2, 1781.
1-91	" Samuel,	June 27, 1784.
1-91	" Elizabeth,	Dec. 10, 1786.
1-91	" William Channing,	Feb. 10, 1789.
1-91	" Susannah,	Nov. 28, 1792.
1-70	GILBERT William Nicholas Magdelene, son of Jean Nicholas and Catherine Anne Audinet, his wife, came from Guadeloupe, W. I., born May 4, 1802.	
1-70	" John, James, Mary, Nicholas,	May 27, 1804.
1-70	" Frederick, Elizabeth, Edward,	Oct. 11, 1810.
1-89	GIBSON Jane S., of John B. and Lillis,	April 6, 1809.
1-89	" John B., Jr.,	Dec. 15, 1810.
1-89	" Henry,	April 11, 1812.
1-89	" Sarah, D.,	Jan. 9, 1814.
1-89	" Harriet Newell,	Feb. 22, 1816.

1-106	GILPIN	Elizabeth Miller, of John B. and Mary,	May 14, 1805.
1-106	"	William,	Oct. 27, 1806.
1-106	"	Henry Addington,	May 13, 1808.
1-106	"	John Bernard,	Sept. 4, 1810.
1-106	"	Charles Barring,	Aug. 3, 1812.
1-106	"	Susan Barring,	June 14, 1814.
97	GLADDING	Cory, of Joseph and Priscilla,	Dec. 10, 1732.
97	"	Jonathan,	April 29, 1735.
125	GODDARD	Margaret, of Daniel and Mary (born Dartmouth, Mass.), Nov. 13, 1718.	
125	"	———,	Feb. 18, ———.
125	"	John,	——— ——, 1723-4.
79, 125	"	Daniel,	——— ——, 1725.
79, 125	"	James,	Aug. 8, 1727.
79, 125	"	Susannah,	July 19, 1729.
125	"	Mercy,	July 4, 1733.
125	"	Stephen,	Aug. 22, 1735.
125	"	Elizabeth,	March 15, 1738.
126	"	Thomas,	Aug. 19, 1740.
126	"	Henry,	Aug. 30, 1744.
126	"	Mary, of Daniel and Ruth, 2w.,	Aug. 14, 1749.
126	"	Bradford,	Nov. 19, 175—.
97	"	Abigail, of John,	Sept. ——, 1734.
125	"	Samuel, of Daniel and Ruth,	July 12, 1753.
186	"	Daniel, of John and Hannah,	April 24, 1747.
186	"	Solomon,	Jan. 23, 1748-9.
176	"	Townsend, of John and Hannah,	Oct. 27, 1750.
72	GODFREY	Mary, of John and Elizabeth,	March 23, 1701.
72	"	John,	Jan. 31, 1703.
72	"	Caleb,	July 17, 1706.
72	"	Elizabeth,	May 21, 1709.
5	GOLDSMITH	Sarah, of —— and Rebecca,	May 11, ———.
5	"	Joseph,	Nov. 13, 1701.
178	GOLDTHWAIT	Samuel, of Samuel and Amey,	Sept. 26, 1761.
178	"	Charles,	Aug. 14, 1763.
178	"	William,	Jan. 24, 1765.
178	"	Elizabeth,	May 19, 1767.
178	"	Elizabeth,	d. same month.
178	"	son,	——, 1768.
178	"	Joseph,	——, 1769.
178	"	———	Jan. 26, ———.
33	GOODSPEED	———, of Samuel and Ma———,	Aug. 4, ———.
10	GOULDING	Thomas, of Robert,	——, ——.
10	"	George,	July 30, 1685.
87, 130	"	Elizabeth, of George and Mary,	July 16, 1713.
87, 130	"	Penelope,	May 7, 1715.
130	"	Mary,	Oct. 18, 1719.
130	"	George,	Feb. 28, 1723-4.
62	"	Gould Daniel, of Thomas and Elizabeth,	Dec. 18, 1696.
62, 127	"	dau. of Daniel and Mary,	Nov. 19, 1720.
62, 127	"	Priscilla,	Aug. 15, 1722.
62, 127	"	Daniel,	Jan. 20, 1723-4.
127	"	Mary,	Jan. 1, 1726-7.
79, 127	"	Jeremiah,	Nov. 1, 1728.
79, 127	"	Thomas,	Feb. 25, 1730-1.
64, 127	"	Ann,	May 29, 1733.
127	"	Wait,	Jan. 3, 1735-6.
127	"	Bathsheba,	July 28, 1738.
152	GRAFTON	Benjamin Chanders, of Nathaniel and Elizabeth,	Feb. 27, 1748-9.
134	GRANT	Elizabeth, and Alexander and Abigail, born at Halifax, N. S., Jan. 17, 1763.	
134	"	Abigail Cheeseborough,	Sept. 16, 1765.
107	GREENE	Thomas, of Benjamin and Niobe,	Jan. 30, 1743-4.
107	"	Penelope,	Aug. 21, 1746.
107	"	Deborah,	Oct. 12, 1748.

107	GREENE	Ann, of Benjamin and Niobe,	Nov. 22, 1750.
107	"	Nathaniel,	May ——, 1755.
107	"	John,	Sept. 27, 1757.
107	"	Mary,	—— 17, 1760.
107	"	Elizabeth Pelham,	May 17, 1763.
1-67	GREENMAN	Job,	Dec. 22, 1742.
1-67	"	Lucy (Brayman), his wife, b. Walpole, Mass.,	Sept. 9, 1743.
1-67	"	William, of Job and Lucy,	Aug. 27, 1766.
1-67	"	Jeremiah,	April 12, 1768.
1-67	"	Josiah,	Nov. 27, 1771.
1-67	"	John,	May 16, 1774.
1-67	"	Israel,	July 27, 1776.
1-67	"	Silas,	Oct. 22, 1788.

Note.—First two born Swansey, Mass., next Oblong, N. Y., three last Newport.

197	GREGORY	Grace, of Henry and Hannah,	May 26, 1754.
197	"	Patience,	May 6, 1757.
2-56	GRIER	William, of Patrick and Ellen	bap. Feb. 27, 1825.
1-123	GUILD	William Burrows, of William and Sarah B.,	Nov. 27, 1830.
1-123	"	Adeline,	Feb. 19, 1836.
2-36	"	Henry Goodwin, of William and Abby De Wolf,	June 5, 1850.

H

234	HADWIN	——, of —— and Elizabeth,	Aug. 28, 1753
234	"	dau.,	Feb. 20, 1755.
234	"	son,	Jan. 29, 1757.
234	"	——,	Nov. 13, 1758.
234	"	dau.,	Dec. 6, 1760.
234	"	dau.,	May 11, 1763.
234	"	dau.,	April 8, 1765.
234	"	son,	March 24, 1767.
82	HALL	William, of George and Eliza,	Jan. 20, 1726.
82	"	Edward,	April 14, 1730-31
156	"	Sibal, of Jeremiah, and Elizabeth,	Aug. 17, 1755.
156	"	William,	Sept. 18, 1756.
156	"	Bethia,	Nov. 5, 1759
156	"	Deborah,	Sept. 4, 1761.
156	"	Joseph,	June 23, 1764.
28	HAMMETT	Thomas, of John and Sarah,	April 11, 1712.
19	"	John, of John and Sarah,	Oct. 10, 1705.
19	"	Mary,	—— 11, ——.
84, 129	HAMMOND	John Arnold, of Elnathan and Mary,	Feb. 9, 1730-31.
129	"	Abigail,	Sept. 20, 1733.
129	"	Abigail,	d. Jan. 15, 1733-34.
129	"	Elnathan,	Jan. 17, 1735-36.
129	"	Elnathan,	d. Dec. 4, 1737.
129	"	Abigail,	Feb. 15, 1736-37.
129	"	Elnathan,	May 11, 1738.
129	"	Joseph,	April 13, 1739.
164	"	Joseph,	d. May 21, 1740.
164	"	Nathaniel,	June 2, 1740.
164	"	Mary,	Sept. 22, 1741.
164	"	Elizabeth,	May 25, 1743.
164	"	Susanna,	June 18, 1744.
1-27	"	Benjamin, of Thomas and Rebecca,	March 17, 1755.
1-27	"	Thomas,	June 16, 1757.
227	"	John, came on board ship Liberty Oct. 9, 1772, died Dec. 28, 1772, on coast of Africa.	
1-44	"	Phebe,	Jan. 15, 1775.
1-44	"	Elizabeth,	Dec. 6, 1775.
1-44	"	Ann,	April 24, 1777.
1-44	"	John Paine,	Oct. 20, 1779.
1-44	"	John Paine,	d. March 16, 1780.

1-44	HAMMOND	William, of Thomas and Rebecca,	Dec. 29, 1781.
1-44	"	Benjamin,	Dec. 22, 1783.
1-44	"	Joseph,	Sept. 22, 1786.
1-44	"	Sally,	March 29, 1789.
1-44	"	Sally,	d. June 30, 1815.
1-44	"	Paine,	June 20, 1791.
1-44	"	Phebe, mother of above children, died, aged 67 years, Dec. 28, 1814.	
1-49	"	Nancy, of William and Lucy,	Aug. 16, 1780.
1-49	"	Polly,	April 8, 1782.
1-49	"	James,	Sept. 30, 1784.
1-49	"	Lucy,	March 21, 1786.
1-49	"	Lucy,	d. Nov. 29, 1787.
1-6	"	Thomas,	died July 29, 1782.
1-6	"	Rebecca, his wife, died Dec. 22, 1781.	
144	HAMPTON	Henry, of John and Mary (Davis),	Dec. 24, 1732.
160	HANDY	Ann, son of James and Mary,	——, 1746.
160	"	Penelope,	——, 1749.
160	"	John,	——, 175—.
160	"	George,	——, 1754.
160	"	Joseph,	——, 1756.
160	"	Hannah,	April 15, ——.
160	"	Mary,	June 15, 1759.
160	"	dau.,	Jan. 26, 176—.
160	"	James,	Jan. 19, 1766.
67	HANNAH	William, of William and Martha,	Feb. 14, 1711-2.
27	HARRIS	John, of John,	Feb. 12, ——.
78	HART	John, of Josiah and Neoma,	March 3, 1728.
193	"	Dinah, of Naptate and Sheporah,	April 30, 1761.
193	"	Love,	Sept. 14, 1762.
193	"	Isaac,	Nov. 5, 1763.
193	"	Sarah,	Jan. 9, 1765.
193	"	Rebecca,	Nov. 20, 1766.
193	"	Son,	April 30, 1768.
193	"	Daughter,	—— 30, 1771.
154	HARVEY	James, of Seth and Ruth,	Aug. 10, 1747.
154	"	Benjamin,	April 17, 1749.
154	"	Seth,	Sept. 19, 1751.
97	HASEY	Abial, of Jacob and Johanna,	April 18, 1736.
97	"	Ebenezer,	Feb. 28, 1737-8.
97	"	Jacob, of Jacob, 2d, and Margaret,	March 12, 174—.
8	HASTINGS	John, of George and Dorothy,	May 30, 1692.
8	"	Benjamin,	—— 12, 1697.
76	HATCH	Jane, of Nathaniel and Comfort,	March 29, 1727-8.
76	"	Nathaniel,	Dec. 25, 1729.
76	"	Susanna,	April ——, 1732.
76	"	Susanna,	d. Nov. 28, 1732.
192	"	Samuel, of Samuel and Hannah,	Feb. 4, 1759.
192	"	John,	May 4, 1761.
1-65	HATHAWAY	Jane, of Abner and Amey,	April 21, 1796.
1-65	"	Abner,	March 25, 1799.
156	HAWKINS	Stephen, of James and Anne,	June 29, 1744.
156	"	Susanna,	Sept. 14, 1747.
222	HAYDEN	John, of James and Deborah,	7m. 24, 1756.
222	"	Rebecca,	11m. 27, 1758.
125	HAZARD	Stephen, of Fones and Marian,	May 18, 1740.
125	"	Nicholas,	Aug. 12, 1741.
2-26	"	Henry Holt, of George M., and Almira,	July 11, 1848.
1-51	HIDDEN	William, of James and Betsey,	July 15, 1798.
31	HIGGINS	Richard, of Richard and Edith,	Dec. ——, ——.
31	"	Anna,	Sept. 6, 169—.
31	"	Anna,	d. Oct. 26, 1699.
31	"	Ephraim,	Aug. 24, ——.
31	"	Henry,	April 16, ——.
31	"	Anna,	July 22, ——.

31	HIGGINS	Amey, of Richard and Edith,	May 29, ——.
31	"	William,	Nov. 25, ——.
31	"	Elizabeth,	May 4, ——.
109	HILL	Timothy Peckham, of Timothy,	Nov. 15, 1748.
109	"	Benjamin,	March 28, ——.
196	"	Lydia, of Joseph and Lydia,	June 13, 1764.
196	"	Priscilla,	Nov. 19, 1765.
196	"	John,	Sept. 19, 1767.
1-87	"	Haley Maria, of Bernard and Sally,	July 30, 1807.
1-87	"	John Wheaton,	Oct. 8, 1808.
1-87	"	Elizabeth,	April 13, 1810.
1-87	"	Sarah,	April 8, 1812.
1-87	"	Caroline,	Oct. —, 1813.
1-87	"	Caroline,	d. March 9, 1819.
1-87	"	Peace,	Jan. 27, 1816.
1-87	"	William Bernard,	Nov. 15, 1817.
1-87	"	Caroline,	Feb. 15, 1820.
1-87	"	Henry Clarke,	Nov. 8, 1821.
1-87	"	James,	Feb. 19, 1824.
1-87	"	Hannah,	Sept. 3, 1826.
1-89	"	Caroline, died,	March 9, 1819.
1-89	"	Hannah, died at Providence,	Jan. 30, 1832.
1-89	"	Peace, died,	March 23, 1836.
1-89	"	Peace Ann, of James and Peace (Slocum), died,	Sept. 1, 1836.
36	HOLMES	John, died	Oct. 1, 1712.
2	HOOKEY	——, of Stephen and Sarah,	d. Aug. 26, 1701.
16	"	William, of Stephen and Mary,	May 11, 1709.
67	"	Stephen, of Stephen, Jr., and Elizabeth,	Nov. 6, 1724.
67	"	Daniel,	April 6, 1728.
139	"	William, of William and Rebecca,	Feb. 1, ——.
139	"	Nathaniel,	——, 1740.
139	"	Sarah,	——, 1742.
94	HOULTON,	of John and Susannah,	May, 3, 1733.
112	"	Ann,	Feb. 20, 1739-40.
112	"	Mary,	——, 27, 1741-2.
112	"	Nathaniel,	June 13, 1744.
144	HOWARD	Ann, of Martin,	Aug. 15, ——.
107	HOWELL	Walter Williams, of Luke and Ann,	Jan. 1, 1763.
107	"	Mary,	Nov. ——, 1766.
107	"	Elizabeth,	Nov. ——, 1766.
106	HOWLAND	Lucy, of Joseph and Martha,	July 19, 1740.
1-123	"	Susan, of Benjamin B. and Phebe C.,	May 7, 1818.
1-123	"	Sarah Jane,	Aug. 12, 1820.
1-123	"	Sarah Jane,	d. May 22, 1846.
1-123	"	Mary Jones,	Oct. 2, 1824.
1-123	"	Phebe C., wife of Benjamin B., died aged 57 years, Sept. 30, 1849.	
2-16	"	Henry, died aged 92y. 5 m., July 9, 1843; 5th generation from John Howland of the Mayflower.	
113	HOXSIE	William, of Giles and Elizabeth,	June 30, 1765.
1-98	"	Gideon, of Benjamin and Elizabeth,	Dec. 23, 1788.
1-14	HUDSON	Catherine, of Thomas and Deliverance,	Jan. 8, 1768.
158	HUGHES	Elizabeth, of Thomas and Elizabeth,	Sept. 23, 1763.
2-55	"	Ann Maria, of Patrick and Maria,	Feb. 22, 1854.
2-55	"	Edward,	Dec. 31, 1855.
2-55	"	Bridget, 2d wife of Patrick,	d. Aug. 7, 1866.
144	HULL	Merebah, of Samuel and Merebah,	May 11, 1756.
216	HUNTINGTON	John, of John and Elizabeth,	Dec. 18, 1742.
221	HUXHAM	John, of John and Elizabeth,	May 16, 1753.

I

1-18	IRISH	John, of Benjamin and Martha,	May 5, 1784.
1-18	"	George,	Oct. 1, 1786.
1-18	"	Mary,	Nov. 2, 1788.

1-18	IRISH Sarah, of Benjamin and Martha,	Feb. 21, 1791.
1-64	" George, of Jedediah and Sarah,	March 25, 1802.
1-64	" William Cornell,	Sept. 8, 1803.
1-64	" James,	July 4, 1806.
1-64	" Joseph,	July 4, 1806.
1-64	" Joseph,	d. Sept. 17, 1808.
1-64	" Joseph 2d,	Nov. 12, 1808.
1-64	" Elizabeth C.,	March 9, 1805.
1-64	" Perry C.,	Oct. 5, 1810.
1-64	" William C.,	Aug. 13, 1812.
1-64	" Albert,	Jan. 8, 1815.
2-74	" Joseph, of James and Susan,	Dec. 5, 1838.

J

2-67	JACK Sarah Burroughs (Hudson), wife of Alexander, died, aged 49 years, Feb. 8, 1827.	
2-67	" Alexander, died aged 64 years,	Feb. 28, 1843.
2-67	" Rebecca (Vose), widow of Alexander, died aged 76 years, Jan. 8, 1857.	
28	JAMES Joseph, of William and Susannah,	Feb. 24, 1697.
10	" William,	died Oct. —, 1697.
161	" Sarah, of Peter and Sarah,	Feb. 4, 1741-42.
161	" Peter,	Sept. 1, 1743.
161	" Esther,	April 23, 1745.
239	" William, of William and Hannah,	Jan. 13, 1742-43.
239	" Rebecca,	March 15, 1744-45.
239	" Ann,	Oct. 4, 1746.
173	JEFFERSON Sarah, of ——, and Elizabeth,	Feb. 18, 1746-47.
173	" Elizabeth,	June —, 1748.
4	JEFFRIES Thomas, of Jethro and Mehith,	April 11, 1679.
221	JENKINS Robert Griggs, of Robert and Susanna,	May 4, 1755.
25	JERSEY John, of Jacob and Content,	d. July 11, 1708.
25	" Damaries,	Aug. 14, 1711.
25	" Damaries,	d. Jan. 19, 1711-12.
41	JOHNSON Joseph, of Joseph and Sarah,	Aug. 20, 1708.
41	" Sarah,	Feb. 27, 1711.
41	" Rebecca,	Feb. —, 1707.
94	JOHNSON ——, son of Joseph and Hannah,	——.
94	" son,	——.
94	" son,	—— 22, 1724.
94	" son,	—— 24, 1726.
94	" son,	—— 14, 1728.
94	" son,	—— 18, 1731.
94	" Obadiah,	Feb. 4, 1732.

K

230	KEATLEY Seetonius, of Andrew and Mercy,	May 21, 1749.
230	" Jennette,	April 19, ——.
230	" Mary,	Oct. 23, 1757.
230	" Temple,	July —, 1759.
221	KEELING Elizabeth, of Thomas,	Aug. —, 1755.
220	KELLY John Callender, of Erasmus and Mary,	Dec. 14, 1771.
219	KENNICUT John, of Daniel, and Honora,	Jan. 5, 1742.
219	" Daniel,	July 6, 174–.
219	" ——,	——.
219	" ——,	d. Nov. —, 1744.
219	" William,	Oct. 4, 1746.
219	" Phebe,	Dec. 21, 1746.
219	" Phebe,	d. Aug. 27, 1752.
219	" Elizabeth,	May 5, 1753.
219	" Lydia,	May 8, 1755.

2-50	KILVEY Michael, of John and Bridget,		July 25, 1853.
2-50	" Susan,		Dec. 15, 1855.
2-50	" Bridget,		Nov. 15, 1857.
96	KING Matthew, of Matthew and Abigail,		Oct. 14, 1725.
96	" John,		Sept. 13, 1728.
96	" Abigail,		July 3, 1731.
103	" Benjamin, of Benjamin and Mary,		June 11, 174—.
103	" Mehitable,		Aug. 8, ——.
103	" Samuel,		Jan. 24, ——.
103	" Mary,		Sept. 18, ——.
1-119	KNOWLES James Lyon, of William and Ann,		April 8, 1810.
1-119	" Hannah Lyon,		March 18, 1814.
1-32	KNOX Thomas Parker Robert Andrew, son of Thomas and Elizabeth, July 18, 1789.		

L

179	LADD Joseph, of William and Sarah,		July —, ——.
179	" William,		Aug. 10, 1769.
179	" John Gardiner,		—— —, 1770.
179	" Elizabeth,		Aug. 21, 1772.
219	" Mary, of John and Lydia,		July 14, 1744.
1-137	" John Howard, of Uriah W., of Lebanon, Conn., and M. Catherine (Burdick), his wife, born at Newport, Oct. 20, 1849.		
1-17	LANGLEY John Sinkings, of John and Elizabeth,		July 5, 1770.
1-17	" Joshua Hacker,		May 10, 1772.
23	LANGWORTHY Abigail, of James,		Sept. 20, 1707.
23	" Mary,		Feb. 27, ——.
23	" James,		April 11, 1711.
30	LAWTON George, of Job and Priscilla,		Feb. 1, 1713-4.
231	" Robert, of George and Hannah		—— —, ——.
231	Mary,		Jan. —, ——.
231	" George,		Feb. 5, ——.
231	" Joseph,		Nov. 1, 1748.
231	" Benjamin,		Nov. 17, ——.
231	" Jonathan,		Oct. 31, 1754.
231	" James,		Sept. 20, 1755.
231	" Job,		July 24, 1758.
231	" Elizabeth,		June 2, ——.
111	" Arnold, of Isaac and Hannah,		June 4, 1761.
222	" Mary, of Robert and Marcy,		Nov. 25, 1761.
222	" Elizabeth,		Nov. 22, 1763.
222	" George,		June 16, 1766.
1-99	" George, of Robert and Dorcas, born at New Shoreham, July 27, 1767.		
1-102	" Joseph Coggeshall, of Jeremiah and Mary,		Jan. 6, 1802.
1-120	" Susan Ann, of Joseph C. and Ruth B.,		May 21, 1830.
90	LEACH Ann, of Thomas and Sarah,		4m., 29, 1710.
90	" Thomas,		5m., 25, 1712.
90	" Mary,		12m., 16, 1713.
90	" John,		8m., 10, 1715.
90	" Joseph,		5m., 29, 1717.
90	" Sarah,		4m., 24, 1719.
90	" Elizabeth,		——. 31, 1720.
90	" dau.,		12m., 22, 1721.
90	" Benjamin,		3m., 2, 1723.
90	" son,		7m., 30, 1725.
90	" son,		d. —— 29, ——.
90	" son,		d. 7m., 30, ——.
228	LEVY Judith, of Horam and Grace,		Sept. 4, 1769.
228	" Moses,		March 4, 1772.
101	LILLIBRIDGE Jesse, of Edward and Esther,		Aug. 3, 1740.
17	LLOYD Henry, of Henry,		Aug. 6, 1709.
74	LOYALL Meriam, of John and Sarah,		Sept. 18, 1728.

243	LUTHER	Elizabeth, of Paul and Mary,	March 30, 1771.
1-69	LYMAN	Anne Maria, of Daniel and Mary,	Nov. 13, 1782.
1-69	"	Harriet,	March 6, 1784.
1-69	"	Peggy,	Nov. 24, 1786.
1-69	"	Polly,	Oct. 7, 1788.
1-69	"	Eliza,	May 29, 1790.
1-69	"	Thomas,	Dec. 20, 1791.
1-69	"	John Wanton,	May 10, 1793.
1-69	"	Daniel,	Sept. 28, 1794.
1-69	"	Henry,	Nov. 18, 1795.
1-69	"	Louisa,	April 16, 1797.
1-69	"	Sally,	Feb. 14, 1799.
1-69	"	Julia Maria,	Aug. 30, 1801.
7	LYNDON	Josias, of Josias and Abigail,	Aug. 17, 1613.
7	"	dau.,	April 2, 1618.
228	LYON	Katherine, of Matthew and Susanna,	May 13, 1737.
228	"	Margaret,	May 1, 1740.
1-4	"	Nicholas, of Joseph and Mary,	April 18, 1777.
1-4	"	William,	Oct. 31, 1779.
1-4	"	Joseph,	Aug. 16, 1781.

M

195	MAGEE	Mary, of John and Phebe,	May 2, 1759.
195	"	William Fairchild,	March 23, 1765.
130	MALBONE	Peter, of Capt. Godfrey and Katherine,	June 24, 1720.
130	"	Peter,	d. May 27, 1738.
130	"	Godfrey,	Sept. 25, 1722.
130	"	Godfrey,	d. Sept. 5, 1723.
130	"	Godfrey,	Sept. 3, 1724.
130	"	Elizabeth,	Dec. 9, 1726.
130	"	Aliph,	Dec. 26, 1728.
130	"	Mary,	Feb. 14, 1730-1.
130	"	Thomas,	May 17, 1733.
130	"	John,	Aug. 21, 1735.
130	"	Katherine,	Oct. ——, 1737.
130	"	Deborah,	Nov. ——, 1744.
168	MANCHESTER,	of Thomas and Jane,	Nov. 28, 1736.
139	"	Sarah, of Thomas and Jane,	May 4, 1740.
139	"	Sarah, 2d,	June 10, 1741.
1-40	MANNING	Mary Clannan, of Edward and Patience,	Feb. 26, 1765.
177	MARCHANT	Henry, of Henry and Rebecca,	Nov. 6, 1765.
177	"	Henry,	d. Jan. 8, 1766.
177	"	Sarah,	—— 18, 1767.
178	"	Henry,	July ——, 1768.
178	"	Henry,	d. ——, 1770.
178	"	William,	——, ——.
178	"	Elizabeth,	Nov. 20, 1770.
178	"	William,	July 25, 1772.
178	"	Elizabeth,	Nov. ——, 177—.
77	MARK	Holland, of Nathaniel and ——,	Nov. 9, 1728.
5	MATTINDALE,	son of Isaac and Godsgift,	May 28, 1693.
5	"	son,	Aug. ——, 1695.
5	"	son,	1697.
5	"	son,	1698-9.
10	"	Ann,	Sept. 3, 1700.
10	"	Mary,	Jan. ——, 1703-4.
1-39	MARTIN	Joseph, of Joseph and Hannah,	May 21, 1789.
1-39	"	George,	May 6, 1790.
2-69	MARVIN	Lucy Temple, of Joseph D. and Anne	June 14, 1864.
2-69	"	Elizabeth Breese,	May 26, 1868.
43	MARYATT	Samuel, of Samuel and Margaret,	March ——, 1719-20.
126	"	Samuel, of Samuel and Elizabeth,	April 21, 1742.
126	"	Elizabeth,	Jan. 24, 1744-5.

NEWPORT—BIRTHS AND DEATHS.

126	MARYATT Mary, of Samuel and Elizabeth,		Feb. 5, 1747-8.
	Note.—Also recorded on Page 154.		
155	" Henry, of Samuel and Ann,		Jan. 11, 1754.
155	" James,		Aug. 21, ——.
155	" Ann,		Nov. —, 1759.
120	MAWDSLEY Robert, of John and Sarah,		Feb. 21, 1755.
120	" John,		Nov. 3, 1761.
	MAXON Elizabeth Ward, of Caleb and Mary,		Sept. 11, 1783.
120	" William Bliss,		Aug. 21, 1785.
120	" Joshua Babcock,		Dec. 12, 1788.
120	" John,		June 25, 1792.
120	" Content,		Feb. 19, 1795.
120	" Mary, of Caleb, and Mary 2d wife,		March 27, 1808.
118	" Judith, of John and Lucy,		Sept 13, 1749.
118	" John,		April —, 1751.
118	" Caleb,		Nov. —, 1752.
179	" Mercy of Jonathan and Lydia,		Jan. ——.
179	" dau.		May 21, 1762.
72	MAXWELL Dorcas, of Samuel and Hannah,		Feb. 7, 1725.
72	" Phillip,		July 23, 1726.
91	" Squire,		Sept. 3, 1729.
91	" Jane,		Sept. 23, 1731.
26	" Mary William, of William and Rebecca,		Oct. 15, 1709.
113	McALPINE Samuel Sturges of Samuel and Mercy,		July 26, 1764.
113	" John,		Jan. 10, 1766.
113	" Lydia,		April 11, 1767.
2-18	MELVILLE Thomas, of David, b. Boston,		—, 1697.
2-18	" David,		b. Boston —, 1709.
2-18	" And others.		
2-18	" Jane (Vaughn), wife of David, died, aged 34 years, Oct. 4, 1734.		
2-18	" Elizabeth (Vaughn), wife of David, died, aged 31 years, Dec. 10, 1738.		
2-18	" Mary, of David and Elizabeth, died, aged 2 months, —, 1736.		
2-18	" Lovelace, died aged 17 days,		—, 1738.
2-18	" Francis, of David and Lydia,		April 12, 1740.
2-18	" Francis,		d. Aug. 17, 1740.
2-18	" Timothy,		June 19, 1741.
2-18	" Timothy,		d. Aug. 17, 1742.
2-18	" David,		Nov. 5, 1742 or 3.
2-18	" David,		bap. Nov. 6, 1743.
2-18	" David, died, aged 42 years,		—, 1751.
2-18	" Elizabeth, his wife, died about —, 1749.		
	Note—Buried at Dartmouth, Mass.		
2-19	" David,		born Nov. 5, 1742.
2-19	" Lydia, of David and Elizabeth,		Aug. 3, 1769
2-19	" Samuel Thurston,		—, 1771.
2-19	" Samuel Thurston, drowned in the Taa, China,		Oct. 17, 1792.
2-19	" David,		March 21, 1773.
2-19	" Polly,		March 20, 1775.
2-19	" Polly,		d. Sept. 10, 1794.
2-19	" Elizabeth,		Dec. 5, 1777.
2-19	" Eunice Thurston,		Sept. 4, 1781.
2-19	" Eunice Thurston,		d. Aug. 29, 1819.
2-9	" Sarah Anthony,		May 23, 1784.
2-9	" Avis,		—, 1788.
2-9	" Avis,		d. May 22, 1792.
2-19	" David, died, aged 62 yeas, Dec. 18, 1804.		
2-19	" Elizabeth, his wife, died, aged 54 years, Dec. 1, 1803.		
2-19	" Elizabeth Thurston, of David and Patience,		Nov. 25, 1813.
2-19	" Henrietta Easton,		Nov. 20, 1815.
2-19	" Mary Catherine,		Feb. 25, 1818.
2-19	" Sarah Matilda,		Feb. 16, 1820.
2-19	" Benjamin Sherman,		Feb. 10, 1822.
2-19	" Samuel Thurston,		July 24, 1824.
2-19	" Geo. Washington Tew,		Sept. 4, 1826.

1-99	MESSER Thomas, born Coventry, Warwick co., Eng.,	Oct. 11, 1767.
1-94	MILES Mary, of George and Sarah (Brown),	Dec. 31, 1810.
17	MILLERD John, of John and Elizabeth,	Feb. 28, 1708.
221	MILLER John, of John and Elizabeth,	Nov. 7, 1754.
221	" Nathan Bull,	March 16, 1757.
221	" James Ruth,	May 25, 1760.
221	" Margaret, died aged 20 days,	Aug. 15, 1761.
221	" Christian,	Oct. 9, 1762.
221	" Christian,	d. Aug. 22, 1764.
221	" William,	July 27, 1764.
99	MITCHELL Sarah, of John and Lois,	April —, 1721.
1-81	" John, of Samuel,	—.
1-81	" Anna Christiana,	May 15, 1774.
114	MONROE William, of John and Abigail,	June 2, 1750.
114	" Ann,	Nov. 10, 1753.
1-60	MOORE William, of Henry and Mary,	Sept. 16, 1798.
1-60	" Martha Matilda,	Sept. 9, 1800.
1-60	" Fanny,	April 27, 1802.
1-60	" John Yeomans,	Aug. 25, 1803.
1-60	" Mary,	Feb. 27, 1805.
1-60	" Samuel Pickering,	Sept. 5, 1806.
1-60	" Harriet,	March 27, 1808.
1-60	" Charles,	Nov. 9, 1809.
2-68	MORAN John, of Timothy and Elizabeth,	Feb. 11, 1868.
2-68	" Mary,	June 26, 1870.
2-68	" James,	Feb. 7, 1872.
166	MORSE William, of Joseph and Mary,	—, 1730.
166	" Sarah,	March 2, 1746-7.
166	" John,	Oct. 17, 1749.
108	MULHOLLAND Henry Hesper, of John and Elizabeth,	Oct. 2, 1742.
8	MUMFORD, son of John and Peace,	Aug. 25, 1699.
36	" Mary,	Dec. 12, 1715.
175	" Nathaniel, of Richard and Sarah,	June 20, 1730.
182	" George, of Stephen and Mary.	April 29, 1748
182	" Mary,	May 21, 1750.
145	" William, of Paul and Mary,	Feb. 3, 1770.
1-35	" Elizabeth, of Joseph and Mary,	Jan. 26, 1789.
1-35	" Mary,	May 12, 1790.
1-35	" Phebe,	March 21, 1792.
1-35	" Samuel,	Sept. 12, 1796.
1-35	" Sarah,	July 15, 1798.
1-35	" Sarah Remington, of Benjamin B. and Hannah,	Jan. 4, 1798.
1-35	" Augustus George,	Nov. 6, 1800.
1-35	" Augustus George,	d. May 1, 1802.
1-35	" Abby Maria,	March 17, 1803.
1-35	" William Oliver,	July 18, 1804.
1-35	" Benjamin Augustus,	July 17, 1806.
1-35	" James Anthony,	Sept. 1, 1808.
1-35	" Hannah Cottrell,	March 22, 1810.
1-35	" John Remington,	Dec. 12, 1811.
1-35	" Mary Ann Shrieve,	Oct. 25, 1813.
1-35	" Oliver Remington,	May 28, 1815.
1-35	" Peter Remington,	Dec. 25, 1816.
1-35	" George Morris,	Nov. 24, 1818.
4	" Anne, of John,	April 28, —.
26	" Stephen, of Stephen and Mary,	June 20, 1698.
26	" Son,	Dec. 4, 1699.
26	" Son,	— 20, 1701.
26	" Dau.,	— 18, 1703.
26	" Dau.,	April 18, 1707.
26	" Son,	Sept. 24, 1708.
26	" Elizabeth,	Aug. 22, 1711.
11	" Son, of John and Peace,	March 6, 1703-4.
11	" Son,	April 15, 1707.
11	" Dau.,	— 18, 1709-10.

N

26	NAPTOLI Abraham, of —— and Rachel,	——, 1695.
4	NEWBURG Su-key, of Benjamin,	October 19, 1700.
1-63	NEWTON John Bigeley, of Simon and Elizabeth,	August 14, 1800.
50	NICHOLS Mary, of Jonathan, and Elizabeth,	Jan. 8, 1707.
50	" Hannah,	Sept. 21, 1709.
50	" Jonathan,	Oct. 24, 1712.
50	" Robert,	May 20, 1715.
50	" Elizabeth,	July 15, 1717.
50	" Sarah,	June 17, 1719.
50	" Joseph,	March 5, 1723.
50	" Benjamin,	March 5, 1723.
162	" Benjamin, of Jonathan and Sarah,	March 13, 1724.
162	" Sarah,	Aug. 7, 1726.
162	" Jonathan,	Dec. 22, 1728.
162	" William,	Jan. 30, 1730.
162	" George,	June 23, 1734.
162	" Mary,	Sept. 23, 1743.
121	" Hannah, of Jonathan and Mary,	Jan. 8, 1738-9.
121	" Jonathan,	Nov. 13, 1740.
121	" George,	Dec. 25, 1743.
121	" Thomas,	Dec. 9, 1746.
121	" Ruth,	Feb. 26, 1743.
108	" Elizabeth,	March 9, 1750-1.
165	" Andrew, of Andrew and Rachel,	June 10, 1739.
212	" Robert, of —— and Elizabeth,	Feb. 28, 1745-6.
212	" Jonathan,	Sept. 22, 1749.
212	" Benjamin,	April 25, 1754.
212	" Joseph,	May 24, 1762.
54	NICOLLS Thomas, of Jonathan and Mary	May ——, 1721.
54	" son,	March 5, 1723.
54	" son, of Robert and Mary,	—— 18, ——.
54	" Sarah,	—— ——.
202	NORTHAM Joseph, of John and Mary,	Nov. 18, 1754.
202	" Mary,	Sept. 4, 1756.
202	" Sarah, —— and Sarah, 2d wife,	July 7, 1764.
202	" Rachel,	Feb. 17, ——.
202	" Stephen Thomas,	May 25, 17——.
201	" Ann,	March 25, 1773.
201	" John,	Jan. 28, 1775.
5	NOYCE Ann, of James and Ann,	March 16, 1704.
11	" daughter,	April 18, 1705-6.

O

4	ODLIN Lydia, of John and Lydia,	Jan. 29, 1701-2.
49	" John, of John and Elizabeth,	March 12, 1718-9.
5	" dau. of John and Lydia,	Aug. ——, ——.
1-50	OLYPHANT Ann, of David and Ann,	Aug. 24, 1786.
1-50	" Ann,	d. Aug. 30, 1737.
1-50	" Ann, 2d,	Oct. 27, 1787.
1-50	" David Washington Cincinnatus,	March 7, 1789.
63	OSBORNE Edward, of Henry and Margaret,	March 20, 17——.
63	" Henry,	—— 23, ——.
63	" John,	April 2, 1728.
1-51	" Elizabeth, of William W. and Hannah,	Aug. 10, 1774.
1-51	" Isaac Senter,	Nov. 30, 1735.
1-51	" William W.,	Aug. 28, 1784.
1-51	" Catherine Read,	April 23, 1737.
1-51	" Polly James,	April 1, 1789.
1-51	" Sylvanus Folger,	Dec. 4, 1794.
1-51	" Sally,	April 22, 1796.
1-51	" James Atkinson,	May 4, 1801.
1-51	" Martha G.,	April 7, 1804.

135	OTIS Abigail, of Jonathan and Catherine,		Sept. 4, 1746.
135	" Katherine,		July 4, 1748.
135	" Mary,		March 1, 1750.
135	" Susanna,		May 14, 1752.

P

1-103	PALMER John H., of John and Sarah,		Aug. 14, 1813.
40	PANNY ——, of Christopher and Elizabeth,		April 16, ——.
164	PARTELOW John, of John and Anne	March 28, ——.	Rec. 1745.
198	PATE Priscilla, of Robert and Priscilla,		Feb. 3, 1756.
198	" Abigail,		Jan. 5, 1758.
101	PAUL Joseph, of Joshua and Sarah,		Nov. 11, 1750.
120	" Sarah,		—— 19, ——.
115	PEABODY Elizabeth, of Benjamin and Abigail,		Oct. 2, 1746.
57	" John, of Joseph and Sarah,		Dec. 12, 17—.
57	" Rachel,		May, ——.
57	" Eliza,		—— 26, ——.
57	" Sarah,		—— 13, ——.
2-44	" George Edwin, of Edwin and Catherine,		July 31, 1835.
2-44	" Charles Henry,		May 3, 1837.
2-44	" Robert Stuart,		March 25, 1839.
2-44	" Mary Kate,		March 1, 1841.
2-44	" Clara Elizabeth,		Feb. 5, 1843.
2-44	" Frank Deller,		Dec. 21, 1845.
2-44	" Kate Friend,		June 24, 1849.
2-44	" Harry Morton,		June 13, 1852.
1-17	PEARCE Mary, of Isaac and Sarah,		Feb. 4, 1786.
1-17	" Isaac,		June 30, 1788.
1-62	" Barton, of Giles and Sarah,		Sept. 1, 1800.
1-62	" Mary Ann,		Jan. 26, 1804.
1-62	" Phebe,		March 11, 1805.
1-94	" Susan,		March 8, 1811.
44	PECKHAM John of John and Sarah,		June 9, 1763.
28	" ——,		——, 1671-2.
28	" ——, and Mercy,		Aug. 19, 1695.
28	" Jeremiah,		Nov. 20, 1697.
28	" Sarah,		Sept. 29, 1703.
28	" ——,		May 2, 1705.
28	" ——,		Jan. 24, 1706-7.
69	" son, of John and Sarah,		April 11, 1688.
3	" son, of Thomas and Hanah,		June 28, 1700.
74	" Mary, of William and Mary,		Sept. 7, 1704.
74	" William,		Sept. 3, 1706.
74	" Dorcas,		July 3, 1709.
74	" Henry,		Feb. 26, 1711.
74	" Elisha,		May 8, 1716.
62	" Joseph, of Joseph and Mary,		Sept. 22, 1705.
69	" ——, of Isaac and Barbara,		May 1, 1712.
69	" Isaac,		Oct. 20, 1713.
69	" Sarah,		Oct. 6, 1715.
69	" Benjamin,		Oct. 19, 1717.
69	" Ruth,		July 22, 1719.
69	" Clement,		May 20, 1721.
69	" Stephen,		March 6, 1722-3.
69	" Son,		July 11, 1725.
94	" Mary, of Thomas,		Jan. 23, 1734 (?).
133	" Elizabeth, of Peleg and Elizabeth,		Dec. 22, 1740.
133	" Peleg,		Dec. 1, 1743.
133	" Thomas,		June 20, 1747.
243	" William, of Isaac and Ruth,		——, ——.
243	" Henry,		June 24, 1757.
243	" Ruth,		Jan. ——, 1759.
243	" Mary,		Feb. ——, 1761.

1-97	PECKHAM	Mary, of Jeremiah, of Benoni,	Sept. 11, 1769.
2-24	"	Isaac C.,	b. May 14, 1801.
1-115	"	Benoni, of Jeremiah and Elizabeth,	Aug. 15, 1804.
1-81	"	Abigail Cross, of Richard M. and Elizabeth,	Oct. 1, 1805.
1-81	"	Joseph Mumford,	Dec. 2, 1807.
1-81	"	John Parker,	Aug. 23, 1810.
1-81	"	Hannah Elizabeth,	Feb. 3, 1813.
1-96	"	Rebecca Ann, of Clement and Mary,	March 19, 1811.
1-96	"	David Pinnegar,	June 28, 1813.
1-96	"	William Pinnegar,	Sept. 13, 1815.
1-96	"	Benjamin Hall,	Feb. 18, 1818.
2-39	"	Anna Brown, of Job A. and Elizabeth,	May 24, 1831.
2-39	"	Henry Swan,	April 24, 1833.
2-39	"	Edward Wickham,	Nov. 10, 1835.
2-39	"	Job Almy,	Feb. 10, 1838.
2-39	"	James Swan,	Jan. 28, 1840.
2-39	"	Alexander,	April 15, 1842.
2-39	"	Alfred,	Aug. 15, 1845.
2-39	"	Elizabeth Swan,	Aug. 28, 1848.
2-39	"	James Swan,	April 21, 1852.
1-127	"	Perry M., of Perry M. and Abby,	Jan. 2, 1833.
177	PECK	Benjamin Gold, of William A. and Mehitable,	Oct. 8, 1753.
177	"	Mary Dinely,	Nov. 2, 1755.
73	PELHAM	Herming, of Edward, Jr., and Arabella,	Dec. 3, 1718.
73	"	Elizabeth,	Oct. 20, 1721.
73	"	Penelope,	May 23, 1724.
77	"	Edward, frees Mercy, a colored servant,	July 25, 1726.
1-57	PERRY	Elizabeth, of George and Abigail,	June 18, 1782.
1-57	"	Mary,	April 15, 1784.
1-57	"	Eleanor,	May 1, 1787.
1-57	"	Eleanor,	d. Oct. 3, 1792.
1-57	"	Frances,	Aug. 29, 1789.
1-57	"	Nancy,	Nov. 25, 1791.
1-57	"	Edward,	March 12, 1793.
1-57	"	George,	March 6, 1795.
1-57	"	Eleanor, 2d,	Jan. 25, 1798.
1-57	"	William,	July ——, 1806.
1-45	"	Abigail,	Feb. 9, 1793.
1-45	"	James,	Sept. 20, 1795.
1-45	"	Phebe,	Jan. 31, 1797.
1-45	"	Mary Ann,	Feb. 8, 1798.
1-45	"	Harriet,	Aug. 1, 1799.
1-45	"	Harriet, 2d,	Jan. 5, 1801.
1-45	"	Catherine Briggs,	March 22, 1803.
1-97	"	Christopher Grant, of Oliver H. and Elizabeth C.,	April 2, 1812.
1-97	"	Oliver Hazard,	Feb. 23, 1815.
1-97	"	Christopher Raymond,	June 29, 1818.
1-97	"	Elizabeth Mason,	Sept. 15, 1819.
20	PETERS	——, of John and Sarah,	Jan. 18, 1713-4.
1-93	PETER	——, of Rouse and Mary,	6m., 13d, 1803.
1-93	"	James,	3m., 24d, 1805.
69	PHILLIPS	Barbara, of John and Rebecca,	March 15, 1687-88.
230	"	Gilbert, of Eleanor,	April 10, 1732.
144	"	Elizabeth Ann, of Caleb and Elizabeth,	May 18, 1755.
1-83	PICKERING	Eliza Carpenter, of Benning and Nancy,	Nov. 22, 1806.
241	PINKNEY	Jarvis, of Jarvis and Lydia,	July 29, 1744.
241	"	Lydia,	March 5, 1746.
87	PITMAN	John, of Joseph and Mercy,	March 26, 1719.
87	"	Mary,	Jan. 1, 1721.
87	"	Samuel,	Jan. 15, 1723-24.
87	"	Martha,	Oct. 9, 1725.
87	"	Joseph,	May 19, 1729.
182	"	Abigail, of Samuel and Rebecca,	———.
182	"	Joseph,	———.
182	"	Sanders,	———.
182	"	Mary,	———.

185	PITMAN Samuel, of Samuel and Rebecca,		Jan. 22, ——.
182	" Moses,		March 11, 174—.
182	" Peleg,		Aug. 14, 174—.
182	" Bridget,		Dec. 11, 17—.
128	" Hannah, of Moses and Martha,		Aug. 18, 1734.
173	PINNEGAR Mary, of Edward and Martha,		March 18, 1771.
14	POCOCK, dau. of John and Rebecca,		—— —, 1689.
174	POPE Mary, of Francis and Freelove,		Nov. 24, 1735.
174	" Sarah,		June 10, 1742.
174	" Mary,		died March 8, 1748-49.
214	" Sarah Experience, of Ezra and Sarah,		Nov. 9, 1762.
213	POTTER Hannah, of Thomas and Hannah,		Sept. 30, 1741.
222	" James C., of James and Mary,		March 25, 1754.
222	" Thomas,		Feb. 21, 1756.
222	" Mary,		May 12, 1758.
222	" Joseph,		Feb. 17, 1760.
222	" Ann,		July 9, 1761.
1-68	" James C., of Henry T. and Eliza,		Aug. 24, 1808.
1-68	" Mary,		July 20, 1811.
1-68	" Ruth,		Aug. 26, 1813.
2-55	POWERS Sarah Jane, of John and Mary W.,		April 23, 1857.
2-55	" John Henry,		Feb. 26, 1859.
2-55	" Mary Elizabeth,		Aug. 4, 1861.
3-4	PRESTON Lewis, of Lewis, and Abigail,		Nov. 22, 1697.
4	" Martha,		April 6, 1699.
4	" John,		Feb. 26, 1700.
213	PRICE Mary, of James and Penelope,		Feb. 27, 1763.
213	" Penelope,		Oct. —, 1766.

Q R

2-66	RANDOLPH Richard K., son of Peyton and Lucy (Harrison, of Gov. Benjamin) born Oct. 19, 1781, died March 20, 1849.	
176	RANKINS Jane, of John and Mary,	June 10, 1737.
2-61	READ Eleazer, Sr., July 22, 1728, d. April 9, 1803.	
2-61	" Hannah, March 22, 1724, d. May 13, 1759.	
2-61	" Isaac, of Eleazer and Hannah,	March 22, 1747.
2-61	" Elizabeth,	Nov. 29, 1749.
2-61	" Elizabeth, (m. Tilley),	d. Jan. 3, 1836.
2-61	" Eleazer, Jr.,	Aug. 19, 1751.
2-61	" Eleazer, Jr.,	d. Nov. 9, 1826.
2-61	" John,	March 22, 1753.
2-61	" John,	d. Feb. 26, 1830.
2-61	" David,	March 15, 1755.
2-62	" Hannah,	March 27, 1757.
2-62	" William,	April 6, 1759.
2-62	" William,	d. Aug. 26, 1826.
2-62	" Eleazer, Jr.,	Aug. 20, 1774.
2-62	" Eleazer, Jr.,	d. at sea. Feb. 20, 1817.
2-62	" Elizabeth (Murphy),	Dec. 17, 1780.
2-62	" Elizabeth (Murphy),	d. June 8, 1867.
2-62	" Oliver,	May 18, 1797.
2-62	" Oliver,	d. Sept. 20, 1798.
2-62	" Elizabeth M.,	Aug. 28, 1798.
2-62	" Penelope,	March 10, 1800.
2-62	" Penelope,	d. Oct. 1, 1800.
2-62	" Oliver,	July 14, 1801.
2-62	" Samuel M.,	July 25, 1803.
2-62	" Samuel M.,	Died at sea.
2-62	" Henry,	March 15, 1805.
2-62	" Henry,	Died at sea.
2-63	" John M.,	March 8, 1807.
2-63	" John M.,	d. March 18, 1807.
2-63	" Catherine,	Feb. 1, 1809.

2-63	READ	Eleazer J., of Eleazer and Hannah,	May 30, 1811.
2-63	"	Eleazer J.,	d. Aug. 25, 1844.
2-63	"	Phebe A.,	July 28, 1815.
2-63	"	Mary M.,	April 28, 1812.
2-63	"	Mary M.,	d. Sept. 24, 1849.
2-63	"	Oliver, born July 14, 1801	
2-63	"	Clarissa Gardiner, his wife, July 13, 1799.	
2-63	"	Clarissa Gardiner, his wife, d. Sept. 23, 1835.	
2-63	"	Catherine Hammett, his 2d wife, April 11, 1811.	
2-63	"	William Gardiner, of Oliver and Catherine,	Oct. 11, 1823.
2-64	"	Anges Matilda (Clarke), 1st wife of William Gardiner Read, Oct. 23, 1826.	
2-64	"	Agnes Matilda,	d. Dec. 9, 1849.
2-64	"	Kate W. (Taylor), 2d wife of William Gardiner Read, Jan. 21, 1829.	
2-64	"	Kate W.,	d. Nov. 20, 1852.
2-64	"	Oliver C., of William G. and Agnes M.,	Nov. 21, 1849.
2-64	"	Kate Wilson, of William G. and Kate W.,	Nov. 16, 1852.
2-64	"	William G., Jr., of William G. and Emeline G.,	Aug. 22, 1856.
2-64	"	Ellen Sturges,	Aug. 18, 1858.
1-47	"	Oliver, born Warwick, Dec. 25, 1743.	
1-47	"	Mary Sherman, his wife, born Newport, Jan. 1, 1741.	
1-47	"	Amey, of Oliver and Mary,	Sept. 2, 1766.
1-47	"	Abigail,	Aug. 26, 1768.
1-47	"	Catherine,	Feb. 4, 1770.
1-47	"	Catherine,	d. June 21, 1788.
1-47	"	Robert,	June 3, 1773.
1-47	"	Oliver,	Oct. 14, 1775.
1-47	"	Oliver,	d. at Batavia.
1-70	"	Mary Ann, of David and Anne,	bap. Nov. 7, 1794.
2-65	"	Hannah Elizabeth, of Oliver and Clarrissa,	Feb. 7, 1825.
2-65	"	Hannah Elizabeth, died at Middletown,	April 22, 1843.
2-65	"	Henry,	Feb. 25, 1827.
2-65	"	Edwin Oliver,	April 25, 1829.
2-65	"	Neddie, of Edwin Oliver and Fanny,	Oct. 30, 1866.
2-65	"	Frank,	May 22, 1868.
2-65	"	Frank,	d. July 14, 1869.
2-65	"	Gardiner,	May 22, 1868.
22	RECORDS	Mary, of John and Virtue,	Sept. —, 1711.
37	"	John,	Aug. 26, 1717.
53	REDWOOD	William, of Abraham and Mehitable	April 14, 1697.
53	"	William,	d. Oct. 25, 1712.
53	"	Mary,	March 3, 1699.
53	"	Ann (b. Antigua),	Sept. 7, 1700.
53	"	Sarah (b. Antigua),	Dec. 19, 1702.
53	"	James Longford (b. Antigua),	— 9, 1706.
53	"	James Longford (b. Antigua),	d. Oct. 27, 17—.
53	"	Abraham (b. Antigua),	April 15, 1709.
86	"	Mehitable, of Abraham, of Antigua, W. I., dau. of James Longford, dec., died 4m. 20d., 1715. Buried in Friends Burial Ground.	
86	"	James Longford, of Abraham and Mehitable, died aged 18 y., 5 m., 18 d.,	Oct. 27, 1724.
127	"	———, died at Salem, Mass.,	Jan. 11, 1728.
1-20	"	William, of Abraham and Martha, died aged 50 years (no issue), (also 30),	May 16, 1784.
1-74	REMINGTON	Hannah R., of John and Sarah,	April 5, 1775.
1-74	"	Benjamin,	June 4, 1777.
1-74	"	Abigail,	Sept. 5, 1779.
1-74	"	Peter T.,	April 7, 1783.
46	RHODES	Samuel, of William and Sarah,	Sept. 18, 1701.
46	"	Sarah,	March 13, 1704-5.
46	"	Mary,	Nov. 12, 1709.
83	"	Samuel, of William and Mary,	Sept. 30, 1725.
104	"	Rebecca, of Samuel and Rebecca,	Oct. 4, 1750.
1-49	"	Christopher, Jr., of Christopher and Ann,	Oct. 15, 1801.

1-49	RHODES	William Hammond, of Christopher and Mary, 2d w.,	May 11, 1805.
1-49	"	Alfred,	Feb. 5, 1807.
1-49	"	Mary Ann,	Jan. 23, 1809.
1-40	RICHMOND	Mary Hardy, of Gideon and Hannah,	April 18, 1786.
1-40	"	Gideon,	April 27, 1797.
45	RIDER	Thomas, of John and Sarah,	Jan. 22, 1706.
45	"	Elizabeth,	Feb. 10, 1708.
45	"	John,	Aug. 26, 1710.
45	"	Sarah,	Aug. 8, 1713.
45	"	William,	March 26, 1715.
91	"	——, dau. of Thomas and Best,	——, 1730.
220	"	Lydia, of Joseph,	Sept. 7, 1755.
2-22	"	William Henry of William B. and Jane Wilson (Swan),	Nov. 5, 1838.
22	ROBINSON	Susannah, of John and Mary,	Feb. 9, 1712.
212	"	John Tyrrell, of James and Mary,	Sept. 28, 1748.
212	"	Sarah Ann,	Aug. 31, 1745.
212	"	Dr. James,	died Nov. 29, 1745.
82	RODMAN	Hannah, of Clarke and Ann,	Jan. 9, 1723.
82	"	Daniel,	Sept. 4, 1721.
71	"	Mary,	May 18, 17—.
71	"	Joseph,	Feb. 20, 1723-4.
71	"	Thomas,	June 5, 1726.
71	"	Samuel,	April 16, 1738.
210	"	Anna, of Joseph and Mary,	March 18, 1746.
210	"	Hannah,	May 29, 1749.
210	"	Clarke,	April 10, 1750.
114	"	William, of William and Lydia,	March 8, 1758.
114	"	Elizabeth,	May 13, 1760.
114	"	Mary,	March 14, 1762.
1-87	"	Hannah, of Elisha and Mary,	Aug. 28, 1804.
1-87	"	Hannah,	d. Nov. 2, 1804.
1-87	"	Hannah Amanda,	March 10, 1807.
24	ROGERS,	——, dau. of Joseph and Mary,	—— 15, 1710.
64	"	James, of John and Sarah,	——, 9, 1714.
64	"	Isaac,	April 4, 1716.
105	"	Thomas, of Thomas and Content,	Dec. 6, 1733.
105	"	Josias,	Oct. 27, 1737.
125	"	Sarah, of James and Charity,	Oct. 18, 1735.
125	"	John,	——, 1739.
125	"	Abi,	Feb. 12, 1741-2.
125	"	dau.,	Oct. 5, 1744.
125	"	James, of James and Abigail,	Jan. 15, 1750-1.
125	"	Mary,	April 28, 1755.
125	"	James,	Feb. 19, 1757.

S

16	SABIN	——, son of Jonathan and Catherine,	Sept. —, 1711.
16	"	Benjamin,	Sept. 23, 1715.
16	"	Joseph,	March 21, 1808-9.
54	"	Benjamin,	d. Sept. 22, 1716.
54, 55	"	Benjamin, 2d,	Aug 14, 1717.
54, 55	"	Katherine, wife of Jonathan,	d. Sept. 1, 1717.
67	"	Elizabeth, of Jonathan and Elizabeth,	Nov. 19, 1724.
47	SANFORD	Mary, of William and Grizzle,	Dec. 19, 1714.
47	"	Margaret,	June 10, 1716.
50	"	Elizabeth, of Eben and Mary,	Aug. 11, 1717.
37	"	John, of William and Experience,	Feb. 9, 1718.
183	"	Mary, of Esbon,	——.
183	"	Eneus,	——, 1721.
183	"	Woodward,	——, 1723.
183	"	Hannah,	——, 1725.
183	"	Esbon,	——, 1728.

183	SANFORD	Peleg, of William and Experience,	——, 1730.
183	"	Benjamin,	—— —.
183	"	Lydia,	——, 1735.
183	"	Joshua,	Aug. —, ——.
183	"	Joseph,	Sept. —, ——.
184	"	Elizabeth, of Peleg and Sarah,	Sept. 19, 1722.
184	"	Sarah,	July 8, 1724.
184	"	Frances,	May 15, 1726.
184	"	Sarah, wife of Peleg,	d. ——, 1726.
184	"	Peleg,	d. May 6, 1730.
131	"	Sarah, of Joseph and Lydia,	Sept. 22, 1723.
131	"	Joseph,	—— 24, 1725.
131	"	Daniel,	Aug. 5, 1729.
131	"	Martha,	July 10, 1732.
131	"	John,	——, 1735.
131	"	Odlin,	—— 24, 1738.
72	"	Grizzell, of William and Grizzell,	June 9, 1726.
102	"	Lydia, of Joseph, Jr., and Esther,	March 15, 1753.
102	"	Simon,	Jan. 22, 1755.
217	"	Susanna, of Benjamin,	Nov. 4, 1754.
217	"	Mary,	Feb. 1, 1756.
217	"	Daniel,	Jan. 26, 1758.
239	SAYER	Abigail, of Joshua and Austress,	July 8, 1741.
239	"	Benjamin,	June 20, 1742.
239	"	Joshua,	Feb. 10, 1745-6.
239	"	Austress,	Sept. 23, 1747.
239	"	Ann,	Dec. 1, 1749.
239	"	Elizabeth,	April 18, 1753.
239	"	Lewis,	Aug. 6, 1755.
1-8	"	John, of Benjamin and Jane,	Dec. 10, 1757.
1-8	"	Rebecca,	Jan. 17, 1760.
1-8	"	Lydia,	Nov. 24, 1761.
1-8	"	Benjamin,	July 31, 1764.
1-8	"	Phebe,	Feb. 28, 1766.
1-8	"	Joseph,	Dec. 9, 1768.
1-8	"	Mary,	July 13, 1770.
1-8	"	William,	Jan. 31, 1772.
1-8	"	Son,	April 4, 1773.
1-8	"	George,	Oct. 7, 1774.
1-8	"	Paul, (b. Jamestown),	April 7, 1780.
173	"	Peter, of Benjamin and Sarah,	Feb. 27, 1764.
173	"	Joshua,	July 8, 1765.
1-100	ST. HLAIZES	Lewis, born Nantes, France,	May 23, 1764.
192	SCOTT	John Cookson, of John and Sally,	Jan. 31, 1774.
10	SEABEAN	Henry, of Jonathan,	—— ——.
243	SEABURY,	dau. of John and Hannah,	Feb. 25, 1735.
1-64	"	Thomas Mumford, of Thomas and Elizabeth,	April 12, 1793.
184	SERGANT	Mary, of William and Mercy,	Sept. 16, 1751.
232	SERVAT,	son of Daniel and Abigail,	May 20, ——.
232	"	son,	Feb. 22, 1745-46.
10	SHAW	John, of Thomas and Martha,	Oct. 26, 1693.
10	"	Martha,	Sept. 28, 1696.
1-53	"	Thomas, of Banania and Elizabeth,	March 24, 1796.
1-58	"	Isaac,	Oct. 23, 1800.
1-78	"	Lucy Ann, of William and Susanna,	March 12, 1803.
220	SHERBOURNE	Henry, of Benjamin and Lucy,	Aug. 3, 1748.
220	"	Abiah,	May 7, 1750.
220	"	Hannah,	March 12, 1753.
220	"	Oliver,	Jan. 7, 1755.
220	"	Benjamin,	Feb. 27, 1757.
220	"	David,	Feb. 19, 1759.
55	SHEFFIELD	Mary, of James and Katherine,	Sept. 21, 1716.
55	"	Katherine,	Feb. —, 1717.
55	"	Sarah,	June 13, 1720.
55	"	James,	Sept. 30, 1721.

76	SHEFFIELD	Ruth, of James and Katherine,	Oct. 21, 1724.
76	"	Elizabeth,	Dec. 1, 1727.
99	"	Samuel, of James,	July 15, 1736.
184	"	Elizabeth, of John and Martha,	——, 1739-40.
220	"	Martha, of Nathan and Martha,	Dec. 10, 1764.
220	"	Benjamin,	Sept. 19, 1771.
1-27	"	Ruth Nichols, of Aaron and Mercy,	April 28, 1875.
1-27	"	Mary Nichols,	April 28, 1785.
80	SHERMAN	George, of Benjamin and Mary,	Feb. 22, 1706-7.
80	"	Isaac,	June 9, 1709.
80	"	Joseph,	June 1, 1712.
80	"	George,	Aug. 7, 1713.
163	"	Patience, of Robert and Katherine,	Jan. 30, 1731.
163	"	Patience,	d. May 26, 1739.
163	"	Mary,	Oct. 25, 1733.
163	"	Robert Taylor,	July 31, 1735.
163	"	Benjamin,	June 1, 1737.
163	"	Benjamin,	d. July 23, ——.
163	"	Elizabeth,	July 4, ——.
163	"	Katherine,	July 3, ——.
163	"	George,	Sept. 28, 174—.
163	"	George,	d. May 26, 174—.
163	"	Patience,	Dec. 24, 1743.
163	"	Hannah,	Nov. 24, 1747.
163	"	Isaac,	Feb. 16, 1748-9.
163	"	Abigail,	Dec. 25, 1750.
176	"	Elizabeth, of Peleg and Phebe,	Feb. 21, 1744.
176	"	Samuel,	June 16, 1749.
178	"	Benjamin, of Peleg and Patience,	May 9, 1764.
178	"	George,	May 9, 1764.
2-54	"	Edward T., of Jonathan and Elizabeth,	Feb. 4, 1840.
75	SHRIEVE	John, of Daniel and Sarah,	Nov. 12, 1726.
1-82	SILLIMAN	Mary Amelia, of Gold Selleck and Hepsa.	Aug. 13, 1802.
1-82	"	Augustus Ely,	Feb. 2, 1804.
1-82	"	Augustus Ely,	d. Nov. 4, 1805.
1-82	"	Benjamin,	Sept. 14, 1805.
1-82	"	Augustus Ely, 2d,	April 11, 1807.
1-82	"	Harriet,	Jan. 11, 1809.
1-82	"	Henry,	May 10, 1811.
1-82	"	Anneliza,	May 10, 1811.
155	SILVESTER	Christopher, of Joseph and Mary,	April 5, 1742.
155	"	Amey,	July 22, 1743.
155	"	Joseph,	Sept. 2, 1745.
155	"	Henchman, of Joseph and Mercy, 2d w.,	March 17, 1755.
113	SIMMONS	Martha, of Edward and Mary,	April 1, 1754.
113	"	Jonathan,	July —, 1755.
174	SIMPKINS	Mary, of John and Susanna,	Dec. 22, 1738.
174	"	Ann,	Sept. —, 1747.
2-50	SIMPSON	Agnes Mary, of Samuel F. and Celia,	Nov. 2, 1852.
2-50	"	Joseph,	Nov. 14, 1853.
2-50	"	Florence,	Sept. 16, 1856.
2-50	"	Edmund T.,	July 17, 1858.
2-50	"	Samuel Engs,	Aug. 21, 1859.
2-50	"	Peter B.,	April 9, 1861.
197	SINGLETON	Henry, son of Hannah ——, by one Thomas Singleton of Philadelphia, Pa.,	Oct. 9, 1763.
193	SISSON	Gideon, of Gideon and Mary,	Dec. 1, 1763.
193	"	James,	July 1, 1765.
193	"	William,	April 13, 1767.
1-128	"	Olney Tripp, of Robert C. and Mary Ann,	Sept. 13, 1835.
1-128	"	William Henry,	Feb. 18, 1839.
1-128	"	Rhoda Frances,	Feb. 1, 1841.
2-40	"	James Edward,	April 21, 1845.
2-40	"	Cynthia Ann Perry,	Oct. 25, 1847.
129	SKINNER	William, of Francis and Catherine Ann,	Dec. 14, ——.

NEWPORT—BIRTHS AND DEATHS.

129	SKINNER	Samuel, of Francis and Catherine Ann,	June, ——.
129	"	Edward,	July 12, 1742.
129	"	Francis,	Sept. 20, 1744.
34	SLOCUM,	son of Giles and Mary,	11m. 30d., 1706.
34	"	—— son,	7m. 3d., 1707.
34	"	——,	7m. 20d., 1709.
34	"	——,	8m. 15d., 1711.
34	"	Benjamin,	11m. 30d., 1714.
63	SMITH	Elisha, of Edward and Elizabeth,	July 17, ——.
63	"	Mary,	April 27, 1702.
63	"	Elisha,	Sept. 9, 1703.
63	"	Sarah,	June 7, 1705.
63	"	Phebe,	July 10, 1707.
63	"	Edward,	Oct. 4, 1709.
63	"	Hannah,	June 21, 1711.
60	"	Mary, of Peleg and Jemima,	Sept. 13, 1712.
60	"	Sarah,	Oct. 25, 1714.
60	"	William,	April 3, 1717.
60	"	Hannah,	Feb. 4, 1719-20.
60	"	Benjamin,	Oct. 12, 1722.
60	"	Abigail,	Jan. 11, 1724-5.
64	"	Dorcas, of Edward and Elizabeth,	July 20, 1714.
64	"	Henry,	Feb. 10, 1715-16.
64	"	William,	April 7, 1718.
64	"	Ann,	March 2, 1719-20.
97	"	Joseph, of Joseph,	Aug. 11, 1738.
210	"	Hannah, of Benjamin and Hannah,	Oct. 21, 1738.
210	"	Joseph,	Oct. 22, 1741.
210	"	William,	July 6, 1743.
160	"	Elizabeth, of Edward and Elizabeth,	June 23, 1744.
160	"	Elisha,	April 6, 17—.
160	"	Edward,	Jan. 22, 174—.
181	"	Arthur, of George and Sarah,	May 26, ——.
181	"	Ruth,	July 5, 1750.
181	"	Ruth,	d. Oct. 13, 1730.
181	"	Ruth, 2d,	July 15, 175—.
181	"	Sarah,	March 30, ——.
106	"	Sarah, of Samuel and Ann,	June 11, 1753.
106	"	Judeth,	April 27, 1763.
192	"	Ann, wife of Samuel,	d. —— 17, 1770.
1-50	"	William Grant, of William and Magdalen,	Sept. 12, 1790.
1-50	"	George Gibbs,	Nov. 20, 1795.
2-50	"	Mary L., of Philip B. and Patience H.	Dec. 6, 1852.
186	SOULE	Merebah, of Henry and Barbara,	Nov. 18, 1743.
186	"	Gideon,	March 2, 1744-45.
186	"	Nathaniel,	Jan. 7, 1746-47.
186	"	Henry,	Oct. 30, 1748.
186	"	Henry,	d. Sept. 19, 1750.
186	"	Jonathan,	June 2, 1750.
186	"	Jonathan,	d. Sept. 22, 1751.
187	"	Sarah,	Dec. 13, 1751.
187	"	Henry,	Nov. 16, 1752.
192	SOUTHWICK	Elizabeth Ann, of Solomon and Ann,	April 10, 1770.
192	"	John G.,	March 30, 1771.
192	"	Mary,	July 30, 1772.
192	"	Solomon,	Dec. 25, 177—.
1-79	SPEARE	Mary, of James and Sarah,	Sept. 22, 1794.
1-79	"	James, Jr.,	June 26, 1796.
1-79	"	John,	July 13, 1798.
1-79	"	William,	May 2, 1800.
1-79	"	William,	d. Aug. 16, 1801.
1-79	"	Elizabeth,	July 7, 1802.
1-135	SPENCER	Thomas Aldrich, of Micah and Sarah Ann,	March 10, 1838.
135	SPOONER	Rebecca, of Thomas and Rebecca,	Aug. 2, 1743.
135	"	John,	April 23, 1745.
135	"	Thomas,	March 8, 1747.

135	SPOONER	Judith Padock, of Thomas and Rebecca,	Nov. 5, 1749.
135	"	Rosanna,	March 21, 1751.
135	"	Alies,	March 2, 1753.
1-103	SPRAGUE	Abigail H. of Jordan and Rebecca,	May 18, 1815.
1-103	"	Mary B.,	Oct. 7, 1817.
101	SPRINGER	John, of Jonathan and Ann,	July 17, ——.
196	STACY	Thomas, of Thomas and Sarah,	March 18, 1770.
196	"	Martha Jarsey,	April 21, 1772.
196	"	Sarah Jarsey,	Feb. 12, 1774.
196	"	Ann,	Jan. 5, 1776.
2-57	"	Deborah, of William T., died aged 38 years,	Jan. 7, 1844.
17	STANTON	Henry, of John and Mary,	June 25, 1688.
20-49	"	Mary, of Henry and Mary, (b. Jamestown),	May 30, 1708.
20-49	"	Mary,	d. Aug. 21, 1708.
20-49	"	Alice,	8m., 17, 1709.
49	"	May 2d,	3m., 6, 1712.
49	"	Catherine,	8m., 28, 1713.
49	"	Hannah,	7m., 25, 1716.
49	"	Henry,	3m., 22, 1719.
49	"	Joseph,	March 30, 1724.
50	"	son of Capt. John and Mary.	June 25, ——.
217	STERNS	Willard, of John and Rachel,	April 26, 1746.
217	"	John,	Nov. 19, 1747.
217	"	Willard,	Aug. 9, 1749.
217	"	Martha,	Oct. 7, 1750.
217	"	Hannah,	Aug. 16, 1752.
217	"	Joseph,	April 3, 1754.
217	"	Benjamin,	Feb. 8, 1756.
217	"	Isaac,	Nov. 21, 1757.
217	"	Simon,	Sept. 17, 17—.
67	STEVENS	John, of Nicholas and Rachel,	April 30, 1725.
131	"	Mary, of Robert and Elizabeth,	Sept. 17, ——.
131	"	John,	March 13, 1740-1.
131	"	Robert,	July 14, 1742.
131	"	Robert, 2d,	July 13, 1743.
133	"	Ann, of William and Ann,	March 28, 1743.
134	"	Sarah,	Feb. 4, 1744-5.
134	"	William,	Oct. 1, 1748.
134	"	Mary,	May 10, 1752.
134	"	Philip,	April 17, 1755.
134	"	Phebe,	July 26, 1759.
1-63	"	Sally of Thomas and Ann,	Sept. 19, 1776.
1-63	"	Ann,	Jan. 3, 1778.
1-63	"	Abigail,	Feb. 4, 1780.
1-63	"	Samuel,	Sept. 14, 1781.
1-63	"	William,	Sept. 10, 1783.
1-63	"	John,	Jan. 24, 1786.
1-63	"	Thomas,	Oct. 6, 1788.
1-63	"	Fanny,	Nov. 25, 1790.
1-63	"	Eliza,	Dec. 3, 1792.
1-63	"	Gardiner,	Dec. 1, 1794.
1-63	"	Robert,	May 25, 1797.
1-95	"	Mary Elizabeth, of John and Susannah,	March 27, 1808.
1-95	"	Elizabeth Ann,	Aug. 21, 1809.
1-95	"	John,	Feb. 5, 1811.

Note.—1st born Portsmouth.

189	STILES	Ezra, of Rev. Isaac and Keziah,	Nov. 30, 1727.
189	"	Elizabeth (Hubbard), of John and Elizabeth, his wife,	July 3, 1731.
189	"	Elizabeth, of Ezra and Elizabeth,	April 17, 1758.
189	"	Ezra,	March 11, 1759.
189	"	Kezira,	Sept. 29, 1760.
189	"	Emily,	April 21, 1762.
189	"	Isaac,	Aug. 10, 1763.
189	"	Ruth,	Aug. ——, 1765.
111	STOCKMAN	Sarah, of Jacob and Ann,	Feb. 13, 1748-9.

111	STOCKMAN	Mary, of Jacob and Ann,	Dec. 6, 1751.
111	"	William,	Jan. 24, 1755.
111	"	Anne,	Aug. 7, 1757.
111	"	John,	March 21, 1760.
111	"	Jacob,	March 1, 1763.
111	"	Iriphena,	Sept. 9, 1765.
111	"	Isaac,	Sept. 4, 1768.
111	"	Samuel,	Sept. 4, 1768.
1-34	STODDARD	William,	Nov. 15, 1747.
1-34	"	Joshua, Jr.,	April 7, 1755, d. Sept. 10, 1761.
2-48	SULLIVAN	Timothy, of Thomas and Jane,	bap. ——, 1822.
2-48	"	Thomas,	d. Sept. ——, 1850.
25	SWAN	——, of Samuel and Dorothy,	Feb. 23, 1710-11.
19	"	dau.,	Feb. 23, 1710-11.

Note—This probably refers to the same birth.

25	"	Hannah,	d. July 12, 1711.
55	"	Elizabeth, of William and Ann,	Sept. 19, 1717.
55	"	William,	May 10, 1719.
55	"	Richard,	Aug. 1, 1721.
55	"	Henry,	Sept. 17, 1723.
55	"	Ann,	Oct. 7, 1727.
162	"	Mary, of John and Hannah,	June 13, 1734.
184	"	John, of Alexander and Elizabeth,	Aug. 25, 1748.
184	"	Gustavus,	June 17, 17—.
184	"	Catherine,	July 26, 17—.
184	"	Alexander,	Aug. 2, 1749.
1-101	"	Richard, (b. Newport), Nov. 26, 1775.	
1-101	"	Elizabeth (Brown, b. North Kingstown), his wife,	April 6, 1778.
1-101	"	Merian,	Sept. 14, 1804.
1-101	"	William,	Dec. 18, 1805.
1-101	"	Elizabeth,	Nov. 14, 1807.
1-101	"	Richard,	Sept. 22, 1809.
1-101	"	James C.,	May 6, 1811.
1-101	"	Edwin J.,	May 27, 1812.
1-101	"	Henry,	June 5, 1814.
1-101	"	Sally Centre,	Dec. 21, 1815.
1-101	"	Jane Wilson,	Jan. 21, 1817.
1-101	"	Caroline Louisa,	Feb. 6, 1819.
192	SWEET	Sarah, of John and Hannah,	March 12, 1753.
166	"	Sarah, of James and Ann,	May 11, 1739.
166	"	James,	June 16, 1745.

T

215	TANNER	James, of James and Hannah,	April 9, 1772.
215	"	Sarah,	March 13, 1773.
40-165	TAYLOR	Catherine, of Robert and Patience,	March 6, 1712-3.
165	"	James,	July 18, 1716.
165	"	James,	May —, 1717.
29, 165	"	Elizabeth,	Aug. 29, 1718.
29, 165	"	Patience,	Nov. 14, 1720.
165	"	Robert,	Dec. 11, 1722.
165	"	Robert,	——, 1723.
216	"	William, of Thomas and Patience,	March 27, 1730.
216	"	Sarah,	——.
216	"	Elizabeth,	Aug. 7, 1737.
216	"	Edward,	April 20, 1741.
216	"	Patience,	——, 1742-3.
216	"	Catherine,	—— 17, 1744-5.
216	"	Margaret,	Dec. 5, 1747.
216	"	Mary,	Nov. 24, 1751.

Note.—Last two born in Virginia.

165	"	Mary, of Robert and Elizabeth,	July 9, 1741.

165	TAYLOR Robert, of Robert and Elizabeth,	July 27, 1742.
165	" Elizabeth, wife of Robert,	d. Aug. —, 1742.
165	" son of Robert and Rebecca,	Oct. 3, 1743.
165	" ——,	May 9, 1745.
165	" Benjamin,	Sept. 27, 1746.
165	" John,	Dec. —, 1748.
165	" Rebecca,	Nov. —, 1750.
165	" Nicholas,	——, 1753.
165	" Patience, 1st wife of Robert,	d. Dec. —, ——.
221	" Elizabeth, of John and Hannah,	Nov. 26, 1755.
1-99	" Edward Easton, of Joseph Wanton and Ruth,	May 24, 1792.
1-67	" Barton, of Humphrey, and Sarah,	July 4, 1801.
2-53	TEARNEY Charles, and Catherine (Lawton's) children—	
2-53	" Ellen,	Feb. 28, 1856.
2-53	" Anne C.,	May 10, 1858.
2-66	" Catherine, widow of Charles, (late a private, Co. C, 2d Reg., N. Y. H. A.),	died March 8, 1871.
2-61	TEFFT Charles W., of John and Keturah,	d. May 18, 1870.
2-61	" Keturah B., of Charles W. and Mary C. (Heath),	d. Feb. 19, 1863.
160	TELFAIR Ann, of Archibald and Mehitable,	March 19, 1722-3.
1-49	TERPAND Olimpe, of Francis and Louisa,	Sept. 23, 1796.
5	TEW ——, of Major ——, and Sarah,	Feb. 12, 1701-2.
28	" son of Henry and Sarah,	Dec. —, 1703.
28	" son,	March 11, 1706.
28	" son,	Feb. —, 1709-10.
28	" son,	Oct. 26, 1711.
42	" Henry, of Henry and Ann,	Jan. 23, 1704-5.
42	" Amey,	May 18, 1707.
42	" Amey,	d. Dec. 23, 1708.
42	" Ann,	Nov. 2, 1709.
42	" Elizabeth,	May 13, 1711.
42	" Elizabeth,	d. July 2, 1711.
42	" Edward,	Aug. 8, 1712.
42	" Amey,	June 1, 1714.
42	" James,	Sept. 2, 1715.
42	" Edward,	Sept. 4, 1717.
42	" Edward,	d. Sept. 3, 1719.
42	" ——,	Sept. 21, 1719.
28	" Edward, of Henry and Dorcas,	Jan. 28, 1710-11.
28	" son,	———.
41	" Elisha,	Feb. 25, 1714-15.
41	" Darius,	Feb. 27, 1714-15.
41	" Paul,	March 27, 1715.
41	" Henry,	d. April 26, 1718.
107	THOMAS George, of Portsmouth, states that his son ——, was born in Newport, Nov. —, 1694.	
2-11	THORNDIKE George Knight, of Israel and Anna T.,	Feb. 11, 1840.
24	THURSTON Daniel, of Daniel and Mary,	Sept. 25, 1687.
24	" John,	June 10, 1692.
24	" Edward,	Sept. 1, 1693.
24	" Benjamin,	March 25, 1697.
24	" James,	July 15, 1698.
24	" Peter,	July 3, 1704.
24	" dau.,	Jan. 19, 1689.
24	" dau.,	March 9, 1690.
24	" dau.,	Jan. 18, 1694.
14	" Edward, of Edward and Elizabeth,	Sept. —, 1702.
14	" Elizabeth,	April —, 1705.
14	" Abigail,	Nov. ——.
126	" Samuel, of Edward and Elizabeth,	——, 1724.
126	" Abigail,	Jan. 4, 1725-6.
126	" Abigail,	d. March 28, 1726.
126	" Edward,	Jan. 12, 1728-9.
126	" Benjamin,	Nov. 20, 1732.
122	" John, of Latham and Mary,	Oct. 27, 1750.

122	THURSTON	Latham, of Latham and Mary,	Sept. 21, 1732.
122	"	Abigail,	May —, 1735.
109	"	Serah, of Benjamin and Sarah,	May 25, 1729.
109	"	Mary,	June 19, 1730.
109	"	Benjamin,	Aug. 6, 1731.
109	"	Hephzibah,	Dec. 25, 1736.
108	"	Mary, wife of Latham,	d. Sept. 30, 1737.
108	"	Latham, of Latham and Mary, went to sea Nov. 23, 1737, and never heard from.	
104	"	Mehitable, of Jonathan and Lydia,	Nov. —, 1743.
104	"	Samuel,	July 5, 1745.
104	"	Lydia,	—, 1749.
173	"	Edward, of Edward, Jr., and Mary,	— 2, —.
173	"	Elizabeth Norton,	— 12, 1768.
156	TILLEY	Nathaniel, of Nathaniel and Susannah,	Aug. 19, 1755.
156	"	Mary,	May 4, 1760.
156	"	Sarah,	June 19, 1764.
156	"	James,	Sept. 5, 1765.
156	"	James,	d. March 2, 1800.
156	"	Thomas,	March 16, 1767.
156	"	William,	Dec. 26, 1769.
156	"	Elizabeth,	Feb. 27, 1771.
156	"	Dorcas,	June 25, 1772.
156	"	Abraham D.,	May 29, 1775.
156	"	Patience,	Aug. 6, 1776.
156	"	John T.,	April 5, 1778.
156	"	George,	Nov. 8, 1780.
156	"	Benjamin,	Sept. 7, 1782.
156	"	Ann,	March 21, 1784.
1-46	"	Mary, of Thomas and Mary,	July 28, 1791.
1-46	"	Thomas Rogers,	Sept. 14, 1793.
1-46	"	Elizabeth,	Feb. 12, 1797.
1-46	"	James,	Oct. 27, 1800.
1-46	"	Rebecca T.,	May 8, 1802.
1-46	"	George S.,	April 7, 1805.
1-46	"	Catherine M.,	May 30, 1806.
1-46	"	William,	Aug. 25, 1809.
1-60	"	Sally Robinson, of John S., and Margaret,	Jan. 12, 1800.
1-60	"	John Taber,	Feb. 22, 1803.
1-60	"	Ann Boutin,	Mar. 11, 1809.
2-48	"	William Lovie, of Thomas S., and Anna E.,	May 29, 1843.
2-48	"	Abby Rider,	July 14, 1855.
1-68	TILLINGHAST	Nichols Paris,	Jan. 21, 1742.
1-68	"	Catherine (Taylor) his wife,	Feb. —, 1744-5.
1-68	"	Elizabeth, of Nicholas P. and Catherine,	April 12, 1768.
1-68	"	Elizabeth,	d. Sept. 24, 1789.
1-68	"	Deborah,	Aug. 25, 1769.
1-68	"	Deborah,	d. July 29, 1796.
1-68	"	Patience,	Mar. 10, 1771.
1-68	"	Patience,	d. Sept. 20, 1772.
1-68	"	Patience Taylor,	Jan. 18, 1774.
1-68	"	Catherine,	May 2, 1775.
1-68	"	Catherine,	d. Nov. 12, 1777.
1-68	"	William Taylor,	Aug. 30, 1776.
1-68	"	William Taylor,	d. Nov. 25, 1777.
1-68	"	William Edward,	Feb. 14, 1780.
1-68	"	William Edward,	d. Aug. 28, 1781.
1-68	"	Sarah (Almy), 2d wife of Nicholas Paris; b. Feb. —, 1756, died March 12, 1787.	
1-68	"	Catherine,	March 22, 1783.
1-68	"	Sarah Coggeshall,	March 8, 1784.
1-68	"	Thomas Coggeshall,	April 23, 1787.
1-68	"	Thomas Coggeshall,	died same day.
1-68	"	Nicholas Paris, removed to Charlestown, Brooke Co., Va., Sept. —, 1798.	
1-111	"	Abby Greene, of John and Mary Ann,	Sept. 4, 1792.

1-111	TILLINGHAST	William, of John and Mary Ann,	Oct. 20, 1797.
1-111	"	Clarke Sanford,	Dec. 28, 1799.
1-111	"	Joseph Sanford,	Sept. 5, 1802.
1-111	"	Martha Russell,	Oct. 24, 1806.
1-111	"	Lydia Gardiner,	May 22, 1809.
1-111	"	Mary Sanford,	April 28, 1811.
1-111	"	Ann Elizabeth,	Feb. 26, 1815.
3	"	Sampson Benjamin, of Benjamin and Elizabeth ——,	Dec. 7, 1708-9
99	TOWNSEND	Hannah, of Job and Rebecca,	June 20, 1728.
99	"	Sarah,	March 8, 1729.
99	"	Susannah,	Nov. 29, 1731.
99	"	Mary,	—— 10, 1733.
99	"	P——,	Jan. 22, 1734-5.
99	"	Edward,	—— 13, 1736.
99	"	Thomas,	Jan. 30, 1742-3.
37	TOWER	Mary, of William and Mary,	May 27, 1715.
116	TOMAN	Thomas, of John and Ruth,	Dec. 20, 1769.
87	TROWBRIDGE	Mercy, of John and Ruth,	Nov. 30, 1726.
76	"	George,	May 25, 1732.
5	TREBY	of Peter and Ruth,	Feb. 18, 1687-8.
5	"	Elizabeth,	June 4, 1679.
177	"	Mehitable, of Peter and Mehitable,	Nov. 24, 1716.
2-36	TURNER	Sarah Catherine, of Henry E. and Anna E.,	May 6, 1845.
2-36	"	Anna Stevens,	Sept. 30, 1846.
2-36	"	Joseph Lincoln,	Oct. 1, 1848.
2-24	"	William Jones, of Peter and Sarah J.,	Oct. 26, 1846.
2-25		Daniel,	Jan. 20, 1848.
2-33	"	Hattie Foster (b. Kittery, Me.),	Sept. 12, 1849.
2-51	"	John Henry, of Joshua and Sophia,	May 23, 1857.
92, 105	TWEEDY	Nathaniel, of John and Mercy,	June 20, 1733.
92, 105	"	Mary,	Dec. 18, 1734.
105	"	William,	July 15, 1736.
105	"	Elizabeth,	Oct. 24, 1737.
105	"	Sarah,	April 28, 1739.
105	"	John,	July 14, 174—.
235	"	Mary, of —— and ——,	Nov. 1, 1741.
235	"	Jane,	June 16, 1743.
235	"	Freelove,	Dec. 21, 1744.
235	"	Samuel,	May 4, 1746.
235	"	Crawford,	April 15, 1748.
235	"	Amey,	Nov. 27, 1749.
1-7	"	Freelove Sophia, of William and Catherine,	March 5, 1763.
1-7	"	Catherine,	Dec. 13, 1766.
1-7	"	Elizabeth Honeyman,	July 7, 1776.

U

90	UNDERWOOD	John, of Philip and Mary,	July 24, 1731.
95	"	Nicholas, of Daniel and Mary,	July 24, 1734.
75	UPDIKE	Lodowick, of Daniel, and Anstres	July 12, 1725.
75	"	Mary,	April 11, 1727.
75	"	Gilbert,	May 9, 1729.
75	"	Wilkins,	May 9, 1729.

V

90	VAUGHN	Rebecca, of Daniel and Rebecca,	9m. 30d., 1715.
66	VERNON	Ann, of Samuel and Elizabeth,	Jan. 23, 1707-8
66	"	Elizabeth,	Aug. 4, 1709.
66	"	Samuel,	Sept. 6, ——.
66	"	Esther,	Aug. ——, ——.
66	"	Daniel,	Aug. ——, ——.
66	"	Thomas,	May 31, ——.

66	VERNON William, of Samuel and Elizabeth,	Jan. 17, 1719.
66	" Mary,	Dec. 23, 1721.
103	" Elizabeth, of Samuel and Amey,	April 24, 1738.
103	" William,	Aug. 3, 1739.
103	" William,	d. Saturday following.
103	" Amey,	Sept. 12, 1741.
103	" Amey,	d. Aug. 28, 1742.
103	" Mary,	Feb. —, 1742-3.
103	" Samuel,	Feb. 17, 1744-5.
103	" Amey,	July, —, 1746.
103	" Amey,	d. same month.
103	" Amey,	Nov. 19, 1747.
103	" William	July 21, 1749.
103	" William,	d. Sept. 1, 1749.
1-31	VICKERY Daniel, of Joseph and Mercy,	Oct. 22, 1756.
1-31	" Thomas,	Nov. 7, 1759.
1-31	" Joseph,	Jan. 30, 1762.
1-31	" Esther,	July 8, 1764.
1-31	" Mary,	Nov. 8, 1766.
1-31	" Hannah,	June 13, 1769.
1-31	" John,	June 17, 1771.
1-31	" Hugh,	Sept. 10, 1773.
1-31	" Martha,	March 24, 1778.
1-31	" Jeremiah,	Jan. 19, 1780.
1-68	VILETT Capt. John,	d. at St. Thomas, W. I., —, 1797.
1-68	" Elizabeth Tillinghast of Capt. John and Patience,	July —, 1796.
195	VINALL Elizabeth, of William,	——.
195	" William,	——.
195	" Sarah,	June 29, 1754.
195	" Mary Ann,	June 6, 1758.
2-17	" VINTON Francis, of Francis and Elizabeth,	Nov. 16, 1842.
2-20	" Henry Gilliatt,	March 29, 1844.

W

2-51	WAGNER Elizabeth, of John and Mary A.,	May 22, 1852.
2-51	" John B.,	Feb. 2, 1855.
67	WALKER John, of Richard and Hannah,	Feb. 2, 1701.
67	" Anna,	Jan. 20, ——.
67	" David,	March 4, 1706.
67	" Mary,	July 2, 1708
89	WANTON Joseph, of Gideon and Mary,	9m. 5d., 1720.
89	" Mary,	5m. 6d., 1722.
89	" Gideon,	6m. 24d., 1724.
89	" Sarah,	11m. 31d., 1725.
89	" Sarah,	d. 3m. 8d., 1729.
89	" Edward,	7m. 26d., 1727.
89	" Edward,	d. 10m. 25d., 1729.
89	" John,	5m. 5d., 1729.
89	" Edward,	5m. 23d., 1731.
89	" son,	April 12, 1734.
150	" Michael, of Stephen and Mary,	Sept. 12, 1739.
150	" Samuel,	March 11, 17—.
150	" Samuel, 2d,	Feb. 26, 17—.
150	" Hannah,	May —, 1747.
150	" Mary,	Dec. —, 175—.
150	" Martha,	June 11, 1757.
26	WARD Richard, of Thomas and Amey,	April 15, 1689.
23	" Amey, of Richard and Mary,	Sept 4, 1710.
25	" Amey,	d. Oct. 22, 1710.
45	" Elizabeth,	Feb. 19, 1715.
35	" Amey,	July 21, 1717.
42	" Isabel,	Sept. 19, 1719.
57	" Hannah,	Sept. 24, 1721.

57	WARD	John, of Richard and Mary,	Aug. 4, 1723.
57-58	"	Samuel,	May 27, 1725.
58	"	Mercy,	June 8, 1727.
58	"	John,	Aug. 15, 1724.
58	"	dau.	April 14, 1729.
58	"	son,	Dec. ——.
58	"	dau.	June 6, 1735.
24	"	dau.	Dec. 10 ——.
23	"	Thomas, of Richard,	Oct. 24, ——.
234	"	Elizabeth, of Henry,	Dec. 11, 1759.
175	"	Richard, of Samuel and Anne,	March 10, 1765.
1-85	"	Elizabeth, of Benjamin and Abigail,	Jan. 6, 1790.
1-85	"	Jonathan Rogers,	May 18, 1794.
1-85	"	Abigail,	Nov. 1, 1796.
1-85	"	Ann,	Nov. 27, 1799.
1-85	"	Priscella Lyndon,	July 21, 1801.
1-85	"	Susannah Clarke,	July 21, 1801.
1-85	"	Benjamin Case,	March 6, 1804.
1-85	"	Cynthia,	March 4, 1806.
3	WEAVER	John, of Thomas,	Aug. 5, 1694.
3	"	Mary,	July 7, ——.
3	"	Hannah,	13 years old, ——.
3	"	Benjamin,	11 years old, ——.
3	"	Maria,	9 years old, ——.
3	"	Peleg,	8 years old, ——.
3	"	Joseph,	5 years old, 25th of ——.
3	"	Jonathan	2 years old, June 3, 1713.
44	"	Elizabeth, of John and Alice,	March 1, 1712.
44	"	Thomas,	Oct. 3, 1713.
44	"	Julie,	March 21, 1715.
44	"	Mary,	May 9, 1718.
44	"	Kate,	March 11, 1719.
138	"	Patience,	April 14, 1716.
138	"	Mary,	Feb. 23, 1721.
138	"	Thomas,	July 6, 1723.
127	"	Christopher, of Benjamin, Jr., and Deborah,	April 30, 1741.
127	"	Deborah,	Aug. 23, 1742.
144	"	Hannah, of Ichabod and Hannah,	Dec. 3, 1746.
207	"	Frances, of James and Rebecca,	June 14, 1763.
207	"	James,	July 8, 1767.
1-25	"	Sarah Holmes, of Thomas, Jr., and Jane,	June 30, 1784.
1-25	"	Lucy Wells,	March 3, 1786.
1-25	"	Anna Potter,	May 3, 1788.
1-25	"	Alice,	Jan. 31, 1791.
1-25	"	Thomas,	April 19, 1793.
1-25	"	Jane,	Jan. 7, 1796.
1-25	"	Mercy,	Feb. 2, 1798.
1-25	"	William Henry,	Sept. 6, 1801.
1-25	"	Fanny Caroline,	July 23, 1804.
126	WEBB	Deborah, of Samuel and Deborah,	Aug. 20, 1739.
126	"	John,	June 24, 1740.
231	WEEDEN	Samuel, of Thomas and Mary,	May, 19, 1759.
203	"	James, of Samuel, Jr., and Abigail,	Oct. 30, 1760.
14,45	WEEKS	Elizabeth, of Joshua and Abigail,	Sept. 20, 1708.
45	"	Samuel,	April 29, 1712.
175	WELDON	Eleazer, of Jonathan and Mary,	May 4, 1741.
1-118	WENCH	Henry, of Henry and Ann,	Oct. 19, 1812.
1-118	"	Albert Coggeshall,	Sept. 22, 1807.
3	WESTGORTH	Katherine, of Robert and Sarah,	Dec. 23, 1684.
3	"	George,	April 24, 1688.
3	"	son.,	Feb. 19, 1689.
3	"	dau.,	Feb. 25, 1692.
175	WETHERELL	Samuel, of Timothy and Sarah,	Sept. 5, 1739.
175	"	Joshua,	Nov. 4, 1741.
175	"	Timothy,	Sept. 5, 1744.

175	WETHERELL	Job, of Timothy and Sarah,	Feb. 17, 1746-7.
175	"	Samuel,	Oct. 14, 1749.
175	"	Joseph,	April 22, 1752.
165	WHALING	William, of Jeffrey and Sarah,	Dec. 10, 1746.
165	"	Sarah,	Dec. 22, 1748.
1-132	WHEELER	Hannah Mary, of Cyrel C. and Hannah M.,	March 31, 1828.
1-132	"	George Richard,	Nov. 25, 1832.
1-132	"	Hannah Mary (Hazard, of Richard and Hannah) wife of Cyrel C., Oct. 24, 1801.	
112	WHITE	Elizabeth, of Thomas,	Aug. 18, 1756.
112	"	John,	Nov. 5, 1757.
112	"	Thomas,	Feb. 24, 1760.
1-44	"	William, of Noah and Rhoda,	July 15, 1777.
1-44	"	Elizabeth,	March 28, 1779.
1-44	"	Susannah,	Feb. 9, 1782.
1-44	"	Simeon,	March 16, 1785.
1-44	"	Nicholas,	Oct. 7, 1786.
1-44	"	Pardon,	Feb. 17, 1788.
1-44	"	Roby,	Jan. 21, 1795.
0-000	WHITHEAD	Samuel, of Samuel and Elizabeth,	Sept. 27, 1719.
1-44	"	Elizabeth,	Jan. 7, 1720.
71	WILBOUR	Mary, of Peleg and Arnold,	Jan. 18, 1721-22.
71	"	John,	Dec. 24, 1723.
71	"	Ruth,	Feb. 24, 1724-5.
78	"	Ann,	June 24, 1728.
201	"	Peleg, of John and Mary,	June 23, 1758.
201	"	Mary,	March 3, 1760.
197	WICKHAM	Thomas, of Thomas and Hannah,	April —, 1736.
197	"	Sarah,	Oct. 4, 1737.
197	"	Samuel,	Feb. 25, 1742.
197	"	Rebecca,	June 16, 1744.
197	"	Charles,	April 22, 1748.
140	"	Elizabeth, wife of Benjamin; b. London, Eng., Aug. 1, 1714, died at Newport, Oct. 13, 1741.	
140	"	Elizabeth, of Benjamin, and Elizabeth,	Sept. 7, 1736.
140	"	Deborah,	Feb. —, 1740.
140	"	Benjamin, of Benjamin and Mary,	Jan. 18, 1746-7.
140	"	John,	Jan. 9, 1748-9.
140	"	Frances,	June 5, 1754.
140	"	Mary,	June 7, 1756.
140	"	Samuel,	Oct. 13, 1758.
140	"	——,	Sept. 26, 1760.
107	"	Thomas, of Thomas and Elizabeth,	Nov. 7, 1763.
134	"	Hannah, of Samuel and Thankful,	Sept. 25, 1765.
1-19	WIGHTMAN	John, Jr., of John,	Oct. 29, 1733.
72	WIGNEL	Austress, of John and Mary,	March 19, 1723.
162	WILKEY	Thomas, of Peter and Elizabeth,	May —, 1744.
1-74	"	Peter Collins, of Samuel, and Huldah (b. Dartmouth), March 10, 1797.	
1-74	"	Elizabeth Ann,	April 16, 1802.
1-74	"	Hannah Southwick,	Oct. 12, 1804.
1-74	"	Samuel James,	March 24, 1809.
1-74	"	Henry Bliven,	Nov. 3, 1811.
64	WILLIAMS	Palgrave, of Palgrave and Elizabeth,	Sept. 19, 1704.
64	"	John,	Sept. 29, 1707.
1-80	"	Alexander —— 1725,	died Jan. 7, 1775.
1-80	"	Experience, wife of Alexander, Oct. —, 1718, died May 15, 1796.	
1-80	"	John, Nov. 7, 1760.	
1-80	"	Sally (Chadwick) his wife, Jan. 27, 1765.	
1-80	"	Robert, of John and Sally,	April 22, 1786.
1-80	"	Sally,	Feb. 21, 1788.
1-80	"	Thomas Chadwick,	Dec. 1, 1789.
1-80	"	William Earl,	March 10, 1792.
1-80	"	Elizabeth,	Feb. 26, 1794.
1-80	"	John,	Aug. 16, 1796.

1-80	WILLIAMS	John, of John and Sally,	d. Oct. 18, 1797.
1-80	"	Richard Fell,	July 19, 1798.
1-80	"	Richard Fell,	d. June 23, 1805.
1-80	"	Polly,	March 21, 1800.
1-80	"	Ann,	Feb. 18, 1802.
1-80	"	John,	April 28, 1804.
1-80	"	Susan,	Jan. 1, 1806.
41	WILSON	Mary, of Benjamin and Ann,	Oct. 23, 1717.
41	"	Benjamin,	Nov. 27, 1719.
41	"	William,	Feb. 1, 1725.
83	"	Jonathan, of Jonathan and Hannah,	Jan. 22, 1729.
83	"	Jonathan, Sr., died —, 1729.	
162	"	Joseph, of Ambrose and Mildred,	March 15, 1734.
162	"	Mary,	July 25, 1736.
162	"	John,	Sept. 28, 1738.
1-39	WRIGHTINGTON	Margaret, of Thomas and Sarah,	Oct. 12, 1729.
1-39	"	John,	Sept. 16, 1731.
1-39	"	Elizabeth,	Sept. 16, 1733.
29	WRIGHT	Elizabeth, of John and Abigail,	May 13, 1709.
29	"	Abigail,	Jan. 17, 1712-3.
29	"	Gideon,	Dec. 23, 1715.
29	"	Tabitha,	Dec. 23, 1715.
241	"	Ann, of Benjamin and Ann,	May —, 1767.
241	"	Samuel,	March 19, 1769.
241	"	Benjamin,	Aug. 20, 1771.
133	WYATT	John, of Standfast and Alice,	Sept. —, 1750.
133	"	Joseph,	—, 19, 1752.
133	"	Damarias,	June 19, 1764.

X Y Z

1-75	YEAMANS	Mary, (b. South Kingstown),	Nov. 8, 1779.
1-75	"	Elizabeth,	Sept. 14, 1782.
1-75	"	Nathaniel,	July 26, 1784.
1-75	"	Samuel,	Feb. 14, 1786.
1-75	"	Abigail,	Nov. 13, 1787.
1-75	"	Martha,	July 8, 1790.
1-75	"	Deborah,	March 16, 1792.
1-75	"	John,	Oct. 13, 1793.
1-75	"	James,	Nov. 14, 1795.
180	YOUNG	Elizabeth, of Charles and Patience,	Aug. 26, 1762.

(The family name of the following persons has been lost from the records.)

1-3	"	Mary,	Aug. 31, 1763.
1-3	"	Abigail,	April 20, 1767.
1-3	"	Joseph,	Aug. 2, 1770.
1-3	"	Ann,	Aug. 11, 1781.

www.ingramcontent.com/pod-product-compliance
Lightning Source LLC
Chambersburg PA
CBHW062131160426
43191CB00013B/2268